COMPELLED
TO
WITNESS

PRAISE FOR *COMPELLED TO WITNESS*

"Marilyn Yalom shows us the underside of the French Revolution as seen up close through women's eyes. It is a view that we don't often get and one that is absolutely essential to understanding the impact of that still troubling event."

—LYNN HUNT
Annenberg Professor of History, University of Pennsylvania.
Author of *The Family Romance of the French Revolution*

"History is made up of seating arrangements: hence Marilyn Yalom's view of the French Revolution from the women who rocked the cradle of the Dauphin, stood guard while Marie-Antoinette shed her body linen before ascending to the guillotine, and stuck their necks out as insurgents is both rare and riveting. Acting as a literary medium with a latter-day feminist eye, Yalom breathes life into these women memoirists and weaves their miniature epics of personal survival into the larger pageant of French history. A wonderful book."

—GAIL SHEEHY
Author of *The Silent Passage*

"Marilyn Yalom is to be congratulated for having focused our attention on the value of women's French Revolutionary memoirs, for understanding women's experiences of revolutionary upheaval, and for interpreting women's central roles in communicating those experiences across generational boundary lines."

—DARLINE GAY LEVY
Associate Professor of History, New York University

"A major contribution to women's history. Thanks to Marilyn Yalom, an American, we French now discover ancestors who have been unknown to us, each with her own role – modest or eminent – played during the maelstrom of the French Revolution."

—ÉLISABETH BADINTER
École Polytechnique de France
Author of *Unopposite Sex*

"Yalom uses her expertise to provide a thoughtful feminist analysis of the French Revolution and the Reign of Terror that followed. . . A unique contribution to historical studies."

—*Publishers Weekly*

"This masterfully crafted book adds a new dimension to our understanding of the French Revolution. . . Scholars and students alike will benefit from this important volume."
—*Library Journal*

"A fascinating study that conveys, as few other accounts have, how differently French women, as opposed to their male counterparts, view the costs of liberty, equality and fraternity."

—MARY MACKEY
San Francisco Chronicle

"Not only gives us a vivid and fresh picture of the French Revolution; it inspires us to rethink the old truism about history being written by the victors. History's victims write too, but their accounts sound different—less glorious and much more like the way we imagine things really happened."

—FRANCINE PROSE

"Yalom's book is accessible and thoughtful, and it has performed valuable service to historical memory by focusing attention on a class of material too often disdained by historians of the revolution, both male and female."

—DORINDA OUTRAM
American Historical Review

ALSO BY MARILYN YALOM

COMPELLED

TO

WITNESS

WOMEN'S MEMOIRS OF THE FRENCH REVOLUTION

MARILYN YALOM

ASTOR & LENOX

Compelled to Witness: Women's Memoirs of the French Revolution
© 2015 Marilyn Yalom. All rights reserved.

ISBN (print edition): 978-0-9860582-2-6

Published by Astor & Lenox, San Francisco, California, USA.

To contact the author or publisher, please visit http://astorandlenox.com. Requests for author appearances, educational and library pricing, and licensing regarding Astor & Lenox titles are welcome.

Cover illustration is *The Intervention of the Sabine Women* (detail) by Jacques-Louis David, 1799. The Louvre, Paris. In this depiction of a legendary event, the Sabine women take center stage to stop a war. David began this painting while he was imprisoned for his activities in the French Revolution. In contrast to his earlier work, portraying women as passive onlookers of men who inhabited the political sphere, this portrayal of women effectively demanding peace on the battlefield reflected both his gratitude to his wife, who secured his release from prison, and his hope for national reconciliation and peace in France.

Previous editions of this work were published under the title *Blood Sisters: The French Revolution in Women's Memory*.

For my children and grandchildren
And Irv, of course

CONTENTS

PREFACE

IN 1987 WHEN I EMBARKED ON A TRIP around the world, I did not plan to write a book about the French Revolution. It was my intention to compile an annotated bibliography of several hundred French women's memoirs published during the past two centuries.

Instead, as I traveled east with my husband to Japan, China, and Bali, my note cards drew me increasingly into one subset of my sample—into the lives of French women whose recorded memories centered around the events of 1789. Whether they were titled "Mémoires," or "Souvenirs," "Récit" or "Journal," or "Several Years of My Life," every autobiography written by a French woman in the last decade of the eighteenth or the first half of the nineteenth century was, to some extent, about the Revolution. I had stumbled into one of history's untapped mines.

Arriving in Paris in the spring of 1988, I found my French friends already sharing the bicentennial frenzy. They were lining up on both sides of the revolutionary divide, most extolling the social and political benefits bequeathed by the Revolution, others lamenting its violent excesses, and a few others still grieving the loss of the monarchy! As a foreigner, I was not obliged to commit myself to either the left or the right. My position could remain that of a feminist scholar concerned with the experience of women. I wanted to know how French women, as distinct from their male counterparts, had remembered the Revolution.

That question became the crux of a book written in French under the title *Le Temps des orages; Aristocrates, bourgeoises, et paysannes racontent* (Paris: Maren Sell, 1989). I am much indebted to publisher Maren Sell and to senior editor Michael Taylor for the realization of that project. For *Compelled To Witness*, I extended my research so as to identify and study the entire published corpus of women's memoirs of the Revolution. In both books, however, the basic aims were similar: to restore to the historiography of the Revolution the vision of its women.

I am grateful to many people and institutions for their support. At the top of the list are the scholars, staff, and associates of the Institute for Research on Women and Gender at Stanford University—fellow travelers over the past years when this book was evolving. The Stanford Biographers' Seminar, under the direction of Barbara Babcock and Diane Middlebrook, and the Stanford Seminar on the Enlightenment and Revolution, under the direction of John Bender and Keith Baker, were valuable intellectual arenas. A month at the Rockefeller Foundation's Center for Research in Bellagio, Italy, a travel grant from the American Council of Learned Societies, and a stay at the Museum of the French Revolution at Vizille, France, greatly stimulated my work at crucial points of research and writing.

Stanford Institute scholars Susan Bell, Karen Offen, Edith Gelles, and Will Roscoe read various chapters of this book, as did John Felstiner of Stanford and Mary Felstiner of San Francisco State University. My very deep thanks to each of them for precious time and criticism. Linda Orr at Duke University offered helpful comments on the Mme de Staël chapter. William Tuttle of the University of Kansas supplied constructive counsel and personal encouragement on numerous occasions.

Philippe Martial, Director of the Library of the French Senate, opened the resources of that library and his home to me whenever I had the good fortune to be in Paris.

As always in my life, my writing affected the members of my family, first and foremost, my husband, Irvin Yalom, who read and critiqued every chapter. Our sons Benjamin, while a Stanford senior, offered useful comments on the first and last chapters, and Reid, a professional photographer, helped select and photograph the illustrations.

I am particularly grateful to Steven Fraser, Executive Editor of Basic Books, and to Director of Publishing Terence Clarke and Publisher Ivory Madison of Astor & Lenox, for their intelligent suggestions and graceful orchestration of the editing process.

Madame de Genlis, prolific writer, educator, and governess of the Duc d'Orléans's children. © *Harlingue-Viollet*

1

INTRODUCTION: MEMORY AND MEMOIRS

Dans ce temps d'horrible mémoire tout Français était complice ou victime.
("In that time of horrible memory every French person was either an accomplice or a victim.")
— Comtesse de Bohm, 1830

"WE ARE IN THE CENTURY OF MEMOIRS," Mme de Fars Fausselandry proclaimed in 1830 on the first page of her autobiography. This assertive octogenarian had witnessed at close hand the ostentation of court life under Louis XV and XVI and the tragic convulsions of the French Revolution. She had survived the gruesome prison massacres of September 1792, which had taken the lives of hundreds of prisoners, including her influential uncle, the Abbot Chapt de Rastignac. She had seen her mother mount the scaffold for having corresponded with an émigré son. She had outlived almost all the famous revolutionary leaders and then Napoleon and even Louis XVIII, who was restored to the throne in 1814. Who more than she had the right to recount the agony endured by the generation of 1789?

Mme de Fars Fausselandry was not alone in her literary mission; more than a thousand people consigned their memories of the Revolution to some form of writing that was eventually published. Most of these were men, but a significant number—about eighty—were women.[1] Many had experienced the deaths of their loved ones in war, prison, or exile, and had barely escaped with their own lives. They had emerged from the Revolution with an urgent need to howl out their losses and cry for justice. The more they had suffered, the more they felt compelled to chronicle the past. No one expressed this better than the Vicomtesse de Fars Fausselandry.

Those who have seen only from a distance the bloody scenes of the revolutionary regime . . . will not understand why the voice of revenge makes itself heard so imperiously in my heart; but those who grieve for their lost father, mother, their dearest relatives, for those who were sacrificed on the scaffold, shot down at Lyons, drowned at Nantes; who during months longer than years, have seen death hover over their heads, those people will understand the exultation of a soul for whom age has carried off only a tiny part of her energy. In memory of my uncle and my mother, my heart cries out once more.[2]

Mme de Fausselandry had waited half a lifetime before she took writerly revenge on her enemies. Forty years had not blunted her sorrow and rage, validated once more, after 1815, by a restored monarchy that encouraged accounts of republican atrocities. Many other survivors of the French Revolution waited twenty, thirty, forty, even fifty years before they had acquired sufficient distance to confront their searing memories.[3]

It is not surprising that two-thirds of the women memoirists were aristocrats. At the time of the Revolution, only one out of two French subjects knew how to read, and only members of the upper class were able to write with ease; even here, there were significant differences between men and women, between those raised in cities or the country, and those educated in the north or south.[4] Certainly the preponderance of memoirs written by aristocrats could be attributed solely to class privilege, but there were political reasons as well. After 1815, whether the authors had been ladies-in-waiting to Marie-Antoinette or mere country cousins, their royalist accounts of revolutionary upheaval could count on the official blessings of the restored monarchs, Louis XVIII and Charles X, Louis XVI's more long-lived brothers.

Such was not the case for memoirists with republican sympathies. In 1828, when Charlotte Robespierre began to record her reminiscences of her two famous brothers, Maximilien and Augustin, she risked political sanction. Indeed, the young Albert Laponneraye, who had suggested that she write her memoirs, would go to prison for publishing his own republican convictions. Since the death of her brothers thirty-four years earlier in the carnage of Thermidor (July 10, 1794), Charlotte Robespierre had lived modestly, almost invisibly, bearing a despised name that had become synonymous with the Terror. It is easy to imagine the pleasure of this isolated, impoverished old woman when she was approached and befriended by the twenty-one-year-old Laponneraye. Undoubtedly, he was drawn to Charlotte because of his admiration for the great Maximilien; this would not have offended her, accustomed as she was to viewing herself as "Robespierre's sister." Her memoirs, published in 1835 (a year after her death), focus less on their author than on Maximilien and Augustin, and represent a form of autobiography-cum-biography not uncommon at a time when women were generally conceptualized as "relative creatures."[5] Eighteenth- and nineteenth-century women's memoirs provide many such examples of the ascent to authorship through connection to a famous man.[6] Yet despite the masculine biographical slant of these writings, each narrator found a way of expressing her own feminine identity.

Denis Bertholet, studying nineteenth-century French autobiography, insists that women born before the Revolution who wrote the stories of their lives defined themselves "in relationship to their sex"—that is, they believed in a predetermined female nature and they conformed to prescribed feminine roles.[7] Although it is true that these women did think of themselves largely in terms of their family roles, and did subscribe, *grosso modo*, to the prevailing gender ideology of their time, place, and class, it is misleading to view these authors primarily in terms of their limitations, deficiencies, and lack of individuality. The eighty women autobiographers providing the case studies for the present book are by no means lacking in distinctive personalities and highly varied life experiences, which makes generalizations about a "collective feminine" extremely problematic.

What the memoirists had in common were their prerevolutionary birth dates and their postrevolutionary deaths, and, above all, their membership in the generation of 1789. By "generation," I mean something more than a group bound by strictly chronological ties, but rather, in the sense proposed by the sociologist Karl Mannheim, a cohort of individuals marked by the same dominant political or social events.[8] Thus I include in the generation of 1789 individuals born as early as 1746 and as late as 1788, if, according to their own definitions, the Revolution shaped their life trajectory more than any other historical event. When these individuals looked back on the Revolution from the vantage of old age, they considered it the transforming crucible of their lives. What had happened in between paled by comparison.

Aristocrats and bourgeois women, royalists and republicans, even the few peasant and working-class women who dictated accounts of their experiences, all were bound together by a common nightmare. Whatever their political loyalties—and indeed there were a few unrepentant republicans like Charlotte Robespierre, Elisabeth Le Bas, and Mme Cavaignac in addition to the more numerous antirevolutionaries—a tragic note prevails. The experience of having survived when so many others had perished often produced what we in the twentieth century, in the aftermath of the Holocaust and Vietnam, have labeled "survivor guilt." Their testimonials spring from an inner urgency to bear witness for those who had been silenced, and they derive their haunting grandeur from the pervasive mark of death.

Death is never faceless in women's memoirs. As caretakers of children and the elderly, nurses of the sick and dying, women were enmeshed in a network of human connections, and their most wrenching memories are of friends and family members loved and lost. Their anxious efforts to ward off death and to sustain life constitute a subtext to their narratives.

Most, with the notable exceptions of Mme de Staël and Mme Roland, were not given to political analysis. They had been educated to play the traditional roles of daughter, sister, wife, and mother, deriving their position largely from the status and success of their male relatives. Most had little interest and even less faith in ideological abstractions, especially as they saw them eroded by violence committed in the name of revolutionary principles. They sensed that the noble promises of "liberty, equality, fraternity" and the "rights of man" were not addressed to them but to the fraternity of men in a literal, gendered sense. In France, as in all other Western nations, women had no political status at that time; indeed, French women would have to wait 150 years until the right to vote was granted them, in 1945—roughly a century after "universal" male suffrage had been established, in 1848.

Yet despite their lack of political status, many of the women of 1789 refused to adopt a passive stance. Their stories describe how they participated, individually and collectively, in the revolutionary saga, how they often succeeded in manipulating a political system designed to exclude them. The republican Mme Roland, wife of the minister of the interior, covertly authored her husband's letters and circulars, and would be executed for complicity with the Girondin leaders. The royalist Mme de La Villirouët managed to liberate herself and her coprisoners by virtue of her dogged epistolary efforts, and she subsequently saved her husband's life as well by pleading his case in court. Dressed as a beggar, Françoise Després carried secret messages for the royalist army in the Vendée, often escaping arrest and inspiring her compatriots with her zeal for the counterrevolution. In both royalist and republican camps, several women defied the ban against female soldiering and, disguised as men, bore arms for their causes.[9] Such examples of resourceful female activism, at odds with prevailing gender norms, were by no means unusual in women's first-person accounts of the Revolution.

The memoirists presented in this book offer an extraordinary range of texts and lives, a range that extends from the sixteen-page testimonial of the Widow Bault, wife of the concierge in the prison where Marie-Antoinette spent her last days, to the ten-volume memoirs of the prolific writer Mme de Genlis. The quality of their work is also highly varied. The memoirs of Mme Roland and Mme de Staël have been granted minor status within the literary canon, and several others have also earned critical respect. But even those of the untutored petite bourgeoise Elisabeth Le Bas, wife of the Convention deputy Philippe Le Bas, and the illiterate peasant Renée Bordereau, who dictated and "edited" her life story, are not devoid of literary value, if we understand literature in its broadest sense: as works that interest and move and enlighten us by virtue of their meaningful content and aesthetic integrity. What is certain is that the reader of these texts hears the author's voice and encounters a distinct persona. Ultimately, what makes these memoirists worthy of our attention—in addition to their value as witnesses to the making of history—is the narrator's character that shines through her words just as the director's sensibility permeates a well-made film. If we perceive the intelligence behind the story, the personality of the protagonist, her will and vision, then the story comes alive for us and we begin to care about her destiny.

Life and literature merge in these narratives—life as mangled and transformed by a great cataclysm, literature as constructed through the prism of memory. Certainly memory is subject to retrospective falsification, to the loss and confusion of facts wrought by the passage of time and, more important, by the distortions of a mind intent upon preserving its particular picture of the past. What narrator wants to portray her enemies as righteous and brave, or herself as cowardly and immoral? Autobiographical narrators are invariably self-serving, some more than others, some more successfully than others.

Speak, Memory, the compelling title of Vladimir Nabokov's great autobiography, conveys the essence of the memoirist's task. He or she summons the remembering self, commands its deposition, records its exact words. Those words bear an uncertain relationship to the facts they profess to report. In the pilgrimage from lived experience to recorded experience, many facts disappear or become blurred. Some are lost in the unconscious, while others are consciously censored; many are transformed into fantasied scenarios that take on a remembered reality indistinguishable from factual reality. There is a tendency for all autobiographical storytellers, and especially for survivors, to intensify their experiences and to construct a more artful, more cohesive, and more meaningful narrative out of disparate events.[10] Then, as they are written down, the words of memory undergo further transformation in response to the aesthetics of style. The very sounds they emit as they journey from brain to print alter their final form. When memory speaks, it is notoriously inventive.

We as readers must listen with a third ear when we seek to appraise the "truth" of memory's utterances and the extent to which memoirs are accurate representations of lived events. For the great public happenings, there are sometimes multiple accounts, allowing for collective verification. For personal events known only to the author, we must trust a more subjective guideline: does it ring true? Are there internal verifications within the text that suggest she is acting in accord with her own character? Is she recounting a plausible sequence of events? What does she omit and why? Is the memoir so thoroughly dictated by the narrator's need to justify her actions during the Revolution (as was the case for many men who had formerly been public figures) that it forfeits its historical credibility? Has the work been so heavily "edited" (that is, ghostwritten or rewritten) by a second party as to become a kind of historical fiction?

Assessing memoirs as historical documents is a very challenging enterprise.[11] The Napoleonic scholar Jean Tulard noted in 1989 that historians of the Revolution often have been reluctant to use the memoirs of that period, preferring instead more impersonal documents, but he also asserts that memoirs should not be neglected, because "they help us penetrate, better than the discourses of orators . . . the mentality of an epoch."[12]

Let us grant at the outset that our women memoirists rarely recorded events exactly as they were but as they were later remembered and filtered through distorting sensibilities. They wrote to give meaning and order to uncustomary chaos, to create out of disaster an art of survival and transcendence. As a literary corpus, their personal narratives form a collective expression of women's memory—one that reconstitutes, humanizes, feminizes, and ultimately mythologizes a great national event. The Comtesse de Bohm's epigraph to this chapter summed up the metanarrative: one must have been either a victim or an accomplice of revolutionary destruction.[13]

However simplistic, this Manichean formulation takes on special meaning when applied to women. Because they were primarily ensconced within the domestic sphere, without the rights or responsibilities of public leadership, none (with the possible exception of Mme Roland) had the opportunity of being a destructive "accomplice" on a grand scale. Conversely, all, including Mme Roland, saw themselves as victims, and all, regardless of class, leave records of the connection between victimization and gender. They tell us what it was like to suffer a miscarriage as the result of a particularly bloody street demonstration, or to have to choose between nursing a baby and following a husband to the wars. They describe their resistance to the bald propositions of jailers offering freedom for sexual favors. They remember the threats of brutal soldiers and the intervention of unexpected saviors as they and their children fled for their lives. Their records restore to us, in the words of Benôite Groult, "the very palpitation of life. "[14]

Still, no matter how "personalized" or "feminized" these memoirs are, they also record the great public moments of the Revolution. Whenever possible, the narrator presents her personal account of a major event, thus acquiring the stature of a historical memorialist in addition to the lesser prestige accorded to the "merely" autobiographical. At the time these works were written, memoirs were a far more traditional literary form than the upstart autobiography, the name for which was not coined until 1797 in English and shortly thereafter in French.[15] The older term, "memoir," was already current in both French and English by the seventeenth century to designate records of historical events written from the personal knowledge of the author. "Autobiography" arose in the aftermath of the 1781 publication of Jean-Jacques Rousseau's *Confessions* to describe a new form of self-referential writing, one that emphasized the interior life and psychological development of the author/narrator/ protagonist.

Rousseau's widely documented influence upon his contemporaries and upon subsequent generations cannot be overestimated, and his appeal to literate French women was almost universal. In the 1780s an entire nation had become captive to his vision of women as a regenerative social force issuing from their roles as devoted wives and breast-feeding mothers. Only a few dissenters, like the philosopher-deputy Condorcet, paused to wonder why women were so impassioned of someone who told them they were naturally inferior to men and good only for domestic servitude. Even such strong-willed intellectual women as Mme Roland and Mme de Staël were enthusiastic devotees of Rousseau, though their bold natures and political activities appear today as fundamentally incompatible with the self-effacing feminine ideal he propagated. Yet Rousseau's vision of the feminine was irresistible to women because it validated their desire for love and offered a new model of conjugal happiness. As Annette Rosa phrased it, "In that century when woman had no rights, Rousseau granted her the rights of the heart."[16]

Women memoirists were particularly susceptible to Rousseau's new autobiographical model, despite their ostensible reluctance to speak directly about themselves. As authors, they often oscillate between pages of testimonial fixed determinedly on famous events and personages, and other pages devoted to aspects of their personal lives that have nothing to do with public history. Mme de Candé, for example, interrupts her account of the counterrevolutionary wars at a critical moment when her family had fled to Cholet to tell us about her loving sentiments, as a girl, for a twenty-two-year-old mother. The Comtesse de Bohm adds to her record of imprisonment those moments when, contemplating the forest of Chantilly from her window, she found comfort in nature and the changing seasons. Marie-Victoire Monnard, who had been sent by her employer to gather information on demonstrations in the streets of Paris, interlaced her chronicle of political insurrection and prison massacre with incidents from her work in the linen trade.

This combination of nascent autobiography and venerable memoir, with its special niche for women, is unique to the history of French literature. It produced a transitional mode of expression that would give way in time to the openly self-referential writing practiced by women as well as men in our own time. But long before it was acceptable for women to assume that stance, the Revolution provided an opportunity, as it were, for a prospective author to interweave her private history within *la grande histoire*. No one could deny her entry into the halls of literature with her ticket stamped "eyewitness to the Revolution." She, too, could chronicle the movement of the crowd as it surged into the courtyard of Versailles or assembled peacefully on the Champ-de-Mars. She, too, could recall the sound of the alarm as it announced the threat of foreign invaders. And she, too, remembered the overpowering silence that reigned in Paris after the execution of Louis XVI. Crafting history was a belated way of entering into the Revolution, which had commenced by inviting everyone to take part and ended by denying women official citizenship and even the right to gather in private clubs.[17] And she would craft that history on her own terms.

How women memoirists remembered and recorded the Revolution is the central issue addressed in this book. I shall focus on what they chose to remember and *how* they transformed their memories into memoirs. Oscillating between a public history that had already been charted by many others, and a private history that belonged to each memoirist, these women fabricated their own design. Whatever the factual truth of their activities during the Revolution, they present themselves as they want posterity to remember them. For the most part, they do not want to be remembered as passive figures. Whenever possible, the memoirist portrays herself as an active participant, cheering the Revolution on its course or, more frequently, resisting it. Even if a particular incident recounted proudly by the author seems to a twentieth-century reader to be of questionable significance, clearly that incident had meaning for her. It was her way of claiming a part in the epic drama that had already silenced its principal players.

In each of their stories, a moment occurs when the author "enters on stage," as Mme de Fausselandry describes her own shift in role. These are the moments that, over the years, had taken shape in each woman's memory and coalesced into a personal myth. Each proclaimed to the world: This is how I acted when I was put to the test.

The Revolution, then, must be understood as context and pretext for these women's memoirs. To lay out the context, I begin by describing the first year of the Revolution from the vantage of a cluster of women, many of whom will appear later in this book as the protagonists of their own life stories.

Each of their eyewitness accounts is anchored in both public and private history. On the one hand, they signpost the Revolution as the major reference point for an entire generation and, arguably, for the entire century to come. On the other, they trace personal journeys through that collective happening. All these texts, even the most self-effacing or the most self-centered, are hybrid chronicles that track the convergence of an individual destiny with national destiny. And almost all reflect not only the period from 1789 to 1795, but the following years and decades during which these women internalized the Revolution, assimilated it into their identities, and coopted it so as to create their own revolutionary mythologies.

In this book, their life stories follow a geographical sequence: the first and most numerous are centered around Paris, which was the primary political theater; the second, in the provinces where the Revolution was played out on an equally bloody, if less influential, stage; the third, in the foreign countries that sheltered the thousands of émigrés who had fled their homeland. This grouping reflects the concentric circles of revolutionary upheaval, emanating from Paris, radiating out to Normandy, Brittany, the Vendée, Bordeaux, Marseilles, Nîmes, and Lyons, and spreading as far as Belgium, Holland, England, Germany, Switzerland, Italy, Austria, Spain, Portugal, Scandinavia, Russia, America, and the French islands in the Caribbean and the Indian Ocean. Those close to the center of action in Paris, with greater opportunity to observe the national debates and crucial political events, constitute about 45 percent of our sample. Roughly 30 percent of the women focused on events in the provinces, and of these, an important subgroup concentrated on the counterrevolutionary wars in the Vendée and Brittany. Many of these "provincial" writers and especially the women of the Vendée emerged as autobiographers in spite of themselves, as if they were still astonished by their earlier, unexpected heroics. A cluster of 25 percent emphasized their time in exile; this statistically overrepresented group brought home to France tales of the foreign countries they had visited, thus introducing the relatively new literary genre of travel writing into the memoir-cum-autobiography vessel. (The breakdown into percentages for geographical settings is only an approximation, since a single work may be divided between Paris and/ or the provinces and/or exile.)

Women's memoirs of the Revolution cover a wide population that includes court and provincial aristocrats, bourgeois women from the upper and middle classes, peasants and servants, writers and actresses, a rare painter and a scant few nuns.[18] No other literature in the Western world offers such an early treasury of women recording their personal histories within the context of a great political cataclysm. One hundred and fifty years would pass before the survivor literature of World War II would equal it in number and intensity. I have chosen, whenever possible, to frame the words of these women with a minimum of analysis, in the belief that, whatever their class, level of education, or political loyalties, they speak eloquently of the human, and specifically female, ability to mine disaster for its redemptive ore. To paraphrase Nietzsche, what did not kill them made them stronger—strong enough to fashion from their tragic recollections compelling human dramas.

Whom were they writing for? When we ask this question, we touch upon their deepest longings. "It is for the future that I am writing," wrote Mme Vallon from the department of the Loir-et Cher, summing up the collective hope of all these memoirists.[19] They considered it crucial for their children and grandchildren and future descendants to be familiar with the great upheaval that their country, their families, and they themselves had endured. For example, the Marquise de La Rochejaquelein, the Comtesse de La Villirouët, the Comtesse de Dauger, the Duchesse de Gontaut, the Baronne de Lambert, Mme Millon-Journel, and Mme Vallon specifically dedicated their works to their children; Pauline de Béarn and Mme de La Tour du Pin to their sons; Mme de La Roque to her daughter; Mme de Ménerville and Mme de Loménie to their grandchildren; Alexandrine des Echerolles to her niece; the Comtesse de Boigne to her nephews; and the Baronne Du Montet to her grandnieces and grandnephews. Some expressed the hope that their stories would offer moral lessons, others were simply pleased with the idea that their histories would be known by their descendants after their death. Mme de La Rochejaquelein is particularly eloquent on this matter:

> It is because of you, my dear children, that I have had the courage to finish these memoirs, which I began long before your birth and which I have abandoned twenty times. I have given myself the sad pleasure of telling you the glorious details of your relatives' life and death. Other books might have made known to you the principal actions by which they distinguished themselves, but I thought that a simple tale, written by your mother, would inspire in you a more tender and more filial feeling for their honorable memory.[20]

Conceptualizing themselves as the transmitters of the family history, these women were generally more concerned with their relatives than were male memoirists. Yet, regardless of whether or not they consciously hoped to transmit their histories to their progeny, all who heeded the memoirist's call—women as well as men—responded to what one of them, Angélique de Maussion, called "the secret desire to prolong [existence] through remembrance and to live a few instants in the memory of those who follow them."[21] This desire to gain a measure of symbolic immortality through the efforts of one's pen—to "persist in one's being," in the words of Spinoza, even after one's death—is clearly present in each memoirist. Let us fulfill their desire and be their posthumous audience.

Engraving of the Women's March to Versailles on October 5, 1789. *Collection of Brigitte Lane*

2

THE YEAR 1789, IN WOMEN'S WORDS

ON NEW YEAR'S DAY, 1789, no one in France was expecting a Revolution that would topple the throne. Louis XVI had already ruled for ten years over the most influential nation in Europe. With its 28,000,000 inhabitants —600,000 in Paris alone—France set the style for the rest of the continent. The imperial palace of Schönbrunnn in Vienna had been modeled on the château of Versailles, and Frederick the Great had been inspired by Voltaire to develop a program of "enlightened" politics in Prussia. By the time of the Revolution, French was the official language of the Russian court under Catherine the Great, who spared no effort to amass the great collection of French art hanging today in the Hermitage Museum of St. Petersburg. French influence extended as far as the fledgling United States, which was indebted to its powerful European ally for substantial military aid during the War of Independence.

To be sure, the disastrous state of the French treasury had prompted the king and his ministers to adopt the extremist plan of reassembling the Estates General, which had not met for 175 years. This body of representatives from the three orders of French society— the clergy, the nobility, and the "people" or Third Estate—would be asked to approve a fiscal plan intended to lift the nation out of bankruptcy. But despite the public knowledge that France was on the verge of financial collapse, despite the uncommon hardships inflicted on the people by one of the coldest winters in history and especially by the dearth of wheat, and despite a smoldering antipathy toward the court found in numerous circles, it was unthinkable that the monarchy of France would collapse.

It was, after all, a monarchy whose roots extended back 1,300 years. French royalty had defended itself and its people against formidable enemies: the Huns in the fifth century, Muslim Arabs in the eighth, the English of the Hundred Years War. A proud history of Merovingian, Carolingian, Capetian, and Valois dynasties stood behind the Bourbon kings, of whom Louis XVI was only the fifth to reign. The Bourbons could still be considered a "young" dynasty, with several male heirs promising future sovereigns. No one at the beginning of 1789, and certainly none of the women represented in this book, could have foreseen that the great tree of monarchy would be battered by its own subjects and ultimately felled.

Yet even among the aristocrats peopling the Court of Versailles, irreverence toward the king and queen had grown to sizable proportions by 1789. This was especially true in the circle dominated by Louis XVI's cousin and rival, the liberal-thinking Duc d'Orléans. Mme de Genlis, governess of the Duc d'Orléans's children, as well as his mistress, later recalled the attitude of polite boredom that was fashionable among members of the nobility on the eve of the Revolution:

> You went to pay your respects at Versailles, moaning and groaning all the way: you said over and over that nothing was as boring as Versailles and the Court... . . . Some people in society foresaw troubles and storms, but in general our sense of security was without bounds. . . . We thought of a revolution as something impossible.[1]

If it was "good form," as Mme de Genlis observed, to make fun of the court, one can be sure that she herself, as an arbiter of fashion and a supporter of the Duc d'Orléans, was instrumental in promoting that spirit.

This same attitude is echoed in the memoirs of another highly placed aristocrat, Mme de La Tour du Pin. In 1789, she was a recently married lady-in-waiting to Marie-Antoinette. Decades later Mme de La Tour du Pin looked back to the prerevolutionary period when it had been chic for members of the court "to complain about everything." The officers of the guard resented the obligation to wear their uniforms every day. The ladies-in-waiting and even the ecclesiastics absented themselves from Versailles under the slightest pretext. Although the word "revolution" was never uttered, a "spirit of revolt reigned" in the antechambers of regal authority.[2]

Beyond the court, overt political discourse was everywhere. The Marquise de Villeneuve-Arifat, née de Nicolay, recalled the tedious conversations she was forced to endure at her parents' sumptuous dinners given to entertain such notables as the king's ministers Calonne, Brienne, and Jacques Necker, and Necker's fashionable daughter, Mme de Staël. Progressive Frenchmen "dreamed only of an English government" with a constitutional monarchy and houses of parliament, and they bandied about numerous English terms that were totally unknown in French. The young Mlle de Nicolay had to ask the meaning of such words as "club," "motion," "petition," "majority," and "minority." In a rare display of wit she wrote: "The 'speakers by order' and 'speakers by head' made mine very tired."[3]

Considerably lower down on the social ladder and considerably more radical in their political views, the family of the future Mme Cavaignac entertained some of the most distinguished thinkers and artists of the day, including the poet Andre Chénier, the painter Jean-Baptiste Greuze, and the writer Bernardin de Saint-Pierre. In this household of "hot democrats," the nine-year-old Marie-Julie was imprinted by the ideas that led to her early marriage with the extremist republican deputy Jean-Baptiste Cavaignac.[4]

For the most part, close relatives shared the same political views, though they occasionally joined opposing factions. Such was the case for the actress Louise Fusil, daughter of a royalist father and wife of a republican husband. Torn between the politics of the two men in her family, Fusil took refuge in the common belief that a woman does not have to manifest political opinions, a belief that permitted her to maintain friends in both camps. In retrospect, she placed herself safely "on the side of the oppressed," sometimes republican, sometimes royalist.[5]

During the first months of 1789, the election of the deputies to the Estates General mandated by the king took place throughout the provinces of France. All male nobles and all members of the clergy, as well as those men from the Third Estate who were at least twenty-five years old and on the tax registers, had the right to vote for the representatives from their district. After two and sometimes three rounds of elections, 1,154 deputies were elected -291 for the clergy, 285 for the nobility, and 578 for the people. The women of the three estates shared in the general optimism occasioned by this extraordinary event. Although they themselves were not eligible to vote or to be candidates, they rejoiced in the triumphs of their husbands and fathers, their brothers, sons, uncles, nephews, and cousins. Long after the Revolution, Victorine de Chastenay, Charlotte Robespierre, and Mme de Fars Fausselandry wrote enthusiastically about the victory of "their men."

Victorine de Chastenay was eighteen when the meetings took place in her hometown of Châtillon-sur-Seine to draw up petitions of grievances and choose the deputies. Her father, Erard de Chastenay-Lanty, was elected chief spokesman for the group of provincial nobles with liberal ideas—a position shared, not surprisingly, by his daughter. In her memoirs she recalled the throes of "republican frenzy" to which she was subject during the first half of 1789 and the "sentiment of trusting cheerfulness" that accompanied her family's departure for the capital.[6]

At the same time, in the northern city of Arras, twenty-nine-year-old Charlotte Robespierre rejoiced in the political rise of her brother Maximilien: "All eyes were fixed on my older brother. I should not say all eyes because there were some men . . . who had been shocked by Maximilien's speeches and writing. . . . They couldn't get used to the words *liberty, equality, fraternity*."[7] Despite this opposition, Maximilien Robespierre was sent to Versailles as a deputy from the Third Estate of Arras.

The same spirit of triumphant pleasure was experienced in the Loire valley by Mme de Fausselandry when her uncle, the venerable Abbot Chapt de Rastignac, was chosen to represent the clergy. On the day of his election, his niece watched a huge crowd of people approach his residence: "I was able to distinguish my uncle's carriage, drawn by members of the clergy. His escort was composed of women and children, and the cries of that populace informed me that the Abbot had been named a member of the Estates General."[8]

Mme de Fausselandry and Victorine de Chastenay, like many other women, accompanied their men to Versailles for the assembly of the Estates General. They welcomed the move that would situate them at the heart of political action. By early May, the deputies and their families had descended upon the royal town, straining its resources and producing an atmosphere of heightened festivity.

In that memorable month of May, the future Duchesse d'Abrantès was only five years old. Fifty years later she would evoke the glorious spectacle of the deputies' stately march to the inaugural session: "I still see that immense and joyful crowd cramming the three avenues and lining the route which the deputies followed. I see those well-dressed women, waving their handkerchiefs—a whole population animated by the same feeling and drunk with hope and joy."[9]

On the other side of the wrought-iron gate separating the château of Versailles from the town, Mme de Staël, the only child of the popular finance minister Jacques Necker, also observed the "imposing spectacle" of nearly 1,200 deputies proceeding to church to hear mass on the night of May 5.

> I was placed at a window near Madame de Montmorin, the wife of the minister of foreign affairs, and I abandoned myself, I must admit, to the keenest hope, seeing for the first time in France the representatives of the nation. Mme de Montmorin, whose mind was in no way distinguished, said with a decisive tone, which made an impression upon me: "You are wrong to rejoice. The results will be disastrous both for France and for us."[10]

This cameo conversation between an older, more cynical woman and her twenty-three-year-old, idealistic friend reflects not only the vivid emotions of the moment, but also the sober wisdom of hindsight: within weeks, Mme de Montmorin's apprehensions began to be realized. What had been felt as polite boredom with the court by members of the nobility had been experienced as raging dissatisfaction by other segments of society. The forum provided by the Estates General allowed for the expression of the most profound grievances. Pent-up hostilities flared and spread like wildfire from the relatively contained arena of national finance to the wide-open territory of social and political reform.

On June 17, the Estates General declared itself to be a National Assembly. On June 20, locked out of the Assembly by order of the king, the deputies convened in a nearby hall and swore what has come down in history as the Tennis Court Oath; they pledged to remain together until a national constitution was given to France, with or without the king.

Minister Necker, associated with the liberal forces, was dismissed by Louis XVI and obliged to go into exile to his native Switzerland. In protest, the Parisians, who regarded Necker as their spokesman, took to the streets and, according to Necker's daughter, liberated the prison of the Bastille as a form of retaliation.

> As soon as the news of Monsieur Necker's departure was known in Paris, they barricaded the streets, everyone appointed himself a member of the national guard, put on any kind of military costume, and grabbed the first available arm—a gun, a sword, a scythe, whatever. A huge crowd of men, all with one mind, kissed each other like brothers in the streets, and the army of the people of Paris, composed of more than a hundred thousand men, was formed in an instant as if by a miracle. The Bastille, that citadel of arbitrary government, was taken on July 14, 1789.[11]

The July 14 uprising quickly became the mythic emblem of the Revolution, although only seven persons were found imprisoned at the Bastille. But since their freedom was paid for by the death of a hundred men in battle, it became an immediate symbol of the victory of the people over tyranny.

This sense of victory was not shared by all the deputies at Versailles, however. According to Victorine de Chastenay, "Versailles was in a stupor and the deputies in dread. . . . Blood had been spilled by the people . . . and the King, blessed by the people scarcely three months earlier, was now at war with that same people."[12] In less dramatic language, the July 14 minutes of the National Assembly attest to the deputies' baleful reaction.

But in the streets of Paris, euphoria, rather than horror, was the order of the day. Théroigne de Méricourt, a legendary revolutionary from Liège known for her beauty and daring, joined the celebration at the Palais Royal, one of the principal centers of popular demonstration. "I was at the Palais Royal when they brought the news that it was taken. The public expressed its great satisfaction, many cried with joy shouting that there was no more Bastille, no more *lettre de cachet*." When the king came to Paris a few days later, she went out to greet him, standing among the ranks of soldiers "dressed in white `Amazons,' with a round hat." She had chosen to wear trousers as a way of melding more easily with a crowd which could not be counted on to welcome women. In a rare prefeminist outburst, she injected the theme of women's oppression into the theme of revolution: "I was at ease playing the role of a man because I was always extremely humiliated by the servitude and prejudices under which men's pride keeps our sex oppressed." Yet what impressed her the most was the sense of communalism, the absence of selfishness, "the general air of good will" and egalitarianism. "Rich people in this moment of ferment mixed with the poor and spoke to them as their equals. . . . I saw many who, although in rags, had a heroic air. However little sensibility one has, it is not possible to see such a spectacle indifferently."[13]

Théroigne's reminiscences penned two years after these events bear witness to the fraternal effusion associated with the great moments of the Revolution. They also reveal the entrenched sexist heritage in French society that she clearly recognized and articulated. Along with Olympe de Gouges and Etta Palm d'Aelders — other bold women like herself—Théroigne expressed the hope that the new regime would extend to women some of the rights that were being claimed for men. She would become disillusioned, like the others, and indeed, before the Revolution was over, its excesses would contribute to the mental breakdown that sent her to the Salpêtrière insane asylum for the rest of her life.

Two days after the fall of the Bastille, Necker was recalled by the king. His daughter Mme de Staël joined in the public welcome fit for a conquering hero.

> The entire population of Paris turned out en masse in the streets. One saw women and men at their windows and on the roofs crying out: Long live Monsieur Necker. When he arrived near the City Hall, the cheers redoubled. The square was filled with a multitude of people animated by the same emotion. They all followed the steps of one man, and that man was my father . . . Monsieur Necker then advanced to the balcony and, when he proclaimed in a loud voice the holy words of peace between Frenchmen of all parties, the whole multitude responded enthusiastically. I saw nothing more at that moment, because I fainted from sheer joy.[14]

It is noteworthy that Mme de Staël, who was to become the greatest woman writer of her generation, responded to her emotions in a fashion that would not have been permitted to a man.

A far different picture of Necker emerges from the memoirs of Mme de Ménerville, the daughter, wife, and niece of powerful magistrates. Her writing reflects the hostility of the ultraroyalist faction toward Necker, condemned as an upstart foreigner with ideas inimical to France.

> An imprudent citizen of Geneva, stuffed with arrogance, dreamed that he had the right, the power to impose upon us a kind of English Constitution, of which he himself did not have a complete idea, but which he would improvise on the remains of our ancient monarchy. . . . He thought, in his criminal blindness, that the revolutionary flood would stop at his command as soon as he had attained his intended goal; that he could call out "That's enough!" What a fool![15]

Two weeks after the fall of the Bastille, the Parisian upheaval had spread through the provinces. Rumors were rife among a credulous populace, including the story of a foreign invasion. It was believed that the Austrians, linked to France through Marie-Antoinette's family, were coming to protect the king and queen. At this moment the young Marquise de La Tour du Pin was with her husband in Normandy, where she witnessed a frightening incident beneath her window in the town of Forges:

> Women were crying and lamenting, angry men were swearing and menacing. Others raised their hands to the sky crying out: "We are lost!" In their midst, a man on horseback was making a speech. . . . "They'll be here in three hours, they're pillaging in Gaillefontaines, they're setting the barns on fire, etc. etc." . . .

Since I am not easily frightened, I went down. I mounted my horse and started to trot through the street where little by little a crowd of people gathered who thought their last day had arrived. I spoke out, trying to persuade them that there wasn't a single word of truth in anything they had heard.

In front of the church, Mme de La Tour du Pin tried to convince the priest not to ring the alarm bells. She grabbed him by his cassock to prevent him from moving, but only her husband, arriving on horseback, was able to persuade the clergyman to postpone the alarm.

An hour later, the La Tour du Pin couple encountered a similar scene in the nearby town of Gaillefontaines where they had gone to investigate the rumors. They succeeded in restraining the crowd, but not without comic misunderstanding: one of the citizens insisted that Mme de La Tour du Pin was the queen. She would have been taken away for questioning had it not been for the intervention of a young locksmith who "began to laugh like a madman, telling them that the Queen was at least twice as old as the young demoiselle and twice as fat." On the basis of his testimony, she was allowed to return with her husband to Forges, where they "found the men armed with whatever they could procure and the national guard organized . . . all over France."[16]

This comic-opera version of the organization of the National Guard in Normandy had a somewhat different scenario in the Bourbonnais region southeast of Paris. Alexandrine des Echerolles was eight years old that summer and living in Moulins with her father and aunt. She would later remember that day as her first clear encounter with the Revolution. "From all points messengers arrived who announced that troops of brigands were advancing. . . . The people assembled, named officers to lead the citizens: the National Guard was established. They needed a leader, and my father was chosen."[17]

Mlle des Echerolles concluded, like Mme de La Tour du Pin, that the agitation was only a pretext for arming the people.

During the last two weeks of July, similar scenes occurred throughout France, giving rise to a phenomenon known as "the Great Fear." Without knowing exactly who the enemy was, villagers were roused to ring the alarm, to arm themselves with guns and pitchforks, and to send their children and animals into hiding. One of these country children, Marie-Victoire Monnard from the village of Creil in the Oise, later recalled how she and her sisters were given bread and Brie by their mother as provisions for their time in hiding. "In the attic where we were, there was a little window from which we could see . . . men gathered from several villages, armed with shovels, spades, and flails, prowling around in the fields and unable to find the imaginary enemies they were looking for." After three hours, the girls ate the cheese and ventured home, where they found their mother no less panicked and no further informed than before. "Eight hours after this commotion, everything returned to normal."[18]

The origins of the Great Fear have remained mysterious to this day. They have been attributed to plots by both revolutionaries and counterrevolutionaries, as well as to the notorious "brigands" who rose up periodically in rural France to pillage harvest and home. What is certain is that the Parisian City Council, responding to the increased disorder and looting that took place at the time of the Bastille insurrection, had already voted for the creation of a national citizens' army to be headed by General Lafayette, days before the events described by Mme de La Tour du Pin, Mlle des Echerolles, and Marie-Victoire Monnard.

Another woman who observed the headway made by the Revolution into the provinces was Mme Roland. Thirty-five years old in 1789, living in the vicinity of Lyons with her husband and young daughter, she greeted the Revolution with unambivalent enthusiasm. "The Revolution arrived and inflamed us: friends of humanity, lovers of liberty, we believed it had come to regenerate the human race."[19] Far from the Parisian scene of action that was later to bring them both fame and tragedy, the Rolands lamented the conservative orientation of their fellow Lyonnais, many of whom became Roland's avowed enemies. But in 1789 neither member of the yet-to-be famous couple was in a position to participate in national politics. Mme Roland had a more pressing personal matter to deal with—her husband's nearly fatal illness. "In 1789 I snatched my husband from a horrible sickness; the doctor's prescriptions would not have saved him without my attendance. I spent twelve days without sleeping, without undressing, six months in the anxiety and agitation of his dangerous convalescence."[20] Women's memories of the Revolution are typically interlaced, like this one, with caretaking stories, as well as episodes of pregnancy and childbirth.

During the summer of 1789, while the Revolution was making its way from Paris into the provinces, the royal family was in mourning. The heir to the throne, the first dauphin, was dead at the age of six. According to Mme Campan, the queen's first lady-in-waiting, "that young prince had, in a few short months, been struck down from flourishing health by rickets, which had curved his spine, elongated the features on his face, and rendered his legs so weak that he had to be propped up like an old man when he walked." Mme Campan described the deep suffering of Marie-Antoinette, who two years earlier had lost an eleven-month-old daughter. "That first misfortune had been, according to the Queen, the beginning of all those that followed."[21]

Mourning the loss of two of her original four children, Marie-Antoinette was further saddened by the departure of Yolande de Polignac, who left France with the first band of émigrés on July 17. The Duchesse de Polignac had not only been the queen's closest friend but her children's governess. The king and queen then chose . the widowed Duchesse de Tourzel as the new governess in charge of the four-year-old dauphin and the ten-year-old princess known as Madame Royale. Mme de Tourzel recorded the intrigue she perceived upon assuming her position at Versailles. Not only had many of the servants been "won over by revolutionary factionists," but even many courtiers loyal to the king and queen "were constantly filling their minds with their own disquiet."[22]

The memory of pervasive unrest was shared by the painter Elisabeth Vigée-Lebrun, famous for her portraits of Marie-Antoinette and many well-born aristocrats. For Vigée-Lebrun, the summer of 1789 was a period of increased public hostility toward anyone with visible signs of wealth; members of high society promenading at Longchamp were accosted by members of the popular classes who would jump on their running boards and call out, "Next year, you'll be behind your carriages and we'll be the ones inside!" At her home rough-looking sans-culottes (Parisian supporters of the radical Left) shook their fists at her whenever she appeared at the upper-floor windows. Mme Vigée-Lebrun fell into a condition of nervous despair: "A thousand sinister noises were coming at me from all sides; finally I lived only in a state of anxiety and profound melancholy."[23]

The people's hostility, exacerbated by the rising food prices and the lack of bread, which constituted the major part of their diet, became more and more difficult for the privileged classes to ignore. Yet, according to an incident recorded by the Marquise de La Rochjaquelein, the king remained blind to the people's dire needs. As a seventeen-year-old lady of the bedchamber attendant upon the queen, she had occasion to observe his insensitivity. One day, coming back from a walk, she saw the king and 200 court hunters pass out through the Dragon Gate, whereupon "the people rose up, closed the gate, and threw stones at the hunters." With their minds solely on the hunt, the royal party left the people there "dying of hunger." About "five o'clock, the King came back from the hunt." The starving mob cried out: " 'Long live the King!' And he passed by without stopping instead of telling them to follow him and enter the château. Thus that poor king, always weak and unsure of himself, lost a part of his dignity every day."[24]

The people of Paris, starving while hundreds of guests hunted at Versailles—that is indeed the picture of monstrous economic and social disparity that subsequent analysts have painted as the raw material of Revolution. Whether or not the monarchy was already making changes that would ease the lives of the poor and attenuate the social imbalance, the king's inadequacy to meet the political crisis on its simplest level was plain enough for even a high-born seventeen-year-old to see.

Once again, as on July 14, the people rose up, only this time it was a mob of women. On the morning of October 5, 5,000 women gathered at the City Hall in Paris; they forced their way inside, procured arms, and enjoined the National Guard to accompany them. They marched to Versailles, a day's journey on foot, to demand that bread be made available in Paris and at a reasonable price. This action inaugurated and carried out largely by women led to the immediate result of capturing the king, of removing the royal family permanently from Versailles and bringing them as virtual prisoners to Paris.

Historians have judged the "October Days" as the single most significant activity undertaken by women during the Revolution. Subsistence riots had always provided French women with a form of political expression, but this time it went far beyond their immediate demands for bread. Acting as a group, the women of October proved themselves to be as strong-willed and as fierce as their male counterparts who had made history on July 14. Eyewitnesses—both men and women—have left us graphic accounts of the women's march, reflecting a double fear of mob rule and the rule of women. Male witnesses expressed an archetypal fear of women as hysterical furies, while women witnesses did not want to be identified with those furies in any way. Perhaps they sensed in themselves the female rage they took pains to deny publicly.

Mme de Ménerville, who had been renting a little country house at Boulogne, found herself unexpectedly "on the stage of the events that took place between Paris and Versailles."[25] She heard the menacing sound of the alarm bell, "the cries of the cannibals who were streaming to Versailles by every route, those women drunk with brandy, avid for blood, who wanted to burn aristocrats' houses on the way and drag along everyone who had been brought there by curiosity or by fear."[26] This overwrought depiction of the October march, while undoubtedly based on the author's memories, was colored by her ultraroyalist sentiments and her highly anxious temperament, both evident throughout her memoirs.

When the enraged mob of women reached Versailles, a small group of delegates was chosen to present their demands to the king. The Duchesse de Tourzel recalled the welcome her sovereign accorded them:

> The fishmonger women cried out that they wanted to speak to the King . . . and they could be calmed only by admitting a dozen of them to the presence of that unfortunate prince. His goodness disarmed them, and their opinions were so changed by the time they returned to their companions that they ran the risk of being the victims of their fury.[27]

The King of France was able to calm the fury of a dozen women; he was less successful with the remaining 5,000, who sent the delegates back to demand a written document that would guarantee subsidized bread in Paris.

During the night, this calm was replaced by violence. While the king and queen and their children slept, some members of the mob penetrated into the château, indeed, as far as the queen's antechamber, and massacred the guards before her door. The queen scarcely had time to escape to the king's apartment.

Mme de Staël, also at the château during the night of October 5-6, woke to the clamor of the crowd demanding that the king and his family be removed to Paris. The queen, "pale, but dignified," appeared on the balcony overlooking the Marble Courtyard filled with people bearing arms.

> One could see in the Queen's physiognomy what she feared. Nevertheless, she advanced without hesitating, with her two children serving as safe-guards.
>
> The multitude appeared moved seeing the Queen as a mother; . . . those who that very night had perhaps wanted to assassinate her, shouted her name to the skies. [28]

According to other accounts, the crowd insisted that the royal children be removed and that the queen appear there alone, which she did. Victorine de Chastenay remembered the words "No children!" and then the cries of "Long live the Queen!" after Marie-Antoinette had sent her son and daughter away.29 The queen's courage, here as in other terrifying circumstances, has been attested to by numerous memorialists of both genders. That a mob composed primarily of women should become softened by the sight of the queen with her two children stands to reason; had they not come to demonstrate on behalf of sustenance for their own children? But how can we understand their even greater applause for her reappearance without her royal offspring? This suggests another level of psychology: the queen's heroic response to the threat of violence may have evoked some primordial sense of female bonding. At that moment, the "Austrian," the ultimate representative of the "other," given Marie-Antoinette's foreign birth and royal privilege, may have been perceived as just another vulnerable woman.

Shortly thereafter the royal family began its final return from Versailles to Paris. The Duchesse de Tourzel elegiacally recalled the moment of departure:

> The King entered the carriage at one thirty in the afternoon, leaving with regret the palace he would never see again. He was at the back of the carriage, with the Queen and Madame, his daughter. I was in the front, holding on my knees Monseigneur le Dauphin. . . . What a contrast between their conduct and that of their ancestors!30

Here as elsewhere the Duchesse offers the view from inside; history is made up of seating arrangements within the royal carriage. From the outside, Victorine de Chastenay observed a jubilant crowd accompanying the royal family on its journey back to Paris:

> That odious multitude finally started off to Paris. Some of them carried several loaves of bread stuck on their spears or bayonets; but what was most unbelievable is that the heads of the Queen's guards preceded them.31

Whereas later republican historians, like the great Jules Michelet, described this event as a "festival" with loaves of bread and poplar branches held high by exultant women and children, Mme de Chastenay renders the vision of a terrified bystander, whose eye saw only the blood-stained heads of the guards, which had been severed from their bodies and coiffed at the nearby town of Sèvres in a grotesque gesture of "horrible refinement."32

Her account follows the royal family to the Hôtel de Ville in Paris where the mayor "offered a few sentences to celebrate what he called that happy day, and the family who was without a doubt the most unfortunate in France went to take its rest at the Tuileries."33 After the bloodshed of July 14 and October 5-6, Victorine de Chastenay abandoned her previously held liberal sentiments. Indeed, few members of the privileged classes expressed any sympathy with the mob of women clamoring for bread at the gates of Versailles.

One notable exception was Mme Guénard in her "memoirs" of the Princesse de Lamballe, Marie-Antoinette's most intimate friend. It was not uncommon in the eighteenth and nineteenth centuries for books labeled as memoirs to be written by someone other than the designated subject; thus Elisabeth Guénard, a prolific novelist, had no scruples in titling her work *The Memoirs of Madame la Princesse de Lamballe*, though it was clearly a biography written in the third person rather than a first-person autobiography.34 But when the author came to the episode of the women's march on Versailles, she abandoned the biographer's more distant stance and allowed her personal emotions to break through. By tapping her own maternal sentiments, Mme Guénard was able to find empathy for those poor mothers driven to extreme means to keep their children alive.

> You have to be a mother and have heard your children ask for bread you cannot give them to know the level of despair to which this misfortune can bring you. . . . With children who are hungry and who ask repeatedly and tearfully for food—it seems as if each sound issuing from their chests parched by poverty is the point of a dagger striking their mother's heart. She cannot bear it, and her pain makes her capable of doing anything because she sees nothing, feels nothing, except the imperious law of nature commanding her not to let those perish who owe her their birth.[35]

Aside from this one example, upper-class women writers expressed no sense of solidarity with their beleaguered sisters at Versailles. The barriers erected by class, wealth, and conventional notions of "feminine" behavior did not tumble at the castle gates. Of course, those women of the working class who participated in the march from Paris viewed their actions differently. Their perspective is not found in anything so grand as "memoirs," but it can be gleaned from a seven-page pamphlet titled *An Event at Paris and Versailles* published in the winter of 1789-90 and signed by "The Woman Chéret." It begins:

> Marie-Louise Lenoël, the woman Chéret, residing in the rue de Vaugirard, then occupied at Passy with a highly lucrative market, abruptly left her virtuous mother, abandoned the profit she was about to make, and joined the Lady Citizenesses who were going to Versailles.[36]

Writing alternately in the third and first person, the Citizeness Chéret describes the relentless procession of a resolute female cadre led by a few male heroes of the Bastille. She notes the welcome of the Versailles bourgeoisie, who greeted their arrival "with acclamations of joy, congratulated them on their arrival, and begged them to work for the general good." Selected as one of the deputation of twelve, the Woman Chéret was led with her sister citizenesses into the National Assembly where she refused to be cowed by its supercilious members. She was proud to report that the twelve female deputies obtained the promise that (1) a new prohibition would be laid upon the exportation of grain, (2) wheat would be sold at an honest price affordable to all citizens, and (3) meat would cost only eight sous a pound. With these promises wrested from the Assembly and the king, the Woman Chéret proclaimed that the king merited more than ever the title of "Restorer of the French Nation" which had been bestowed upon him earlier that year, in July, after the fall of the Bastille. She concluded her account with self-satisfied praise for the women "covered with glory" at Versailles and received like "liberators" upon their return to Paris. Clearly the Citizeness Chéret looked back on the October days with great pride. Unlike the upper-class memoirists eager to disassociate themselves from unseemly female behavior, Marie-Louise Lenoël Chéret wanted her contemporaries to know that she had participated decisively in the making of history.

A quite different story of collective female action during the early Revolution concerns the Charity Maternelle (Maternal Charity), a philanthropic organization founded in 1788 to help poor women care for their babies. Related by Mme de Ménerville and her sister

Angélique de Maussion, the story offers a fascinating glimpse of traditional upper-class women's culture responding to the domestic needs of the poor.

Mme de Ménerville and Mme de Maussion were in a good position to observe the workings of the Maternal Charity because their mother, Mme Fougeret, was its founder. With the number of abandoned babies greatly on the increase in the period preceding the Revolution—an estimated 40,000 a year—Mme Fougeret set out to create an organization that would subsidize the care of infants who might otherwise be left at church doors by their destitute mothers.[37]

Mme Fougeret found allies among other powerful women of her class; her honorary patron was none other than the queen. During the winter of 1789-90, with the royal family as quasi prisoners in the Tuileries, Marie-Antoinette called the members of the Maternal Charity to meetings in her still-sumptuous rooms. Mme de Ménerville vividly recaptured the scene:

> I shall never forget the first meeting which took place in the Tuileries January 5, 1790. It was the night before Virginia's birth [Mme de Ménerville's second daughter]. . . . I can still see Madame Necker, very close to the Queen; . . . women from the Court astonished by the people who had been admitted near them; women from the world of banking and finance, adorned and smiling at the change that permitted them to be seated in the presence of the Queen. . . .
>
> Her Majesty wanted two women, the youngest in the group, to give a report. . . . I read, as best I could, two little résumés I had written. The Queen was so good as to come over to me, take me by the hand, encourage me, speak to me about my mother with such praise, about me with such goodness, about my condition (I gave birth the next day) with such interest that it broke my heart.[38]

The birth of her own daughter the day after the meeting merits only a parenthesis in Mme de Ménerville's memoirs, yet that fact surely floods the narrative with a double maternal cast. Aroused by motherly empathy, women like de Ménerville translated their own pregnancies into public works that helped alleviate the conditions of less fortunate mothers. The benefactresses made of their organization an exceptional success story. Between May 1788 and July 1791, the Maternal Charity supported 991 children and assisted almost 1,000 women to give birth at home, of whom only 2 died. By contrast, in the hospitals of Paris (except for the superior Hôtel-Dieu) the mortality rate for birthing mothers was 55 percent.

The reasons for their success were linked to an ideology of child care that was part and parcel of the Revolution itself: the ideology of maternal breast-feeding. Subsidized mothers were required to make a commitment to nurse their children themselves and to raise them at home on their own milk. This code of conduct reflected the widespread influence of Rousseau, who had claimed in *Emile* that a general social reform would result if mothers nursed their own babies, as opposed to the common practice of sending them out to wet-nurses.[39] The Maternal Charity incorporated this Rousseauist doctrine in its entirety, asserting that breast-feeding would "tighten family bonds, attach mothers to their duties, force them to remain in their homes, and thus preserve them from all sorts of disorders."[40] Liberty, equality, fraternity, to be sure, but breast-feeding above all: mother's milk flows alongside the patriot's blood in the mythology of the French Revolution.

In both instances of female collective action—in the women's march on Versailles and in the work of the Maternal Charity—women were motivated by what philosopher Sara Ruddick calls "maternal thinking," defined as "acting in the interest of preserving and maintaining life."[41] Some poor women took to the streets to demand bread for their children, whereas others, in order to feed their newborns, promised to stay in their homes at a far remove from street demonstrations. Upper-class women, who condemned the political intervention of their working-class sisters at Versailles, were willing to subsidize them as domestic breast-feeders. Whatever their differences, and they were legion, the one ideal that most women from all classes held in common was their sense of responsibility for the preservation of their children and other dependents.

When women looked back at the Revolution in their memoirs, they endowed their personal maternal activities with historical significance. To have breast-fed their babies, to have saved them from want, sickness, or an assassin's bullet, to have raised them according to republican or royalist principles—these were seen as integral to the revolutionary drama. For one thing, they were never quite sure where their personal histories ended and national history began.

They had good reason to be confused by what historian Lynn Hunt has called "the unstable boundaries of the French Revolution" in reference to the increasing politicization of private life between 1789 and 1794.[42] Mme de Ménerville's apology at the beginning of her narrative, echoing the position of many other women memoirists, poignantly expresses this blurring of public and private space, especially between one's personal history of survival and national history. "I do not pretend to write the history of the French Revolution," she wrote. "I want to speak only of myself and those close to me. But how can I avoid recounting the events whose fatal influence on the destiny of my family will not cease to be felt until a single descendant no longer remains?"[43]

The collage of texts presented in this chapter was pieced from memories of 1789, memories that derive from highly personal experiences, such as pregnancy and sickness, as well as such highly public events as stately processions and unruly mobs, and often some mixture of both. In each case, a "historic" event was filtered through the memoirist's sensibility and colored by her temperament. And for each of these women, regardless of whether she was forty-three in 1789, as in the case of Mme de Genlis, or only five, as in the case of the Duchesse d'Abrantès, 1789 would remain in her memory as a watershed year dramatically dividing the stream of life.

In the following chapters, many of the women we have encountered only in cameo appearances will return as lead players in their own life stories.

The Duchesse de Tourzel, governess of the royal children, and the Dauphin Louis XVII.
By Danloux. © *Harlingue-Viollet*

3

—————

THE FALL OF THE ROYAL FAMILY: WITNESSED BY THE DUCHESSE DE TOURZEL

AS THE LAST GOVERNESS OF LOUIS XVI and Marie-Antoinette's children, the Duchesse de Tourzel witnessed at close hand the royal family's downfall. She shared their final days at Versailles, their forced move to Paris, their abortive flight from France. In 1792, she experienced the mob's invasion of the Tuileries Palace on June 20, and the decisive insurrection of August 10. She was with her sovereigns when they were first incarcerated in the Temple tower, only leaving their side to be transferred to another prison. No one was better placed to observe the private life of the royal family as it descended the rungs of misfortune, and no one undertook the memorialist's mission with greater dedication. Decades after the deaths of the king, the queen, the king's sister Madame Elisabeth, and the little dauphin who had been Mme de Tourzel's special charge, she retired to a convent to write her memoirs. Jean Chalon, who edited the 1986 edition of this work, calls it the "history of the Revolution seen through the glasses of the Restoration and the eyes of a great and powerful lady."[1]

Of all the women's memoirs on the Revolution, Mme de Tourzel's work comes closest to the conventional model of a self-effacing witness chronicling the lives of the great. Without concealing her unswerving royalist convictions, the Duchess stays properly in the background except for the moments when, as a participant in historical events, it is appropriate for her to come forward. She conceives of "historical events" as any happening within the royal family, be it the first communion of the royal princess or the meals taken by the little dauphin. As for her own history before her tenure as the royal governess, the Duchess says nary a word.

She does not tell us that she was born into the distinguished de Croÿ-Havré family in 1749, a fifth and youngest child, and that she married the Marquis de Tourzel, scion of an equally weighty family, in 1764. Of this union, five children were born; the youngest, Pauline, figures prominently in Mme de Tourzel's memoirs and also authored her own under her married name, the Comtesse de Béarn.[2] Mme de Tourzel's husband, who had been *le grand prévôt* of France, died in a riding accident at court in 1786. Both she and her husband had been highly respected for their devotion to their family, their loyalty to the monarchy, and their deep religious faith. From all accounts, their high moral tone was conspicuous among courtiers better known for their frivolity. Mme Campan, Marie-Antoinette's first lady-in-waiting, praised Mme de Tourzel as "a mother with an irreproachable conduct, who had directed the education of her own daughters with the greatest success."[3]

Mme de Tourzel was appointed to replace the former royal governess, Mme de Polignac, who had gone into exile with the first band of émigrés in July 1789. The new governess's stay at Versailles would be brief. The mob of 5,000 Parisian women congregating at the château on October 5 would not return without "the Baker and the Baker's wife." With the dauphin on her lap, Mme de Tourzel rode away from the colossal castle that, for more than a century, had epitomized absolute power. In Paris, the Tuileries Palace was unprepared to receive its new occupants: with no guards there to protect them, the Duchess barricaded the doors to the dauphin's room with furniture and spent the first night seated beside his bed. In the morning the Tuileries terraces were filled with a crowd clamoring to see the king. "The royal family, and even the Princesses, were obliged to put on the national cockade and show themselves over and over again to the people."[4] Writing long after this event, the Duchess still sounds indignant at the insults visited upon the royal family and the "Princesses"—Louis XVI's elderly aunts—obliged to wear the revolutionary ribbons and to show themselves like marionettes to the public. Henceforth they would live surrounded by the crowd and be subject to its passionate outbursts.

Nonetheless, according to the Duchess's recollection, the year 1790 began on a relatively encouraging note. A deputation from the National Assembly, led by its president Jean Nicolas Desmeuniers, came to present its respects on New Year's Day; the president offered his good wishes to the king and queen, the latter flanked by her two children. He was, the narrator maintains, so moved at their sight that he could not hide his feelings.

> Indeed, nothing was more touching than to see that Queen surrounded by her two charming children. One, still too young to feel the misfortunes that menaced him, bore on his face the stamp of happiness and joy; the young princess, at an age when one should know only those two sentiments, was already beginning the career of sorrow that she has since traveled with so much courage, sweetness, and sensibility. The King had a very special predilection for her; and though he was not demonstrative, he never missed an occasion to reveal the tenderness he felt for her.[5]

Here, as elsewhere, Mme de Tourzel presents the king in the most flattering light: the sentimental father with a soft spot for his daughter, the good prince concerned with his people's well-being, the apostle of harmony and peace.

But peace was clearly not in store for France. The Duchess recalls the upheaval wrought by "brigands" who pillaged châteaux and committed "all sorts of disorders."[6] She reproaches the National Assembly for turning a deaf ear to those popular outbursts of violence, preoccupied instead with projects seen as hostile to the monarchy. She never misses an opportunity to chastise the Assembly deputies, individually and collectively. In her mind, the revolutionary world had consisted of two opposing camps, those who had wished to destroy the monarchy and those, like herself, who had continued to serve the king. The only criterion for judging good and evil was loyalty to the Crown. Her memoirs show no sympathy for the legitimate grievances of the people or the new political ideas that would ultimately transform the face of France.

It was in the incendiary atmosphere of the spring of 1790 that the eleven-year-old daughter of Louis XVI and Marie-Antoinette—the princess known as Madame Royale—made her first communion. Before leaving for the parish church of Saint-Germain l'Auxerrois, she took leave of her parents in an emotional scene dramatically recorded by her governess:

> Madame fell at the feet of the King and Queen to ask for their blessing. The King . . . spoke to her in the most touching manner of the great act she was about to accomplish, and added as he held her in his arms: "Pray, my daughter, for France and for us; the prayers of the innocent can soften celestial anger." The young princess broke into tears, could not say a word, and climbed into the carriage.[7]

The Duchess paints a family picture in the style of eighteenth-century bourgeois paintings—the daughter throwing herself at her parents' feet, the father giving his blessing and invoking divine authority. At the church, the Princess manifested "the most sincere devotion" during a ceremony marked by "the greatest simplicity." Yet for all its domestic flavor and even the queen's "incognito" in church, one wonders how private or apolitical an occasion it could have been when located directly across from the Louvre. Who would have remained hard-hearted at the sight of an eleven-year-old dressed in the virginal white of communion and participating in a ritual so deeply embedded in French history?

During the first six months of 1790, the National Assembly passed numerous decrees that radically altered French society: the suppression of primogeniture and solely masculine inheritance, the abolition of a hereditary nobility, the sale of church property, the establishment of a civil constitution for the clergy. Mme de Tourzel experienced each decree as a desecration. Like her sovereign, she was particularly grieved by the decree of May 22 that gave the Assembly, rather than the king, the right to decide over matters of war and peace. In reviving the political debate surrounding that decision, she scorns the conduct of deputies, like LaFayette, who voted in its favor. She describes LaFayette's exit from the Assembly after the vote and his passage across the Tuileries terrace, accompanied by a boisterous crowd crying "Long live the Nation!" Inside the Tuileries Palace the Queen of France, "in order to avoid hearing that constant noise beneath her window," was obliged, like any other woman, to retreat to less accessible quarters.[8]

During the summer of 1790 the great event was the celebration of the Festival of the Federation, set for July 14 by the Constituent Assembly. (The National Assembly had become the Constituent Assembly on July 7, 1789; it would become the Legislative Assembly on October 1, 1791.) On the first anniversary of Bastille Day, fourteen thousand "federates" were sent to Paris by all the provincial National Guard units to celebrate the new constitution under preparation. Mme de Tourzel's account of this event bears witness to the revolutionary zeal that had invaded France. Despite her personal aversion for republicans, she was obliged to recognize the sense of solidarity expressed by individuals from all walks of life. Many wielded picks and pushed wheelbarrows so as to transform the ground of the Champ-de-Mars into a huge amphitheater.

> Everyone wanted to have a part of the action. . . . Even the ladies had themselves driven there in carriages so they could help fill the wheelbarrows; and everyone who might have passed quietly by the Champ-deMars without stopping ran the risk of being insulted. . . .
>
> There were workers, bourgeois men and women, Carthusian monks and others from different orders, military men, beautiful ladies, men and women from every class and all stations of society. . . . From time to time one heard the repeated cries of "Long live the Nation! Aristocrats to the lantern-posts!" and "ça ira" etc. etc. , labeled patriotic hymns by ladies impassioned of the Revolution. Several of them, even from the highest social class, became so fatigued that they fell sick, and finished by being victims of their patriotic zeal.[9]

If the Duchess's description is tinged with irony, she cannot dispute the widespread optimism associated with the spectacle of the Federation. It began with an impressive procession of Assembly members led by their president and followed by the king and the royal family marching solemnly between two rows of colorful flags. When everyone was in their assigned places, Charles Talleyrand, the bishop of Autun, blessed the flags and celebrated mass. Lafayette, major general of the event, ascended to the altar and gave the signal for the pledge; the king pronounced it out loud and the president of the National Assembly repeated it with a chorus of "three hundred thousand voices." The Duchess does not fail to note that on several occasions "the Queen lifted Monseigneur the dauphin in her arms to show him to the people and the army, who burst out with demonstrations of joy and love for the King and the royal family."[10] For once, the Duchess admits, the crowd, the elected government, and the monarchy acted in harmony, and made of this day one of the great moments of the Revolution.

The following day, the federal representatives presented themselves to the king in a spirit of reconciliation, and the royal family responded with gratitude by dining with them in public. The royal governess notes that the dauphin, "who was still too young, ate his meals in his own room according to his own schedule." But she also adds, proudly, that the federates took great pleasure in seeing the dauphin, who appeared frequently on a little balcony. "He would say a little word to one or the other, and then return to play in the salon, where one could easily see him."[11]

The federal delegates invited the king to come to visit them in their regions of origin. "We shall certainly know how to defend you against your enemies," he was told by the deputies from Dauphiny. Those from Normandy promised they would "always be faithful to their King."[12] The Duchess's conclusion that the king should have profited from such a favorable opportunity to leave Paris is also the judgment of history.[13]

IN 1790 THE KING STILL ENJOYED great prestige and personal liberties, including that of traveling a few miles to the town of Saint-Cloud to take the country air. The little dauphin, according to his governess, enjoyed the less-restricted life at Saint-Cloud and profited both in mind and body from his time away from Paris. She describes him at five years old as having "a natural taste for study" and "a good memory." His governess and tutors, charged with the education of the heir to the throne, supervised his moral deportment as well as his formal lessons:

> We accustomed him to respond by himself to the compliments that were addressed to him, and we preferred to see him give short answers than to suggest ideas that would not have been his own. It was enough to correct them when they were not right. Sometimes that made him quite angry, but he ended up finding a way to respond and got used to saying things on his own that were courteous and kind.[14]

It is certainly the voice of the pedagogue speaking here, an enlightened educator influenced by those eighteenth-century theorists favoring naturalness, sincerity, and the development of one's character through experience rather than rote memory or prescribed rules of conduct. Still, the governess who had earned the nickname of "Madame Severity" was not afraid to correct him from time to time, nor was the dauphin afraid to show the temper of a five-year-old.

Paris, only a few miles away from Saint-Cloud, was a political hothouse fueled by incendiary newspaper articles that attacked the monarchy, the nobility, and the clergy. Political journals sprang up overnight and flourished in France as never before.[15] The historian Robert Darnton estimates that, in the first six months of 1789, 250 new newspapers were founded; this reached a high point the following year, when there were 335 daily newspapers in Paris.[16] The year 1789 also witnessed the appearance of the "fisherwomen pamphlets"—libels written in the voice of the notoriously outspoken female fishmongers—which viciously lampooned the queen, the clergy, the nobility, and everything else detested in the Old Regime.[17]

The revolutionary theater, too, was another ardent battlefield. It ranged from burlesque comedies designed to entertain illiterate crowds, to licentious caricatures of the royal family and its courtiers, to serious drama preaching republican virtues. Yet many actors did not forget their former royal pensions and privileged relationship with the king; several even dared to demonstrate their loyalty, as Mme de Tourzel recounts in the following anecdote:

> They were giving a performance of *Iphigenia* at the Opera; the chorus singing "Let us honor our Queen" was roundly applauded by the royalists, who cried out "encore." There were several boos and murmurs from the opposing party. . . . The opponents' displeasure increased when [the actor] Lainez allowed himself to say: "I think, gentlemen, that every good Frenchman should love the King and Queen" . . . following this remark he was thrown a laurel wreath. . . .
>
> Two days later . . . the revolutionaries, who had bought up all the seats in the orchestra . . . did not let Lainez act until he had trampled under his feet the wreath he had received earlier.[18]

The hubbub around the actor Lainez was part of the general uproar associated with the Assembly's decree requiring priests to pledge allegiance to a civil constitution. Those who refused—and they would be in the majority—would be called "refractories." The king resisted for a long time before he approved this decree, but on December 26 he resigned himself to sanctioning it. Mme de Tourzel describes the events that subsequently took place in the churches during the winter of 1790-91 when the priests were scheduled to take the pledge:

The churches were filled with brigands of the two sexes. . . . and you cannot imagine the scandalous scene. It was greater at Saint-Sulpice than anywhere else. . . . When he [the parish priest] returned to the sacristy after refusing to take the pledge, they all threatened to strike him; one struck him with a fist, another put a pistol to his cheek. The Maréchal de Mouchy, who was at the mass, never left the priest, and even warded off several blows that were destined for him. Monsieur Bailly [the mayor] arrived as usual when the danger was over.[19]

It is unlikely that the Duchess had seen with her own eyes the tumult at Saint-Sulpice, or that she had been present at many of the public places she evokes so convincingly in her memoirs. Still she writes *as if she had been there.* That was her right as a memorialist according to the conventions of her time. And since she writes well, with passionate conviction, she succeeds in creating the illusion of an eyewitness account.

The controversy over the clergy led to very grave consequences for the royal family. Intending to travel to Saint-Cloud to celebrate Easter there with a refractory priest, the king was prevented by the National Guard, who refused passage to his coach, in defiance of the National Guard's own leader, Lafayette. Once again seated in the carriage with the dauphin and Madame Royale, the Duchesse de Tourzel had front-row access to the stage of action. "I was witness to the horrible scene that took place on that cruel day. The National Guard grenadiers, aroused to a sense of danger by the King's departure, revolted, placed themselves in front of the horses, and declared that they would not let the King depart. Messieurs Bailly and Lafayette tried in vain to vanquish their resistance."[20]

According to the Duchess, that day, April 18, 1791, marked the beginning of the king's plans to flee France. By June he would undertake with the members of his family and a few trusted attendants, among them Mme de Tourzel, that fateful flight to Varennes which, more than any other single event, turned the people against him.

The story of this journey commands center position in the Duchess's memoirs, dominating the twelfth of her twenty-four chapters like the peak of a five-act tragedy. The author musters all her literary talent to narrate this decisive event. She begins with the simple, intimate details of her role in the secret departure.

To eliminate any idea of a departure from the minds of my staff, I told them to draw my bath the next day. . . .

Much earlier I had taken the precaution of having my daughter Pauline make a little linen dress and a bonnet so as to dress Monseigneur the dauphin as a little girl if circumstances made that change necessary. We used it with success. When the carriage arrived, the Queen herself went to look to see if everything was calm in the courtyard, and not seeing anyone, she embraced me, saying: "Madame, The King and I put in your hands, with the utmost confidence, all that is dearest to us in the world; everything is ready, leave at once."[21]

The driver of the coach, Count Axel de Fersen (whose reputed liaison with the queen goes unmentioned by the Duchess) had been preparing the royal family's flight for quite some time. He had obtained the Russian passport in the name of the Baronne de Korff destined for Mme de Tourzel and the members of her entourage—that is, the dauphin and Madame Royale disguised as her two daughters, and the king, queen, and the king's sister Madame Elisabeth disguised respectively as her valet, chambermaid, and the children's nanny. It was the Count who drove the king as far as the town of Claye, where they planned to take a relay coach to the border.

Nothing went as planned. The Duc de Choiseul, chosen to lead the first detachment of troops charged with escorting the royal family, was not at the designated rendezvous. The Duchess excused him in her memoirs on the grounds that he had not taken into consideration the unforeseeable incidents that had delayed the king's coach by two hours. But others have been more severe in judging Choiseul. The modern biographer Jean Chalon attributes the failure of the plan, first to "the Duc de Choiseul's inconsistency," and then to "the thoughtlessness of Léonard," Marie-Antoinette's hairdresser.[22] The latter, considered indispensable by the queen even on a flight for her life, took the liberty of dismissing some of the soldiers waiting at Varennes for the royal party!

Recognized at Varennes and obliged to spend the night there, the members of the royal family found themselves in the most embarrassing situation. The king, we are told, "seeing that pretence was useless, declared that he was the King, that he had left Paris to get away from the daily insults they took pleasure in heaping upon him, and that he was not planning to leave the kingdom." While the king and queen struggled for words with the local officials, the royal children, "overwhelmed by fatigue, fell asleep immediately. Their sleep was tranquil and calm, and the contrast between their situation and that of their unfortunate parents was truly heart-rending."[23] Here as elsewhere Mme de Tourzel has one eye on public history and the other on domestic realities.

Drawn into a situation that could not have been more humiliating—indeed, one that resembled nothing so much as the many contemporary theatrical productions and broadsides that buffooned the king and queen—the royal couple "employed every possible means to touch the hearts" of their captors, and to "revive the ancient love of Frenchmen for their King." But they were talking to "hearts of bronze," hardened by two years of antiroyalist sentiments and the king's own colossal blunders.[24]

All along the return trip to Paris, French citizens hurled insults at the royal coach. The time when they had cried out "Long live the King" and accompanied him joyfully on his route was now past history. He had been caught in an act of treason and the people cried out "Long live the Nation!" and other, saucier slurs. At each stop where he had to descend from the carriage to receive the keys to the city, mayors "permitted themselves to reproach him sharply for his departure from Paris."[25] He was treated like a naughty boy, a runaway prisoner.

On the return trip, they encountered the three commissioners from the Assembly sent to bring the king back to Paris: Maubourg, Barnave, an. Mme de Tourzel judged their conduct as if they were engaged in a comedy of manners. "Monsieur de Maubourg conducted himself perfectly during the trip. He was very respectful toward the King." Barnave, too, "was silent and respectful during the whole trip." But Pétion was "talkative and insolent," and behaved "with the most revolting familiarity." Barnave sat in the back "between the King and the Queen, who held Monseigneur the dauphin on her lap," while Madame Elisabeth, the Duchess, and Pétion were seated in the front, and the two women took turns holding Madame Royale on their knees. In these close conditions,

Barnave struck up a long conversation with Madame Elisabeth over the destiny of France. The Duchess's rendition of this scene evokes an atmosphere best described by the

French word *romanesque*, romantic as in fiction. Such was the force of the eighteenth-century novel that it bled into other texts whenever the opportunity arose. The Duchess's fine eye did not miss the tragicomic details of the scene awaiting them at the gate of Paris:

> Following the order of Monsieur de Lafayette, everyone had his head covered; he had also enjoined
> them to remain absolutely silent to show the King, he said, the feelings his trip had inspired. His orders
> were so strictly observed that several scullery-boys without hats covered their heads with their dirty,
> filthy handkerchiefs.[26]

This silent Parisian reception can be seen as a form of decoronation, with the use of head covers directly reversing the prior respectful practice of uncovering one's head in the presence of the king.

The flight provoked unprecedented hostile reactions to the monarchy.[27] Immediately following the king's return, the Legislative Assembly deliberated on the action it should take concerning the royal family and all those who had abetted their escape. Mme de Tourzel was retained in the dauphin's study and forbidden to speak to anyone. She waited for the moments when the queen or Madame Elisabeth went through this room on their way to mass and were able to slip her a few secret messages. In this way and by reading the newspaper *Le Moniteur* at a later date, she was able to reconstruct the Assembly's proceedings.

Three weeks after her return, the Duchess was interrogated. A bailiff conducted her from the dauphin's quarters to her own where she made her deposition. Returning to the dauphin's apartment through the National Guard room, she prepared herself for taunts and insults: "I assumed an air that was more self-assured than what I really felt in the depth of my soul. . . . but I owe it to truth to say that the most profound silence was observed as I passed and repassed."[28] A self-assured air: one would expect no less from "Madame Severity," whose upright demeanor apparently reduced the guardsmen to silence.

After its inquest into the flight to Varennes, the Assembly concluded, in the words of Robespierre, that the king had lost the confidence of the people. The Assembly chose to propagate the belief that the king had been abducted by émigré forces. But henceforth he would be a powerless hostage. He had only to sign, without the slightest protest, the Constitution adopted on September 3, 1791. The Duchess, having been granted her liberty, attended the public ceremony in which the king swore the oath prescribed by the Assembly. "He expressed the deepest desire to reap, as the fruit of the act he had just performed, the return of harmony and peace."[29]

This Constitution was badly received by the conservative deputies in the Assembly; to show their opposition, they withdrew from the hall before the king's arrival. It was badly received by the king's two brothers, the future Louis XVIII and the future Charles X, both enjoying their freedom in exile. It was badly received by the major European powers: Austria, Russia, Spain, Prussia, and Sweden. Yet the king, who "still fancied himself in a position of power in the shadow of the Constitution," was overheard by the Duchesse de Tourzel naively informing the queen that "he was going to do everything in his power to make the Constitution work."[30] This suggestion that the king no longer had any power at all is as close as Mme de Tourzel ever comes to criticizing Louis XVI's lack of political astuteness.

ON APRIL 20, 1792, WAR WAS DECLARED with Austria. The Assembly took exceptional measures: it ordered the deportation of all refractory priests and the creation of a corps of 20,000 National Guardsmen to protect Paris. Louis XVI vetoed these two decrees. At the news of these vetoes, the people rose up, and on June 20, 1792, a mob of armed citizens, commanded by the section chief General Antoine Santerre, appeared before the Assembly. The marchers included soldiers and civilians, men, women, and children, all armed with a variety of weapons and cymbals. A representative of the delegation read an oration that established the will of the people as superior to that of the king. At least 8,000 demonstrators paraded for two hours through the Assembly to the accompaniment of revolutionary music.[31] Afterward, they turned in the direction of the royal residence and invaded the Tuileries Palace. Mme de Tourzel offers a detailed description of that unforgettable day.

> The King, seeing that the doors were going to be forced open, wanted to go out to meet the factionists and try to control them by his presence. . . .
>
> Madame Elisabeth, seeing the danger the King was incurring, did not want to abandon him, and placed herself in the window opening. . . . It was then that she was taken for the Queen. Seeing the factionists move toward her as they cried out: "The Austrian, where is she? Her head! Her Head!" . . . she said to those around her these sublime words "Don't disillusion them; if they take me for the Queen, there may be time to save her."[32]

In the mythology of the French Revolution, the king's sister Madame Elisabeth appears as a saintly heroine. The queen, whose life Madame Elisabeth had tried to save by sacrificing her own, had been whisked off to the council room where General Santerre was parading "his horde." There Marie-Antoinette sat in front of a table, the dauphin on her right and Madame Royale on her left, listening to the insults of a menacing, "roaring crowd that inveighed against her continuously . . . The parade did not end until eight in the evening."[33]

These terrifying experiences were followed by a tearful family reunion. The queen and her children threw themselves at the king's feet. He embraced everyone and expressed to Madame Elisabeth "the most tender sensibility for all she had done for them during that horrible day."[34] Again the vision evoked by Mme de Tourzel is reminiscent of popular engravings and bourgeois drama where virtuous family members are reunited after a close escape from ugly villains. But once again the artistic models fall short in conveying the multilayered dimensions of a national epic in which the distinction between good and bad characters is not so clear-cut.

A month later, the Prussian army was poised to invade the province of Lorraine in order to protect the royal family from the kind of attack it had suffered on June 20. The Assembly declared "the nation in danger." On July 22, the alarm cannon sounded every hour of the day to announce war with the Prussians. The Assembly did everything possible to augment the number of soldiers; it sufficed for a man to be eighteen years old and five feet tall to enroll in the army. Frenchmen were forbidden to leave France. Riots broke out all over the South. In Bordeaux and Limoges, fanatic patriots assassinated several priests who had refused to swear allegiance to the civil Constitution. The Tuileries gardens were closed to the public. The royal family no longer ventured out.

On July 30, troops arrived from Marseilles with arms, baggage, and two cannons. The presence of the notoriously revolutionary Marseillais produced a groundswell of fervor among the people. From the time of the troops' arrival in Paris, Marie-Antoinette was harassed by insults and threats beneath her windows. The Queen of France was reduced to having her little dog sleep under her bed to alert her to the slightest danger.

On August 10, an insurrection organized with the complicity of Pétion, the mayor of Paris since June 15, was directed against the royal family. At the Tuileries, the king had at his disposal 900 Swiss guards, 200 gendarmes, 300 royalist gentlemen, and 2,000 National Guardsmen. The latter would cross over to the side of the insurgents. At ten o'clock in the morning, the king was persuaded to leave the Tuileries and place himself under the protection of the Assembly. After the departure of the royal family and its entourage, including Mme de Tourzel, the insurgents massacred 600 of the 900 Swiss guards, easily recognized by their red uniforms, and a large number of the gentlemen. They spared only the women.

Among those who escaped the massacre, Mme Campan, first lady-in-waiting to Marie-Antoinette, recalled the anguish of that bloody day: the carnage of the Swiss Guards outside the palace and the assassination of the king's gentlemen, whose bodies were then thrown out the windows. The women gathered in the queen's drawing room and all thought that they were on death's doorstep when, as Mme Campan tells it, "a long-bearded man appeared and called out on behalf of Pétion: 'Spare the women; don't dishonor the nation!' " Several minutes later, as she was running toward the stairway, Mme Campan brushed against death once more. A "horrible man from Marseilles" grabbed her, but someone cried out from the bottom of the stairs: "What are you doing there? . . . We don't kill women." The story continues:

> I was on my knees, my executioner released me and said: "Get up, you slut, the nation's letting you off." The coarseness of those words did not prevent me from suddenly experiencing an undescribable feeling which came almost as much from love of life as from the idea that I was going to see my son again and everything that was dear to me. . . . One rarely sees death so closely without experiencing it.[35]

Mme Campan's account of the August insurrection, like the rest of her memoirs, bears the distinct mark of her personality; she is spontaneous, quick-witted, and anecdotal, with an eye for the unexpected even in the midst of bloody tragedy. Where Mme de Tourzel imposes through relentless gravity and distant grandeur, Mme Cam-pan attracts through her unabashed partiality. No one, not even a "horrible man from Marseilles," would have called Mme de Tourzel a slut! And it is unlikely that Mme Campan would have been able to march through a room of National Guardsmen without provoking some kind of impudent response. Together the royal governess and the queen's first lady-in-waiting furnish complementary versions of the same saga, one resolutely epic, the other piquantly anecdotal.

Another memorialist, the Marquise de La Rochejaquelein, saw the August 10 insurrection from outside the Tuileries. Seven months pregnant, she crossed Paris on foot from the Champs-Elysées to the neighborhood of Saint-Germain with her first husband, the Marquis de Lescure. Disguised as a working-class woman, this highly placed aristocrat would succumb to mass hysteria and join the mob in screaming revolutionary slogans. The author is remarkably successful in rendering not only her frenzied personal emotions, but also the eerie vision of Paris at night lit up by the Tuileries in flames.

> Never in my life will the spectacle that presented itself to my eyes leave my head: on the right and left, there were the Champs-Elysées where we knew more than twelve hundred people had been killed that very day; there the densest obscurity prevailed. In front of us was the Tuileries on fire, from which we heard furious cries mixed with gun shot. . . .

> After having gone an enormous distance, we reached the Louvre. Monsieur de Lescure made me follow the streets which had the most people and which were the best lit. We rubbed elbows with all those people carrying spears, most of whom were drunk and howling. I had lost my head to such an extent that I started screaming with them with all my might: Long live the sans-culottes, burn, break the windows! and Monsieur de Lescure could not calm me down nor make me stop screaming. We found the Louvre, which was somber and solitary, and from there the Pont-Neuf bridge where there were quite a few people and a lot of noise. Finally we crossed over to the other side of the Seine.[36]

Mme de La Rochejaquelein had donned the garb of a working-class woman, for fear that any exterior sign of her class would have been dangerous. Was she exaggerating? Not if we are to believe another account, this one written by a true working-class woman. Marie-Victoire Monnard was living near the rue Saint Honore, "at the center of events and close enough to see everything." On the morning of August 10, 1792, a "patrol armed with bloody spears and sabres" made the rounds of the neighborhood, ordering everyone to close their shops.

> In less than three minutes, the shops were closed and the streets evacuated. . . . How many horrors I remember having seen through the blinds, among them, three sans-culottes holding a tall handsome man by the collar of his frock coat. This unfortunate person kept saying: "Take me to the section office," which they refused to do. . . . they gave him a blow on his forehead with the butt of a rifle and finished him off. They took his watch, his clothes, and left him dead.

Peering through the shop blinds, Marie-Victoire saw a further sight that she was reluctant to describe because it brought "shame to our sex." She saw "at least fifteen women, one after the other, climb up on this victim's cadaver, whose entrails were emerging from all sides, saying that they took pleasure in trampling aristocracy under their feet." For six hours, similar massacres took place before her eyes. "On that day in that neighborhood it was enough . . . for one to have been a little well-dressed to be suspected of aristocracy, and to be arrested, assassinated, and then robbed."

During the afternoon, Marie-Victoire was sent by her employer to the Tuileries "to find out what was happening." She saw about 300 cadavers in the street, and revolutionaries throwing from the broken windows of the palace the spoils of their pillage and "the men they had killed." She learned that the king and his family "had taken refuge in the bosom of the representatives of the Nation."[37]

Mme de Tourzel was part of the group taken with the royal family into custody by the Assembly. Within days they would all be sent to the tower of the Temple, originally a monastery belonging to the Knights Templar. Ever faithful to her sovereigns, Mme de Tourzel was ready to follow them to the death, but she had not anticipated that the queen would also ask for her daughter Pauline. She remembers her hesitation at this request:

> I was chilled by her proposition. . . . I trembled at the idea of exposing my daughter, so young and pretty, to the mercy of those madmen. . . .
>
> Monseigneur the dauphin and Madame Royale, who saw my moment of uncertainty, threw themselves at my neck and begged me earnestly to give them their dear Pauline. . . . It was impossible to resist such entreaties; I entrusted my daughter to the hands of Providence.[38]

This self-portrait of the Duchess torn between her loyalty to her sovereigns and her maternal sentiments is the only truly unguarded moment in the memoirs; here she removes her official mask and displays the torment of a mother. In the end, the Duchess's sense of duty and attachment to the royal family prevailed. She seems eager to justify her decision (what if Pauline had perished in captivity?) by designating the royal children, rather than the queen, as the persuasive parties. This suggests both her sensitivity to the children's pathetic situation, as well as their strong attachment to her daughter.

From Versailles to the Tuileries to the Temple—Mme de Tourzel describes these three years with a rare ability to capture both the epic and the commonplace. She notes that on the first night of their captivity, everyone pretended to eat for the sake of form, while the dauphin, seated on her lap, fell asleep in the act of finishing his soup. His governess was always astonished by the boy's facility to fall asleep under the worst possible circumstances.

Their quarters in the Temple tower were adequate if rudimentary: two rooms for the queen, the Princesse de Lamballe, the dauphin, Mme de Tourzel, and Pauline; on another level were lodgings for the king, his guards, and Madame Elisabeth, the latter installed in a "horribly dirty" kitchen.

They established a regular schedule: a morning meeting in the queen's room, meals at designated hours in the space that had been converted into a dining room, a walk in the garden at five o'clock, some reading provided by a little library. But even this restricted life with its semblance of normalcy was short-lived; barely a week after their arrival the royal governess was awakened in the middle of the night to be conducted, with the queen's entourage, to City Hall:

> We got dressed and presented ourselves to the Queen, in whose hands I placed that dear little prince; his bed was carried into her room without his even waking up. . . . Madame Royale was stunned and greatly distressed to see us taken away. Madame Elisabeth arrived from her room and joined the Queen in encouraging us. We embraced those august princesses for the last time.[39]

From this day forth the Duchess was able to express her loyalty to her sovereigns only from a distance. The spotlight shifts from the royal family to the narrator, her daughter, and the queen's beloved friend, the Princesse de Lamballe, carried off to the Prison de la Force, where their story takes on the overtones of a gothic novel. Three female victims are thrown to the mercy of the people of Paris, a volatile mob whipped into violent action by demagogues such as Jean-Paul Marat. Frenzied crowds provide the backdrop to the hasty trials and gory executions that proliferate in Parisian town halls and prisons. Bloodthirsty villains and mysterious saviors—individuals sharply drawn as extreme representatives of good and evil—appear as in a Dickensian novel. A macabre fate is in store for the Princesse de Lamballe during the September prison massacres, but by a series of miraculous vicissitudes, a happy ending awaits the Duchess and her daughter.

Mme de Tourzel recalls the first days in prison as a time of great intimacy between the three women; they had "but one heart and one mind." They tried to keep busy by reading and taking care of their room. The hierarchy of rank did not disappear altogether, since Mme de Tourzel and Pauline had to keep watch over the Princess, who was subject to falling sickness, probably epileptic attacks. Yet, the Duchess remarks that the Princess did not have any nervous attacks in prison, and that "she had not been in such good health for a long time."[40] One wonders whether her nervous condition was somehow kept in check by the probability of imminent death.

The Duchess makes no secret of how difficult it was for the three of them to endure the atmosphere of a prison designated mainly for prostitutes. She disdainfully recalls the "scoundrels and hussies who made abominable remarks and sang detestable songs; the least chaste ears would have been offended by everything they continuously heard, night and day." But soon the three prisoners faced an ordeal of infinitely greater magnitude. Two weeks after their incarceration, on Saturday, September 2, François the jail-keeper told them not to leave their cell: "The foreigners are advancing and that has made everyone anxious in Paris."[41]" Indeed, with the capitulation of Verdun, troops of Austrians, Prussians, and French émigrés had penetrated into France, leading to mass hysteria among certain elements of the French population, all of which would culminate in the September massacres.

The narrator makes this bloodbath the climax of her memoirs. One by one, her companions will be disposed of until she, alone, stands in the spotlight and is judged. In telling this story, she borrows from the novel a number of narrative strategies, including the use of dialogue and the suspenseful withholding of information. The reader follows the eye and ear of the narrator as she recalls the grating sound of the prison door opening one night to reveal the figure of a well-dressed stranger. Following the conventions of fiction, Mme de Tourzel reconstructs their dialogue with a maximum of economy and mystery:

> Approaching Pauline's bed, he said to her:
>
> "Mademoiselle de Tourzel, get dressed immediately and follow me." "What do you want with my daughter?" I asked him with great emotion.
>
> "That isn't your concern, Madame. She must get up and follow me." "Obey him, Pauline. I hope Heaven will protect you."[42]

Thus Pauline de Tourzel escaped from the Prison de la Force, carried off by an unknown man who would return later to save her mother as well.

On Sunday the Princess and the Duchess added special prayers to the ones they habitually recited. Climbing up on the Princess's bed, from which they could view what was happening in the street, they saw "a considerable gathering at the prison door." At the other window overlooking the courtyard, the situation was no more reassuring: "Dismayed prisoners were in a stupor; and a profound silence prevailed, like the harbinger of death." About eleven o'clock, the Princesse de Lamballe was summoned from their room, and Mme de Tourzel followed her, although, as she remarks parenthetically, she herself had not yet been called. They found in the records office a court set up to judge the prisoners. "Each one was conducted by two assassins from the prison, who took them by the arm to massacre them or to save them, according to the judgment meted out." In the courtyard there were many "cut-throats," all badly dressed and half-drunk, menacing in gesture and mien. But Mme de Tourzel also recalls that "there were also several honest people who had slipped among them, and who were only there in the hope of seizing an occasion to be useful to the prisoners, if they could find the opportunity."[43]

She affirms that she did not leave the Princess's side for an instant and that she was seated next to her when they came to take her to the tribunal. The Duchess cannot bring herself to speak of the Princess's horrible death. By other sources, including the memoirs of Madame Royale presented in the next chapter, we know that the Princesse de Lamballe was massacred by the people, and that her head, stuck on the end of a pike, was borne to the Temple to taunt the queen.

As for her own fate, Mme de Tourzel recounts her unexpected salvation at the hands of the unknown man who had already saved her daughter:

> Monsieur Hardy, my rescuer, did not forget me. . . . I was surrounded at that time by people with dreadful faces, who did not hide from me the fate that was destined for me. Monsieur Hardy, who felt I would be lost if they were present at the tribunal, conceived the project of getting them drunk. . . .
>
> Those miserable people who had been made drunk could no longer stand on their legs and were obliged to go home to sleep, and those who remained softened up considerably.[44]

After four hours of waiting and ten minutes of interrogation, Mme de Tourzel heard the cry of "Long live the Nation!" She had been acquitted! Conducted to the prison door, she was surprised to find herself congratulated and embraced by the same men who, a few hours earlier, had been ready to murder her. Three of them accompanied her in the coach to the refuge offered by the Marquise de Lède, and on the way they indicated to the coachman what streets to avoid so as to spare the Duchess the further sight of carnage. Once they had arrived at her destination, they refused the slightest recompense. Here as elsewhere in revolutionary narratives there is a mixture of generosity and cruelty characterizing impassioned "patriots."

The Duchess's rescue was complete when she held Pauline in her arms. Thanks to M. Hardy, the hero of this episode, mother and daughter were reunited and their story ended, at least momentarily, on a happy note.

The royal family had a notably different ending: the king was executed on January 21, 1793; the queen on October 16, 1793; Madame Elisabeth on May 10, 1794; the dauphin dead of unknown causes in the Temple on June 8, 1795. Only Madame Royale escaped from the fatal net woven around her father and mother, her brother and aunt.

Mme de Tourzel outlived the Revolution. She, her son, and four daughters miraculously escaped the guillotine, despite further imprisonment during the Terror.

She survived the reign of Napoleon, who sent her into exile with her son and three of her daughters. When beseeched by Pauline to allow her mother's return after four years in exile, Napoleon finally granted that request. (Pauline de Béarn's memoirs are more informative on this period than her mother's.) In 1815, the restored King Louis XVIII conferred upon Mme de Tourzel the hereditary title of duchess. Shunning Restoration society, she retired to a convent and died in 1832, at the age of eighty-two.

Her memoirs did not appear in print until 1883, when her great grandson, the Duc Des Cars, broke the family interdiction on their publication. As explained in the introduction to this edition, the generation that had lived through the revolutionary period retained a sense of anxiety and "habits of circumspection" that were transmitted to their progeny.[45] Thus it was that Mme de Tourzel's descendants waited more than half a century after her death to make public her testimony to the sovereigns she had served, lost, and mourned.

Marie-Thérèse-Charlotte de France, Madame Royale. Engraved by F. Bartolozzi. From Récit des Evènements Arrivés au Temple (*Paris: Audot, 1823*)

Portrait of Marie-Antoinette, Queen of France, led to her death; drawn by the pen of David, eyewitness to the convoy. *Bibliotbèque Nationale*

4

THE KING AND THE QUEEN IN THE FACE OF DEATH: WITNESSED BY MADAME ROYALE AND ROSALIE LAMORLIÈRE

SEPARATED FROM THE MEMBERS of the royal family in August 1792, the Duchesse de Tourzel was unable to chronicle their last days. This task was left to two other women, the king's daughter and an unschooled servant. When examined side by side, their testimonials offer a diptych of regal tragedy reduced to the dimensions of common human misery.

In 1817, a small book titled the *Private Memoirs on the Captivity of the Royal Family in the Tower of the Temple* was published anonymously in Paris.[1] Its author was easily identifiable as the one surviving member of the family—the Duchesse d'Angoulême, known before her marriage as Madame Royale. Her account of imprisonment in the Temple knelled the successive deaths of Louis XVI, Marie-Antoinette, Madame Elisabeth, and the little dauphin. The king, at least, had the consolation of being surrounded by his loved ones until the very end, whereas the queen spent her last seventy-six days in the isolation of the Conciergerie under the surveillance of unfamiliar servants and hostile guards. One of these servants, Rosalie Lamorlière, offered her reminiscences of Marie-Antoinette's final weeks to one of the queen's early biographers, and thus to posterity.[2] The testimonials of the Duchesse d'Angoulême and Rosalie Lamorlière have contributed significantly to the myth of martyred royalty perpetuated for the past two centuries by many groups and individuals still faithful to the memory of Louis XVI and Marie-Antoinette.

The Duchesse d'Angoulême's slim volume is the sole bona fide account written by one of the deposed Bourbons, though several other "false memoirs" cropped up in the wake of the Revolution. (Those reputedly authored by Marie-Antoinette or Madame Elisabeth are either biographies written by members of their entourage, or extracts of their letters and other personal documents strung together by entrepreneurial editors.) In the fall of

1795, while still in the Temple but finally allowed visitors, the sixteen-year-old princess gave her manuscript to her former governess, Mme de Tourzel, and a copy to Mme de Chantereine, the companion appointed for her by the revolutionary government. Then after her liberation, when she was seventeen, she dictated another copy to her uncle, the restored King Louis XVIII. Despite her request that the manuscript remain unpublished, handwritten copies were widely circulated and eventually found their way into print during her lifetime in numerous pirated versions.[3]

Why, we may ask, did Marie-Thérèse-Charlotte de France, Duchesse d'Angoulême, write her memoirs in the anonymous third person? By feigning to be merely an observer, she avoided the first-person confessional mode that would have been inappropriate for the daughter of Louis XVI and Marie-Antoinette. Caught between her obligation to maintain the dignity of her station and her desire to bear witness to her family's tragic destiny, she assumed the distant voice that allowed her to do both. Undoubtedly Louis XVIII had some hand in the final published version, since he had personally copied and "corrected" the text; his interest in his niece, married in 1799 to the Duc d'Angoulême, his nephew and heir apparent, was hardly devoid of political motivation. As Louis XVIII wrote to the ambassador of Spain, "My niece's long suffering, her courage, her virtues have gathered around her an interest that has turned to love on the part of the French people, of which it is essential to take advantage and appropriate for myself."[4] The publication of her memoirs was undoubtedly part of a larger campaign to "appropriate" the royal daughter for the reigning monarchy.

Her book begins when she was fourteen, with the installation of the royal family in the Temple on August 13, 1792, three days after their eviction from the Tuileries. Initially the king, queen, Madame Royale, the dauphin, and Madame Elisabeth were accompanied by the Princesse de Lamballe, Mme de Tourzel and her daughter Pauline, three chambermaids, and five men in attendance on the king, but on the sixth day of captivity, all the attendants were taken away to the Prison de la Force; only the king's valet de chambre, Jean-Baptiste Cléry, would be allowed to return. In relating the details of their first prison days, the Duchesse d'Angoulême omits any mention of herself and maintains an impersonal voice: "All the members of the royal family spent the day together. The King taught his son geography, the Queen taught him history and had him learn poetry, and Madame Elisabeth gave him lessons in arithmetic. The King had fortunately found a library that engrossed him, and the Queen did fancy needlework."[5]

But the sober tone breaks down as the author recounts the increasing horror of their situation. This gruesome passage was written in the context of the September prison massacres and the murder of the Princesse de Lamballe:

> His Majesty, having asked what was happening [outside], was told by a young officer: "Well! Since you've asked, it's the head of Madame de Lamballe they want to show you." At this news the Queen was seized with horror. . . . The prisoners learned that the people wanted to force the door; and the municipal authorities were only able to prevent them by . . . permitting six of the seditious mob to make a tour of the tower with Madame de Lamballe's head, but on the condition that they would leave at the door her body, which they wanted to drag with them.[6]

Note how the passage captures the event with surprising economy and vividness. In a few horrifying sentences, the king, the queen, the guard, the municipal authorities, the mob, the severed head and body rush past the reader's eye.

As the story of their lengthening captivity and the king's increasing peril continues, more personal emotion seeps into the narrator's voice. Her account of his death is a moving tribute to a beloved father.

> The family learned the sentence on Sunday the 20th [January 1793] from the hawkers who came to cry it out under their windows, at seven in the evening. A Convention decree allowed the Princesses to descend to the King's room. They ran there and found him very changed; he was crying with anguish for them, and not for fear of death. . . . Then he gave excellent religious instruction to his son, enjoining him to pardon those who were sending him to his death, and he gave his blessing as well as to his daughter. The Queen ardently desired that the whole family spend the night with Louis XVI; he refused, making her understand that he needed tranquillity. She requested that she be at least allowed to return the next morning—a request to which he assented. But when they were gone, he asked his guards not to permit them to come down again because that caused him too much pain.

While the women were in their quarters, the king remained with his confessor. Then he slept from midnight to five o'clock "when he was awakened by the drumbeat" that heralded his execution. His daughter's description of his behavior at the scaffold, obviously from hearsay, portrays him as dignified and resolute: "He wanted to speak to the people, but Sanson [the executioner] prevented him by beating the drum." He undressed himself, and his hands were bound with his handkerchief, rather than the common cord. "At the moment when he was about to die, the abbot said: 'Son of Saint-Louis, ascend to heaven.' "

"The morning of this terrible day, the princesses got up at six o'clock," thinking that "they would go down to him, and they still had this hope when the joyous cries of an unbridled mob told them the crime had been consummated."[7] The pages devoted to the king's execution are a curious mixture of personal observation and secondhand chronicle, with oblique references to the story of the crucifixion. Like Jesus, Louis XVI reputedly forgave those responsible for his death, and, following the words of the Gospel, the dreadful act was "consummated." When the blade of the guillotine was about to fall, the attending priest recalled Louis XVI's relationship to his thirteenth-century ancestor, Louis IX. By invoking the name of Saint Louis as he commended Louis XVI to heaven, the priest implied that the eighteenth-century monarch should be canonized as well.

But what distinguishes this version of the king's execution from others is not its hagiographic intent, for that is found in numerous accounts of the monarch's ultimate ordeal; rather, it is the domestic wound bleeding through the text—the image of Louis XVI weeping for his abandoned family, his white lie to the queen concerning their meeting the next morning, and the fear of losing his fortitude in the face of execution. This is the king at his most human and his most sympathetic.

The memoirs continue with a series of further separations and deaths, each rendered with classical clarity, and each imbued with wrenching emotion. On the third of July 1793, the little dauphin was taken away from his mother.

> He threw himself into his mother's arms, emitting loud cries and begging not to be separated from her. The unfortunate Queen . . . did not want to give up her son, and, against the municipal authorities, she defended his bed where she had placed it. But they menaced her with the use of violence. . . . The Queen responded that they had only to kill her rather than to snatch her son from her. . . . Finally they threatened so positively to kill the child if she did not deliver him to them that her maternal tenderness forced her to this sacrifice.[8]

This vignette of maternal-filial separation, like the scenes of the king's separation from his family and Marie-Antoinette's later removal to the Conciergerie, became popular subjects of paintings in the postrevolutionary years. Two of the earliest, painted by Jean-Jacques Hauer in 1794 and 1795, can be found in the Carnavalet Museum in Paris.

Marie-Antoinette's separation from her daughter and sister-in-law on the night of August 2, 1793, was recorded more dispassionately:

> She left after having embraced her daughter, engaging her to preserve all her courage, and enjoining her to take good care of her aunt, and to obey her as if she were a second mother. . . . The young princess was so overwhelmed, and her affliction was so profound to see herself separated from her mother that she did not have the strength to respond. At the end . . . she left without another look at her daughter, for fear of losing her fortitude.[9]

Compared with the tigress defending her son, Marie-Antoinette appears almost detached in her farewell to her daughter. Her stoic behavior leads to unanswerable questions about the nature of the mother-daughter relation. It is perhaps sufficient to recall Mme de Tourzel's references to the king's predilection for his daughter, as well as the queen's intense attachment to her son. In this, the pattern conforms to a common stereotype of paternal and maternal cross-gender preferences.

Even though her mother had been taken away, Madame Royale refused to believe in her death, and none of the municipal authorities was willing to disillusion her. Then she saw her "second mother," Madame Elisabeth, carried off from prison on May 9, 1794, to be executed the following day. Remembered for her sweetness, piety, and great attachment to her family, Madame Elisabeth became for her niece the model of virtue she hoped to emulate. Thirteen months later, on June 8, 1795, her brother's death made Madame Royale the sole surviving member of her family. Her memoirs end with a brief account of the dauphin's death, attributed not to poison, as some had rumored, but to "uncleanliness, joined with the horrible treatment, cruelty, and unparalleled hardships that had been inflicted upon him."[10]

The dauphin's experience in the Temple was the most pathetic of all. Seven years old when he accompanied his parents to prison, already known for his precocious intelligence and effeminate beauty, he was entrusted after his mother's death to a shoemaker named Simon. It is difficult to know to what extent Simon and his wife (who have been accused of all sorts of villainies) were responsible for the deterioration of the little prince, but when the head surgeon of the Grand Hospice de l'Humanité was called in, he found the tenyear-old child in so alarming a condition that he had him moved from his dark cell into a more airy room. These and other last-ditch efforts to keep the prince alive proved futile. At eight o'clock in the morning of June 9, 1795, the dauphin's body was laid out on his bed, and four members of the Committee of Public Safety came to ascertain that the heir to the throne of France was really dead.

After this final loss, Madame Royale spent six more months in prison under conditions that were considerably ameliorated by a regime experiencing pangs of guilt for the "Orphan of the Temple." Mme de La Briche, a wealthy aristocrat who survived the Revolution with comparatively little damage, wrote in her journal that on August 15, 1795, she observed from a distance the daily promenade then accorded to Madame Royale in the company of her newly appointed companion, Mme de Chantereine. Mme de La Briche was one of many fashionable Parisians who ascended to the fourth-floor room rented near the Temple by M. François Hüe, Louis XVI's former valet de chambre, for the sole purpose of observing Madame Royale through a telescope. At seven in the evening, after a four-hour walk from her home, she was rewarded with the following scene:

> I saw Madame come out of the tower. A little dog preceded her and turned back to caress her. Madame de Chantereine followed behind at a distance. Madame was dressed in white; a fichue tied around her head and descending very low on her forehead prevented one from seeing her hair. She carried her head high like her unfortunate mother, which made her appear taller than she is.[11]

Such was the entertainment value of the unfortunate prisoner for those free to circulate in the summer of 1795.

Mme de Chantereine's reports to the Committee of Public Safety portray her new charge as speaking with hesitation and writing with difficulty, since she had been in isolation, without paper, pencil, or ink, for three years. Pauline de Tourzel, granted visitation rights with her mother during this period, wrote in her memoirs that they were surprised to find Madame Royale "beautiful, tall, and strong" despite "three years of unbelievable misfortunes, mortal anguish, and captivity."[12] On December 18, 1795, the day before her seventeenth birthday, she was released in exchange for political prisoners held by the Austrians. She was to live until 1851, a visible reminder of what she, her family, and her country had suffered during the revolutionary cataclysm.

Fragments of her life story are found in the memoirs of many of her contemporaries—those of Mme de Tourzel, her daughter Pauline, Mme Campan, Mme de Chastenay, Mme Vigée-Lebrun, the Baronne d'Oberkirch, Mme de Boigne, and the Duchesse d'Abrantès, among others—and several biographies have traced her mournful fate, which did not turn out to be much happier for the adult than for the child.[13] She was quite literally a pawn of history, both in her tragic teen years, and later in her political alliance to the Duc d'Angoulême, which was a marriage in name only. From all accounts, the inscription she chose for her tombstone, despite its grandiosity, was well merited: "O vos omnes qui transitis per viam attendite et videte si est dolor sicut dolor meus" (All you who pass this way, behold and see if there be any sorrow like unto my sorrow).

IN CONTRAST TO THE CELEBRITY of the Duchesse d'Angoulême, little is known about the memorialist of the queen's last days, the tender-hearted Rosalie Lamorlière.[14] A native of Breteuil in Picardy, she was hired in 1793 as a servant in the Conciergerie, the judicial palace and prison on the banks of the Seine from which the condemned were led to the guillotine. Before her employment there, she had served as a chambermaid to Mme Beaulieu, the mother of a famous actor. According to an informant who visited the Conciergerie during the time of Lamorlière's service, she was unusually beautiful, and through the "delicacy of her attentions, obtained the special affection of the queen."[15]

Unable to write or read, Rosalie dictated her testimonial in about 1837 to the Abbot Lafont d'Aussonne, author of an early biography of Marie-Antoinette.[16] Transforming speech into text, d'Aussonne obviously edited Lamorlière's words: most of the sentences are too well constructed to have come directly from the mouth of an illiterate servant. Yet the metamorphosis of spoken language into print did not entirely erase its oral quality. Vestiges of Lamorlière's voice can still be heard in her seventeen-page chronicle published under the title "Marie-Antoinette's Last Prison."

Servant to the queen in her final hours, Lamorlière later basked in the aura of martyred sainthood that surrounded Marie-Antoinette decades after her death. Already in her lifetime, attention to the queen's person and body had given rise to those polar extremes of idolatry and vilification that have fascinated generations of historians.[17] Fairy princess or fiendish monster, solicitous monarch or vindictive harpy, loving mother or incestuous slut—she was all things to all people and never in moderation. Lamorlière records how the queen's most trifling possessions were treated with awe by both her sympathizers and detractors. Bault, the second concierge under whom Lamorlière served, confiscated the white ribbon given to Lamorlière by the queen for fear it would be damaging to both of them. A small piece of cambric cloth preserved from one of Her Majesty's dresses was fervently covered with tearful kisses by the wife and daughter of the court painter Joseph Boze, when they came to visit him in the Conciergerie prison. The queen's black woolen shoe, surreptitiously passed among imprisoned aristocrats and priests, was also the object of reverent kisses. Rosalie Lamorlière, bearer of these relics, intermediary between Marie-Antoinette and the world outside her cell, witness to the queen's last imprisonment, became herself a kind of fetish. In her later years she was visited in a home for the sick and aged by a number of callers seeking a reflected glimpse of the doomed queen. Mme Simon-Viennot found her at sixty "imposing and still beautiful" with a noble bearing, as if she had somehow inherited the queen's mantle.[18] Even the reputedly proud Duchesse d'Angoulême expressed gratitude to Rosalie Lamorlière for firsthand information about her mother's final weeks, although the Duchess was notoriously curt to Temple and Conciergerie personnel.

Though Lamorlière's testimonial was undoubtedly colored by her designation as the queen's memory-bearer, it nonetheless exudes authentic feeling and credibility. What makes her story so moving, and so credible, are the intimate details of Marie-Antoinette's prison existence. Lamorlière spares us nothing—neither the queen's last bowl of soup nor the vaginal hemorrhaging to which she was subject.

Initially Lamorlière was hired as a servant to Mme Richard, who performed, with her husband, the functions of concierge. For the first forty days, Rosalie merely accompanied Mme or M. Richard when they served the queen breakfast at nine o'clock and dinner at two or two-thirty. One day Mme Richard brought along her youngest child, a son named

Fanfan. With his blond hair and blue eyes, his face was, in Lamorlière's words, "well above his station" and reminded the queen of her own son left behind in the Temple. "She took him in her arms, covered him with kisses and caresses, and began to cry as she spoke to us of M. le Dauphin, who was about the same age; she thought of him night and day."[19] Afterward, to spare the queen pain, Mme Richard did not bring her son.

Judged according to how she treated Her Majesty, a criterion applied to everyone in Lamorlière's story, Mme Richard receives relatively high marks. With the help of the local merchants, some still loyal to the queen, she provided the best possible food: "At the market," Lamorlière remembers, "two or three merchants who recognized the jailer, tearfully gave him the most delicate chickens and the most beautiful fruits: For our Queen, they said." But Mme Richard had to be extremely cautious: any sign of favoring her regal prisoner could result in catastrophe. She did not dare request a piece of furniture to hold Marie-Antoinette's linens and only reluctantly allowed Rosalie to lend a paper box to the queen, "who received it with as much satisfaction as if she had been given the most beautiful piece of furniture in the world." It is with obvious pride that the narrator recalls this event, along with others that demonstrate her usefulness to the fallen monarch.

> The prison regime did not permit us to give her a mirror, and Madame renewed that request every morning. Mme Richard permitted me to lend my little mirror to the Queen. I blushed when I offered it to her. That mirror, bought on the quais, had cost me only twenty-five sous in script! I still can see it: its frame was red and there were Chinese figures painted on each side. The Queen accepted this little mirror as if it were something of importance, and Her Majesty used it until the last day.[20]

To have been the one to lend Marie-Antoinette a mirror in her time of need—the monumental irony of this situation encapsulates all that is grotesquely tragic in her destiny. She whose face had graced the coins of the realm, whose raised eyebrow had cost ambassadors and ministers their posts, whose smile had conferred colossal fortunes and empyrean bliss, whose skin had inspired rhapsodies from Elisabeth Vigée-Lebrun, the greatest portrait painter of the age—this Queen of Queens was now reduced to the reflection provided by a cheap little hand mirror, and indebted to the kindness of a poor servant girl.

This pathetic picture grew even darker after the "Carnation Conspiracy," an abortive attempt to free the queen. For a time she had been allowed visitors, one of whom, the Chevalier de Rougeville, had left behind in her cell a carnation with a tiny note suggesting the possibility of escape. Marie-Antoinette's answer, pricked with a pin on a long slip of paper, was discovered and turned over to the National Convention. Among those who suffered from the royalist plot were M. and Mme Richard, duly imprisoned with their eldest son.

The new concierge Bault (mistakenly called Lebeau in Lamorlière's account) had a reputation as "hard and severe" but the narrator, in her capacity as judge, adds that "he was really not a bad sort." Remaining as a cook in his service, Lamorlière was then confined to the Conciergerie. No longer could she go to the market for provisions, and those that were brought to the prison by the tradesmen were not of the same quality as before. Lamorlière takes care to state that the queen noticed the deterioration of her treatment after the carnation episode but "never uttered a single complaint."[21]

It is this picture of the queen as suffering in silence, courageously enduring all hardships, courteous to her captors, dignified in adversity, that Lamorlière wished to project. Since we have no evidence to the contrary, there is little reason to disbelieve her account. Still, to speak well of the queen was undoubtedly self-serving, especially when Lamorlière could link her own qualities to those of her prisoner. For example: "Madame, who was excessively clean and delicate, noticed that my table linen was always white, and her look seemed to thank me for the delicate attentions I had for her."[22] A concern for cleanliness in the midst of prison squalor may indeed have established a bond between two women of vastly different ranks and destinies.

An even more intimate bond was established in the Queen's final days when she began to experience vaginal bleeding. At thirty-eight, Marie-Antoinette was probably undergoing some form of menstrual irregularity, which Lamorlière attributed to "her sorrows, the bad air, the lack of exercise." Once again Lamorlière presents herself as willing and able to be of unusual service to Her Majesty. "She asked me secretly for some linen and I immediately cut up my chemises and put those strips of cloth under her bolster." The secrecy surrounding menstrual blood, in a prison where every item entering the cell was scrutinized by a succession of guards, could not have been easy to maintain. [23]

Lamorlière relates other favors she performed, such as prolonging her evening housekeeping duties so as to shorten the queen's time alone in the dark. She ironed her cap-strings, and washed her underwear, and cleaned the mold off her shoes. These small attentions must have been highly appreciated by the occupant of a dank stone cell whose narrow windows were boarded up after the Carnation attempt.

Lamorlière's narrative is, for the most part, a loosely constructed series of anecdotes. It manages, nonetheless, to convey the passage of time and a sense of impending doom. In the section relating Marie Antoinette's interrogation and her last three days, the story line is tightened and the narrative rises in dramatic intensity as the queen goes from her cell to the tribunal and ultimately to the guillotine.

Through the eyes of a servant responsible for the queen's sustenance, we witness those bodily rituals that lend an air of the familiar to high tragedy. They punctuate *la grande histoire* with reminders of a common humanity. We are drawn into the drama of the queen's final ordeal as much by the banal details of her physical needs as by the skillful, almost suspenseful, narration of those public events that will seal her fate. Lamorlière's memories of the queen's penultimate day center around the commonplace necessity of providing her with food.

> Finally the dreadful day of October 15 arrived; at eight o'clock in the morning she went up to the court room to receive her sentence, and since I do not remember having given her any kind of food that day, I believe they made her go up on an empty stomach.
>
> During the morning, I overheard several people talking about the session. They said: "Marie-Antoinette will get off; she answered like an angel; they will only deport her."
>
> Around four o'clock in the afternoon, the concierge said to me: "The session has been suspended for three quarters of an hour; the accused is not coming down; go up at once, they have asked for some bouillon."

I immediately took some excellent soup that I had been saving on my stove, and I went up toward the Queen.

As I was going into one of the rooms near her, one of the police commissioners named Labuzière, who was small and flat-nosed, grabbed my soup-tureen from my hands, and giving it to an extremely well-dressed young woman, he said to me: "This young woman has a great desire to see the Capet Widow" . . . and that woman immediately withdrew carrying the half-spilled soup.

I begged and pleaded in vain with Labuzière. He was all-powerful, I had to obey. What must the Queen have thought receiving her soup from the hands of someone she did not know![24]

This melodramatic scene offers a brief respite in the mounting intensity before the queen's final agony.

At a few minutes past four o'clock in the morning on October 16, they came to tell us that the Queen of France had been condemned! I felt as if a sword had been run through my heart. . . .

Around seven in the morning, he [the concierge] ordered me to go down to the Queen and ask if she needed any food. Entering her cell, . . . I saw that she was all dressed in black, stretched out on her bed. . . .

"Madame," I said to her, trembling, "You took nothing to eat last evening, and almost nothing during the day. What do you want to have this morning?" The Queen was shedding abundant tears. "Ma fille, I no longer need anything. Everything is finished for me." I took the liberty of adding: "Madame, I've kept some bouillon and noodles on my oven; you need to sustain yourself. Allow me to bring you something."

The Queen's tears redoubled, and she said to me: "Rosalie, bring me some bouillon." I went to get it; she sat up and could swallow only a few spoonfuls; I swear to God that her body received no other sustenance, and I had reason to believe that she was losing all her blood![25]

Here the focus on food becomes more pathetic. The death sentence has been pronounced, the Queen's life thread is at the breaking point. Stretched out upon her bed, dressed in the widow's black that now prefigures her own end, she gives way to tears of despair. We may smile at Rosalie's attempts to urge Marie-Antoinette to take a few sips of soup, yet there is poignancy in those efforts to stoke the embers of life for a last time.

The last prison ritual to which Lamorlière was privy centered around the queen's dress for the guillotine. She would never forget the sight of Marie-Antoinette changing her blood-stained underwear under the eyes of a male guard.

Her Majesty passed into the little space between the bed and the wall. . . . Indicating that I should stand in front of her bed to block the sight of her body from the gendarme, she bent down and removed her dress so as to change her linens for the last time. The officer instantly approached us and, standing next to the bolster, watched the Queen change. Her Majesty immediately put her shawl back across her shoulders and said to that young man, with great gentleness: "In the name of decency, Monsieur, allow me to change my linen without a witness."

"I cannot consent to that," the gendarme responded brusquely. "My orders state that I have to keep an eye on all your movements."

The Queen sighed, put on her last chemise with all possible precaution and modesty, chose for her attire not the long widow's dress that she had worn in front of her judges, but the white negligée that generally served as her morning dress. . . .

She carefully rolled up her poor bloody chemise and concealed it in one of her sleeves . . . ; then she stuffed that linen into a chink she noticed between the old canvas wall covering and the wall.[26]

This, then, was Lamorlière's last vision of Marie-Antoinette, reduced to the stark necessities of flesh and blood. A tragic portrait of royalty shorn of all adornment, it parallels Jacques Louis David's more famous, similarly elemental, sketch of the queen seated backwards in the cart that drew her to the scaffold. The queen's attempts to preserve vestiges of dignity, like Lamorlière's efforts to feed her charge, constitute a kind of domestic heroics.

However bleak her destiny—and indeed it is difficult to follow the final phase of Marie-Antoinette's life unsympathetically—her courage was uncontested. According to an eyewitness to her execution, the queen descended from the cart "with lightness and promptitude" and ascended the scaffold "with an even calmer and more tranquil air" than she had shown in leaving prison.[27] Displaying the graceful carriage for which she was famous, she seemed to hurry to her end. The executioner cut off her head at twelve-fifteen and showed it immediately to the crowd.

Rosalie Lamorlière, left behind in the Conciergerie, was asked to collect her mirror and cardboard box and ordered to wrap all the queen's personal effects in her bedsheet. Then she went to her room to bemoan the fate of "the best and the most unfortunate Queen who has ever existed."[28]

The hyperbole was not wasted on the Duchesse d'Angoulême, whose largesse softened Lamorlière's last years. When interviewed in the 1830s, Lamorlière reported that she "still enjoyed the kindness of Madame la Duchesse d'Angoulême," through whose good graces she had been admitted to the Hospice des Incurables and received a pension of 200 francs.[29] We do not know whether the desire she expressed to meet her benefactress face to face was ever realized.

THE EMINENT BRITISH HISTORIAN J. M. Thompson, in his classic 1943 book *The French Revolution*, expressed the position of several generations of vehemently antiroyalist scholars when he wrote of the queen's death sentence, "Can it be wondered that, where so much hatred was kept alive by the tradition of Bourbon tyranny, and so many interests threatened by any return of the old regime, there should have been a demand for the completion of the work of January 21st?"[30] That the queen's head was a necessary "completion" of the king's execution is not so readily apparent today.

Both French and American writers contributing to the torrent of words unleashed by the bicentennial of the Revolution have painted a more sympathetic picture of both Louis XVI and Marie-Antoinette, and though many uphold the king's execution on political grounds, few attempt to justify that of the queen. Indeed, the most common view today is that she was led to the guillotine for reasons unrelated to the charges of treason brought against her, not the least reason being that of her sex. Following a line of feminist scholarship that has investigated the pervasive fear of women as a threat to the body politic, and that has simultaneously highlighted the excessive punishments meted out to women who made themselves publicly visible, even nonfeminist historians recognize the overlap between Marie-Antoinette's official condemnation to death and the condemnation of her behavior as a reputedly bad woman, wife, and mother.[31] At her trial, the prosecutor Antoine Fouquier-Tinville pulled out all the stops in portraying her as immoral, greedy, intemperate, indeed as the sexual initiator of her own son. The latter charge, it must be said, was greeted in the courtroom by such incredulity on the part of the women spectators that it almost turned the proceedings in the queen's favor.

Simon Schama, in his best-selling history *Citizens*, links MarieAntoinette's "inevitable sentence" to this "generalized character assassination," and he is quick to point out that she "was not the only woman . . . to be incriminated for conspiring against the Jacobin ideology of obedient wife-motherhood." His description of the queen on her last day, which profits from the list of clothing recorded by Rosalie Lamorlière down to the royal prune-colored shoes, gives a sympathetic cast to the gaunt figure seated erect in an open wooden cart, as sketched by David. This is a far cry from J. M. Thompson's interpretation of that same drawing: a woman "defying death and a hostile mob, with Hapsburg disdain."[32]

The value of records left by Lamorlière and the Duchesse d'Angoulême is not that they are impartial—that would be impossible—but that they are eyewitness accounts, and, as such, they provide the raw data for fresh interpretations. As we study the destinies of Louis XVI and Marie-Antoinette, the sentimental testimonials of a royal daughter and a prison servant counteract the vicious satires found in such newspapers as the *Père Duchesne* and the letters sent from the provinces congratulating the Convention on having accomplished regicide. Close-up views remind us that even kings and queens cry and bleed, and that they are susceptible to posthumous judgments different from the official verdicts that cut short their lives.

Through their executions, Louis XVI and Marie-Antoinette entered the mythic circle reserved for royal victims of revolution. The king stands alongside Charles I of England and the Czar Nicholas II. But who is the counterpart of Marie-Antoinette? Surely no other queen in Western history has given birth to a comparable legend of such arrogant fortune and monumental misfortune. Recently, at a dinner party in France, a retired diplomat took me aside and pleaded: "When you write of Louis XVI, you can say that his death was perhaps necessary for reasons of state, but the Queen—*ah, non!*" And a glow of indignation shone in his moist eyes. This is not the reaction I have found in America, where the Marie-Antoinette of "Let them eat cake" fame (a statement she probably never made) calls forth indignation of another sort. Americans tend to treat Marie-Antoinette with scorn and to believe, without much knowledge of her life, that she got exactly what she deserved.

Despite numerous biographies of Marie-Antoinette in many languages, there is still another one to be written. It would take into account her unusual relationship with her mother, the Empress Maria Theresa of Austria, who sent Marie-Antoinette as a bride to

France when she was only fourteen and thereafter corresponded with her on subjects ranging from her daughter's menstrual periods and sex life to international politics. It would investigate the relationship between Marie-Antoinette and her husband Louis XVI, possibly the only monogamous monarch in the history of France. It would pay attention to her close female friendships with the Corntesse de Polignac, the Princesse de Lamballe, and the painter Elisabeth Vigée-Lebrun. It would restore the important role that motherhood played in her life, after her initial seven-year failure to produce an heir to the throne. And, following the insights of feminist scholarship, it would analyze the political situation of a woman who had power without authority, and whose gender and foreign birth made her liable to extravagant forms of satire and abuse. Before she was out of her teens, rumors were rampant of extramarital relations with both men and women, though it has never been conclusively proven that Marie-Antoinette had even one lover— only Axel de Fersen may have had that distinction. Carolly Erickson's recent biography of Marie-Antoinette vividly evokes the intriguing court ambience, but despite valiant efforts, she does not bring to life the person behind the legend, the daughter, the wife, the mother, the friend, the woman who never belonged to herself.[33] If our only sources for such a biography were the memoirs of all but one of her female contemporaries, Marie-Antoinette would come down in history as a woman worthy of affection rather than the vilification that has colored her popular memory. But the one dissenting voice—that of Mme Roland—undoubtedly represents the more prevalent eighteenth-century view. Let us now turn to her version of the Revolution.

Portrait of Madame Roland on the cover of a bonbonnière in the Musée Carnavalet, Paris.
Reproduced from Ernest F. Henderson, Symbol and Satire in the French Revolution (*New York: Knickerbocker Press, 1912*)

5

THE REPUBLIC VINDICATED
AND VIOLATED:
STARRING MADAME ROLAND

THREE WEEKS AFTER THE EXECUTION of Marie-Antoinette, another prominent woman was carted to the guillotine. She was neither an aristocrat nor a royalist—far from it! Madame Roland and her husband, the minister of the interior from 1791 to 1793, were staunch republicans who had played an important role in hurrying the Revolution along its tempestuous course. Yet in the end, not radical enough for the extreme left, they and their political allies were swallowed up by the hunger for scapegoats that marred the Revolution's last years.

Mme Roland was arrested in connection with Robespierre's 1793 purge of the Girondin deputies, which included her influential husband Jean-Marie Roland de la Platière . While he fled to the southeastern provinces, she remained to confront her husband's enemies; she could not imagine that she, too, would be crushed by the Robespierrists. During her five-month imprisonment, she wrote the work that became the most famous eyewitness chronicle of the Revolution; and of the female contingent, her memoirs are all the more remarkable because so few women expressed republican sympathies.[1] Unlike their royalist counterparts, most republican women deemed it wise to remain silent in print. The few who applauded the Revolution in writing did so—like Mme Roland—while it was still in progress (Théroigne de Méricourt in an Austrian prison, Mme de Genlis in exile) or when they were so old that government reprisal during the Restoration was unlikely (Charlotte Robespierre).[2] Elisabeth Le Bas's manuscript recounting the loss of her deputy husband in the Thermidor coup, Sophie Grandchamp's reminiscences of her friend Mme Roland, and the memoirs of the regicide deputy's wife Mme Cavaignac were not published until the turn of the twentieth century.[3] Only Mme de Staël, living in her native Switzerland, dared praise the Revolution's ideals publicly at the very time when Louis XVIII was hoisting his corpulent form on the throne vacated by Napoleon.[4]

Mme Roland's work has held a dual place of honor for almost two hundred years within the canons of history and literature, though a complete version true to the original text was not published until 1905.[5] At that time, the editor Claude Perroud revealed the complex structure of her manuscripts. In her first set of notebooks, labeled "Historical Notices," Mme Roland set out to collect "all the facts and all the persons belonging to public life" from the period when her husband had been active in revolutionary politics.[6] The second notebooks, called her "Private Memoirs," contained her personal autobiography from childhood through early adulthood. The third set added further "Portraits and Anecdotes" to the public record.

The context in which these singular works were written explains, in part, its tripartite form. Mme Roland's initial goal, as stated on the first page of her work, was to consign to paper the circumstances of her arrest on June 1, 1793. Her husband had fled into hiding, along with many of the twenty-two Girondins accused of having conspired against the Republic. Two months after her incarceration, Mme Roland noted: "I spent the first period of my captivity writing; I did it with such rapidity and in such a happy disposition that before the month was over I had enough manuscript to fill a small-sized book." Unfortunately, as she explained, the notebooks in which this political testament had been written and smuggled out of prison had been thrown into the fire by the person to whom they had been entrusted because he feared his own arrest. "I would have preferred he had thrown me in instead," she wrote with an author's exaggerated sense of loss.[7]

As a form of distraction from the loss of her first manuscript, she began to write a more personal autobiography. The experience of retracing the intimate story of her life from the time of her childhood filled her with unexpected delight: "One lives again a second time when one goes back over all the steps of one's career, and what does one have better to do in prison than to transport one's existence elsewhere through a happy fiction or through interesting memories?"[8] In the midst of this self-reflexive process, she learned that some of her original notebooks had not been destroyed; what remained could be fleshed out with a series of contemporary portraits inspired by the model of Plutarch's Lives, a book she had passionately admired since the age of eight.

The piecemeal nature of her writing did not deter Mme Roland's posthumous editors from grouping all her prison manuscripts together and publishing them under the single word "memoirs." This composite designation would probably have surprised her. She had assigned a much greater value to the "Historical Notices" and "Portraits and Anecdotes" than to her "Private Memoirs" because the former were concerned with public history, whereas the latter was "only" the recollections of a private life.

Mme Roland's assessment of her writing has not been that of history. Posterity has hailed her "Private Memoirs" as her major contribution, and granted secondary status to the rest of her work. The representation of her childhood and early adulthood, following the model of Rousseau's *Confessions*, conveys the burden-free pleasures of youth and the joy of recollection for its own sake.[9]

In contrast, the "Historical Notices" and "Portraits and Anecdotes" are driven by shifting needs and tragic concerns. Thrown into prison the day after her husband's flight from arrest, Mme Roland agonized over the threat to his life and the lives of his fellow Girondins, as well as over her own uncertain situation. Would Robespierre and his henchmen succeed in annihilating the Girondins? What would happen to her only child Eudora, entrusted to the care of friends? And what terrible destiny awaited France and the Revolution in the hands of Robespierre and Danton, belatedly seen as odious assassins?

In her outrage at finding herself in the Abbaye prison, she jotted off numerous letters to protest her detention. To the National Convention (rebaptized as such on September 21, 1792), the Citizeness Roland cried out on June 1: "I have just been snatched from my domicile, from the arms of my twelve-year-old daughter, and detained at the Abbaye by virtue of orders that do not carry any motive for my arrest." To the deputy Jacques Antoine Dulaure, editor of *The Daily Thermometer*, she sent a copy of her letter to the Convention with the request that he publish it in his newspaper. To the new minister of the interior—her husband's former ministry—she asked that it intervene on her behalf. To the minister of justice she wrote on June 8, "I am oppressed; therefore I have cause to remind you of my rights and your duties."[10] The tone in all these letters is indignant and admonishing; even in adversity, Mme Roland refused to be a supplicant.

After the initial shock of her imprisonment and the frenzy of letters it inspired, she settled more philosophically into her situation. Her writing changed its focus, like a camera shifting from a narrow to a wide-angle view. She extended her vision chronologically and embarked upon the history of her husband's involvement in revolutionary politics from the moment of their arrival in Paris in February 1791, when he assumed the duties of special deputy from the region of Lyons, until his resignation as minister of the interior in January 1793. As with many other women memoirists—Charlotte Robespierre, Elisabeth Le Bas, Mme de Staël, and the widows of the Vendean generals, for example—the relationship to a famous man provided her initial literary *raison d'être*. Yet, unlike her sister eulogists, Mme Roland was not yet writing an elegy. At the time of her imprisonment, M. Roland was still alive; there was still hope that they would both ride out what she called "le temps des orages" (the time of tempests).[11] Her account of his contribution to revolutionary history, with her own tucked into the interstices, was intended to justify the Roland couple to their contemporaries and to serve as an exemplum of civic virtue for future generations.

"Historical Notices" begins with an account of her excited return to Paris after a half dozen years in the provinces. From the distance of Lyons, where her husband was an inspector of commerce and manufacture, she had avidly observed the work of the National Assembly. Her letters written during those early years of the Revolution, especially those to the deputy Jean Henri Bancal-des-Issarts, reveal her frustration at being far from the scene of action and a certain impatience with the men of 1789 as she envisioned them based on reports in newspapers and pamphlets. Once resettled in Paris, she gave herself passionately to their oratorical spectacles.

> I ran to the sessions; I saw the powerful Mirabeau, the astonishing Cazalès, the audacious Maury, the astute Lameth, the cold Barnave. I noticed with annoyance on the side of the blacks [the deputies on the right] that kind of superiority in public meetings conferred by the habit of representation, the purity of language, and distinguished manners; but the strength of reason, the courage of honesty, the insights of philosophy, the knowledge of the consulting-room and the facility of the Bar were to assure the triumph of the patriots on the left.[12]

These few sentences suggest the elevated—almost pompous—style characteristic of her writing; they also communicate something of her passion and energy. She and her husband quickly became intimate with a number of the deputies on the radical left, foremost of whom was Jacques Pierre Brissot, the leader of the group called Brissotins in his honor, and simultaneously called Girondins in reference to the Gironde region near Bordeaux from which they had come. They arranged to spend four evenings a week together at the conveniently located Roland flat, an arrangement that suited their hostess perfectly as it favored her "taste for following political discussions." Yet she took care not to cross the boundary into the men's space.

> I knew what role was appropriate for my sex, and I never abandoned it. The meetings took place in my presence without my taking any part in them. Placed outside the circle near a table, I worked with my hands or wrote letters, while they deliberated. But were I to dispatch ten missives—which sometimes happened—I did not lose a word of what was uttered, and sometimes I had to bite my lips so as not to say a word of my own.[13]

Like her contemporary Jane Austen, who hid her manuscripts behind a piece of sewing whenever visitors came into the room, Mme Roland occupied her hands with needlework or letter writing, while her mind raced alongside or ahead of the men deliberating in her presence.

In her memoirs she takes great pains to establish her credentials as a woman supremely happy with her status as a bourgeois wife, and not the meddling harpy her enemies had pictured. Indeed, the image of the nonassertive wife was an essential defense against the accusations of her complicity in the Girondin conspiracies. But there are other reasons as well for her denial of a public role; Mme Roland feared the ridicule attached to publicly visible women. In her "Private Memoirs," recalling her passion for writing and the notebooks she had filled when she was a young woman, she insisted,

> I never had the slightest temptation to become an author; I saw very early that a woman who acquired that title lost much more than she gained. Men do not like her and her own sex criticizes her. If her works are bad, they make fun of her . . . and if they are good, they deny that she wrote them. . . . They pick holes in her character, her habits, her conduct and her talents.

Before her marriage, however, when she was still Mlle Marie-Jeanne (Manon) Phlipon, she had expressed her discontent with her restricted lot in a letter dated February 5, 1776, to her friend Sophie Cannet: "I am truly vexed to be a woman: I should have been born with a different soul or a different sex . . . then I could have chosen the republic of letters as my country."[14] Later, converted to the cult of domesticity by her passion for Rousseau, she followed the path of his heroine Julie, in *La Nouvelle Héloïse*, by marrying a man twenty years her senior and by giving herself unstintingly to wifehood and motherhood. Had the Revolution not catapulted the Rolands into the political arena, she would probably have ended her days in provincial obscurity. But finding herself unexpectedly in a position to express her earlier ambition for a "higher destiny," she seized the opportunity to become a writer, at first behind her husband's name and finally, in prison, under her own.

Sophie Grandchamp, her closest friend in her last two years, claimed that Mme Roland was unhappy with her life before she was able to express herself through her husband's call to office. Grandchamp wrote in her reminiscences that Manon Roland had nourished "a secret ambition . . . to appear on a stage where she could deploy all her talents," and that she was even more eager to assume political power than her husband.[15] Yet in her memoirs Mme Roland not only denied her ambitions but heaped scorn on women who express political opinions "because public discussion is so little suitable for women and those who talk about affairs of state appear to me to resemble old newsmongers."[16] This ridicule of women's political voice contrasts markedly with the articulate republican so apparent in her letters and memoirs.

The minister's wife who had held her tongue in the presence of the deputies of 1791 did not deny herself literary revenge on them two years later. She wrote scathing portraits of the leading figures of her day. Aside from her husband, who is always depicted as the epitome of probity, few rise to the standard of republican excellence she had construed from her reading of Plutarch, Tacitus, and Rousseau. Of the deputies she had observed in the Constituent Assembly and in the privacy of her home, she wrote, "There was only a small number of resolute men who dared fight for their principles, and in the end, they were reduced to Buzot, Pétion, and Robespierre.[17] Despite her later reversal of opinion about Robespierre, she grants that in the first years of the revolution he appeared to be *un honnête homme* (an honorable man). Mme Roland had personal reasons for including François Buzot and Jerome Pétion among the Jacobin elite; Pétion, the mayor of Paris in 1791, was a very close friend and at the moment of her imprisonment, he was one of the fugitive deputies in hiding with Buzot, the man to whom she had given her heart.

Buzot is singled out in Mme Roland's memoirs as one of the rare patriots worthy of sustained respect. Elected to the Estates General in 1789, he became a member of the extreme left group of deputies frequenting the Rolands' Parisian lodgings during the spring and summer of 1791. One of the few allusions to their intimate relationship concerns the letters they wrote one another when each was away from Paris. Mentioning the correspondence she maintained with both Buzot and Robespierre, she noted, "It was more consistent with the former; there existed between us a greater similarity, a greater basis for friendship. . . . It became intimate, inalterable; I shall write elsewhere how this liaison became binding."[18]

This promise of writing elsewhere about her liaison with Buzot is not fulfilled in her extant memoirs. There are only allusions to an unnamed person who had taken possession of her heart. One reference to this mystery lover indicates that she had confessed this love to her husband: "I cherish my husband as a sensitive daughter adores a virtuous father to whom she would sacrifice even her lover; but I found the man who could be that lover. . . . My husband . . . could not support the idea of the slightest change in his dominion; his imagination blackened, his jealousy irritated me, happiness fled far from us." Although Mme Roland never named Buzot as the man responsible for the change in her marital relations, a discerning reader might have suspected from her description of him in the "Portraits and Anecdotes" that Buzot was the unnamed man. Surely the following portrait is more befitting a lover than a statesman.

BUZOT, with his lofty character, proud spirit, and fiery courage, sensitive, ardent, melancholic and lazy, is sometimes given to extremes. A passionate contemplator of nature, nourishing his imagination with all the charms that it can offer, and his soul with the principles of the most affecting philosphy, he seems to be made to taste and procure domestic happiness; he would forget the universe in the sweetness of private virtues with a heart worthy of his own.[19]

That heart worthy of Buzot's could only be hers. Mme Roland does not seem to have been troubled by the existence of a Mme Buzot, dismissed parenthetically as not being on the level of her spouse.

The untold story of Mme Roland's unconsummated love affair was the "not-said" carefully concealed in her memoirs. It had created a breach between husband and wife that was still unreconciled by the time of his flight and her imprisonment. A memoir to perpetuate Roland's glory would be one way of expunging the blemish on her marital record. As a disciple of Rousseau, Mme Roland would not deny the claims of the heart, so long as the lovers did not yield to carnality. She and Buzot would be united only beyond the grave, as she cried out in a final farewell: "And you whom I dare not name! . . . who respected the barriers of virtue . . . will grieve to see me go before you to a place where we shall be free to love each other without crime."[20]

For Buzot, then, her passion would not find fulfillment in this lifetime. For Roland, the injured spouse, there would be compensatory glorification. From prison, Mme Roland wrote to Buzot that her enforced leisure would give her the time to think about him and the opportunity to serve her husband through her writing. Roland would always be depicted as scrupulously honest, remarkably competent, appropriately austere, courageous in the face of injustice whether perpetrated by monarchs or revolutionaries—indeed, he was all that could be desired in a public servant. Her scripted stance toward him was essentially daughterly and deferential. Compared to Mme de Staël's passionate eulogy to her father (see chapter 8), one would think that the roles had been reversed between the minister Roland and the minister Necker, that Jean-Marie Roland de la Platière was Mme Roland's father and Jacques Necker, Mme de Staël's husband.

The exceptional documentary value of Mme Roland's memoirs as a record of revolutionary history begins in February 1791, when Roland was appointed special deputy from Lyons to the Constituent Assembly. Mme Roland cryptically summed up his accomplishments in that capacity: "Roland's mission kept him seven months in Paris; we left that city in mid-September after Roland had obtained for Lyons all that city could desire." Autumn of that year was spent at the Roland family property near Lyons where they were occupied with the grape harvest. When the Constituent Assembly unexpectedly eliminated the position of inspector of commerce held by Roland, he decided to return to Paris to claim his "rights to a pension after forty years of employment." Moreover, Paris was deemed a more suitable location for him to pursue his encyclopedic work on the history of commerce, "at the center of enlightenment among scholars and artists rather than in the depths of the desert."[21] The Rolands returned to Paris in December 1791, and there a much grander, if shorter, destiny awaited them.

According to his wife, Roland had a reputation for both scholarly and administrative work, as well as a firm and fair character. As an active member of the Jacobin Club charged with its correspondence, he had attracted the attention of several prominent deputies, who proposed his name to the king for the position of minister of the interior. Mme Roland asserts that by mid-March 1792, "the intimidated Court was . . . trying to do something that would restore its popularity; . . . it was even willing to take Jacobin ministers."[22]

Her memory of Roland's appointment illustrates the way she interposed her own history in the narration of her husband's career. Relating a conversation with the deputy Brissot two days before Roland was named minister, she suggests her importance as a mediating influence between her husband and official power: "Brissot came to see me one evening . . . asking if Roland would consent to assume that burden; I responded that . . . his zeal and activity would not be repelled by this nourishment."[23]

On March 23, 1792, at eleven in the evening, the minister of foreign affairs, General Charles Dumouriez, arrived at the Roland residence to announce that Roland had been named minister of the interior. Mme Roland claims that, from the start, she had grave misgivings about Roland's serving in the same cabinet as Dumouriez. She recalls her comments to her husband about Dumouriez's duplicitous nature: "There's a man . . . who has a subtle mind, a shifty look and of whom you should perhaps be more distrustful than any one in the world. . . . I would not be surprised if he had you sacked one day." Within months, Doumouriez did indeed betray Roland, just as he later betrayed the entire nation by going over to the Austrians. She contrasts her own psychological acumen with her husband's credulity.

> I saw Roland and Clavière [the newly appointed minister of public contributions] almost enchanted for three weeks concerning the King's dispositions, taking him at his word and rejoicing like good fellows at the way things were shaping up. "Good Lord!" I said to them, when I saw them leaving for the Council in that confident frame of mind, "it seems to me that you are always about to make a stupid blunder."

Not content with this telling conversation from the past, Mme Roland goes on to elucidate the intrinsic differences between monarchy and representative government, and one that provides a good example of her acute intelligence.

> I was never able to believe in the constitutional vocation of a king born under despotism, raised for it and accustomed to exercising it; Louis XVI would have had to have been a man much above the ordinary in his intelligence in order to have sincerely wanted the Constitution that restrained his power, and if he had been that man, he would not have allowed the events to occur that led to the Constitution.[24]

A comparison of this passage with Mme de Tourzel's assessment reveals two absolutely opposed visions: the Duchess presented the reigning sovereign as thoroughly willing to facilitate the transformation from absolute power to a constitutional monarchy. She blamed its failure on evil revolutionaries determined to unseat the king and sweep away all traces of the hierarchical past. Mme Roland, writing only months after the king's death, shows no sign of regret for his execution. Monarchy, in her eyes, was fundamentally inimical to the republic of her dreams, and Louis XVI a thoroughly disposable specimen of kingship.

The story of Roland's first appearance at court is intended to do honor to his austere simplicity and to throw ridicule upon established etiquette. She narrates this event with the ease of a seasoned storyteller.

> The first time Roland appeared at Court, the simplicity of his costume, his round hat and the ribbons which tied his shoes astonished and scandalized all the valets. . . . The master of ceremonies approached Dumouriez with a distressed look, his eyebrows knitted together, his voice low and constrained, pointing to Roland out of the corner of his eye. "Eh, Monsieur, no buckles on his shoes!" "Ah, Monsieur, everything is lost," Dumouriez replied with a sang-froid that would make you die laughing.[25]

Dumouriez comes off quite well in this episode, but elsewhere he is made out to be a devious and decadent courtier. Mme Roland was particularly offended by the open living arrangements with his mistress, Mme de Beauvert, who "did the honors of his table, to the great scandal of sensitive men, friends of morality and liberty." In Mme Roland's view, sexual license was not at all compatible with republican values. She took Dumouriez to task for arranging to deposit with a notary "one hundred thousand pounds from which Mme de Beauvert was to have her share; she was Dumouriez's mistress, a high-class prostitute . . . surrounded by the stinking aristocracy of people without morals." For one given to lofty language, this is strong speech indeed. Her angry outbursts against sexually free women support Dorinda Outram's thesis that Mme Roland, like many of her contemporaries, saw female sexuality as a corrupting force in the public world.[26]

Mme Roland described her own lifestyle as retaining the simplicity and decency of former days. Refusing to be impressed by the magnificent new ministerial lodgings, she remained an industrious housekeeper given to domestic pleasures and scholarly retreats. Twice a week she entertained, once for her husband's colleagues and a second time for other notables in the world of business and administration. In retrospect, hers was the ideal table "where taste and cleanliness reigned . . . and ornamental luxury never appeared."[27]

Soon, however, Roland's incongruity as minister to Louis XVI became all too evident. He was removed from office for opposing the king's refusal to sanction two Assembly decrees calling, first, for the deportation of refractory priests and, second, for stationing 20,000 soldiers around Paris. Roland's efforts to pressure the other ministers to take a collective stand against the king on these matters was unsuccessful, forcing him, as Mme Roland reminds us, to act bravely on his own: "It was appropriate for Roland's integrity and courage to advance alone, and we drafted between the two of us his famous letter to the King."[28] A copy of this "famous letter" of June 11, 1792, excoriating the monarch's bad faith, was sent to the Assembly, then printed and distributed to all the departments of France. The king immediately dismissed Roland, as well as two other ministers.

In narrating this event, Mme Roland made it clear that she was the strategist behind her husband's acts and the chief composer of this well-publicized letter. From her perspective, the letter of June 11 should go down in history as a turning point in the public attitude toward the king, serving to demonstrate conclusively his "determined opposition to the maintenance of the Constitution." "There we were," she wrote, "back in private life."[29] But not for long. The events of the summer of 1792 would drive the king out of office and Roland back in.

Mme Roland's analysis of the political situation during that summer reverses the image of the panorama depicted by Mme de Tourzel. Where the Duchess saw only the baseness of the Assembly and the hand of "factionists," Mme Roland blamed "the treachery of the Court." On the tenth of August—the day of the royal family's bloody eviction from the Tuileries so vividly described from the royalist perspective by Mme de Tourzel, Mme Campan, and Mme de La Rochejaquelein—Mme Roland placed herself on the side of the insurgents. Then and later she maintained that the court itself had provoked the Tuileries invasion by making its own preparations for attack. "One will say," she argued, "that it was to defend itself; but the idea of attacking would never have come to anyone or would never have been taken up by the people if it [the court] had sincerely executed the Constitution."[30] Here Mme Roland echoes the common revolutionary justification for violence as a legitimate response to provocation or as a deterrent to counter-revolutionary violence.

Yet this intransigent republican was not ignorant of the considerable role played by "factionists" in stirring up the people. Her analysis of their tactics had undoubtedly been sharpened by the Rolands' own recent experience as the victims of demagogic onslaughts. She zeroed in on the "factionists" in a characteristically lucid and graphic manner:

> They strike the popular imagination by exaggerated pictures; they flatter the passions of the multitude, always eager to admire the colossal. . . . Certainly, many people of this temper had thrown themselves into the popular party against the court, ready to serve it for its money, then to betray it if it became weaker. The court affected to consider all of those who opposed its views as such types, and pleased itself by mixing them together under the label of "factionists." True patriots let this noisy pack go unfettered like guard dogs, and perhaps were not displeased to make use of them.[31]

Chief among the rabble-rousers that she held responsible for the mounting assaults on the Roland couple in the fall of 1792 were Marat, Danton and his follower, Fabre d'Eglantine, and, finally, Robespierre. During her husband's first ministry, she had received Danton and Fabre regularly at her home. She remembered that "Danton scarcely let a day go by without coming to see me. Sometimes it was for the Council; he would arrive a little ahead of time and pass into my apartment or stop in a little afterwards, usually with Fabre d'Eglantine. Sometimes he came to ask for supper on days other than the ones on which I habitually received." But after the insurrection of August 10, 1792, which she attributed to Danton's hand, and especially after the September prison massacres, for which she held him responsible by default, Mme Roland began to view him as an abominable assassin. An amateur of physiognomy, she saw in his "repulsive and atrocious face" evidence of a thoroughly corrupt and bloodthirsty character. In her mind's eye Danton appeared "with a dagger in his hand, exciting with voice and gesture a troop of assassins more timid or less ferocious than himself."[32]

As for Fabre d'Eglantine, the dramatist deputy credited with having invented the revolutionary calendar, Mme Roland took him apart in one sentence: "Rigged out in a monk's frock, armed with a stiletto, occupied in hatching a plot to discredit innocence or to do in the rich whose fortune he envies, he is so perfect in his role that whoever wanted to paint the most villainous hypocrite would have only to do his portrait in that costume."[33]

Mme Roland recalled that Danton and Fabre stopped coming to visit her at the end of August; they did not, according to her interpretation, want to expose themselves to her "observant eyes" as they plotted the horrors of the September massacres. She inserted at this juncture a flattering portrait of the Roland couple, doubly enhanced by its juxtaposition to the unscrupulous Danton and Fabre pair. In her self-portrait, she emphasized the traits of which she was proudest: the firmness of her principles, her psychological penetration, and her talent as a writer.

They concluded that Roland was a decent man who would have nothing to do with enterprises of their kind; that his wife offered no handle by which they could exert influence on her; that, as firm in her principles [as her husband], she perhaps had that kind of penetration characteristic of her sex of which false people must be especially on their guard; perhaps they also guessed that she could sometimes command the pen, and that, on the whole, such a couple . . . could perhaps harm their schemes and were only fit to be destroyed.[34]

Mme Roland could not wait for posterity to ferret out her merits; she pointed our noses in their direction with a heavy-handedness that has undoubtedly put some noses out of joint. No one has ever accused her of undue modesty.

Roland's triumphant return to office after the August 10 insurrection did not have the happy consequences he and his wife had anticipated. Their enemy was now not the far right but the far left. Though the Rolands had approved of the Tuileries insurrection, they found it impossible to countenance the atrocities committed a few weeks later. Informed of the prison massacres, M. Roland "wrote to the Assembly that letter of September 3, which became as famous as the one he had addressed to the king." In publicly opposing massacre as a revolutionary means, he demonstrated, in his wife's words, the courage to "denounce with equal vigor royal or popular tyranny."[35]

Mme Roland's understanding of the September slaughter probably profited from her own incarceration, first in the Abbaye, then in Sainte-Pélagie. According to her sources, the massacres were part of a "unified plot" carried out by a "small number of executioners." At the Abbaye, there were, she said, barely fifteen of them, sufficing to exterminate hundreds of prisoners. However, her judgment of the tacit complicity of everyone else who failed to oppose the massacres leads to an indictment of all Parisians. "All of Paris," she affirms, "was witness to those horrible scenes. . . . All of Paris allowed them to happen, all of Paris is cursed in my eyes."[36] Her rhetoric expresses the concept of collective guilt that would, in our own century, be applied to the behavior of all Germans during World War II.

Now that the king was effectively out of the way (although he would not be executed until January 1793), the Rolands found themselves increasingly under attack from their former allies. It was Marat, at the behest of Danton, who launched the first offensive. The September 19 issue of Marat's journal *The People's Friend (L'Ami du Peuple, no. 683)* contained a blistering satire of Mme Roland. She remembered her conversation with her husband after its appearance:

"That," I said to my husband, "is pure Danton; he wants to attack you, he begins by circling around you. . . . He is stupid enough to imagine that I shall be sensitive to such foolishness, that I shall pick up my pen to respond; . . . Those people may have some judgment of my abilities, but they do not know how to judge my soul. They have only to slander me as much as they like, they won't make me budge."

She attributed Marat's personal animosity to an incident dating from the beginning of Roland's second ministry, when Roland had refused Marat's request for 15,000 pounds to publish some of his manuscripts. But the force behind Marat was Danton, compared to a skillful master unleashing a "mad dog . . . to run after and bite" his adversaries.[37] The Danton-Roland enmity was, in Mme Roland's view, occasioned by Danton's envy of Roland's growing national power. It had begun to rival Danton's own influence with the Commune of Paris, which was steadily tightening its grip on the entire country.

She remembers a key incident from the Assembly session of September 25, 1792, when both Danton and Roland had been elected deputies—Danton by the Commune of Paris and Roland by the department of the Somme—and both had to choose between their posts as deputies or ministers. Danton rose to question Roland's reappointment as minister of the interior. According to Mme Roland, "his vehemence betrayed his hatred, made him say many ridiculous things and, among them, that the invitation should be addressed to me as well because I was not useless to Roland's ministry." Danton's actual words at that session were: "If you extend an invitation to him [Roland], extend it also to Mme Roland, because everyone knows that Roland was not alone in his department. I, I was alone in mine."[38] Danton knew exactly how to cast aspersions on his rival: given the eighteenth-century mentality that feared the intrusion of women into the polity, a statesman known to share political power with his wife was an easy target for ridicule.

Among the many reasons why Roland had incurred the enmity of the Dantonists, Mme Roland chooses to remember only those that reflect well on her spouse—his popularity, his austerity, and his activities at the Office of Public Opinion, a propaganda agency responsible for sending letters and circulars to the provincial departments. She glorifies this correspondence as an expression of her husband's "enlightened vigilance" and denigrates his detractors as "suspicious and jealous men." What she takes care not to say directly is that she herself was the chief force behind the Office of Public Opinion and the author of many of its publications. Elsewhere, however, she admits as much. Her description of her role as the literary interpreter of her husband's thoughts offers a model of cornpanionate efficiency:

> If it was a question of a circular, of a piece of instruction, of an important public document, we would confer about it according to the trust we had in one another, and, impregnated by his ideas, nourished by my own, I took up the pen which I had more time than he to use. Since we both had the same principles and the same mind, we ended by agreeing on the form, and my husband had nothing to lose by passing [his projects] through my hands.[39]

This favorable judgment of the publications emanating from Roland's office was not shared by his enemies. Increasingly, according to his wife, they represented him as a "dangerous man, . . . a corruptor of public opinion, . . . a conspirator." The Jacobins, ruled by Danton, Robespierre, and Marat, finally succeeded in driving the Rolands from office. Mme Roland's "Historical Notices" ends by blaming this trio for her husband's defeat and the atrocities of the Terror. Her bitterness against Danton and Robespierre would hardly abate during her captivity, and she would greet Marat's assassination on July 14, 1793, with cautious applause, her caution deriving only from the fear—which proved to be well founded—that henceforth he would be seen as a martyr. Of Charlotte Corday, Marat's assassin, Mme Roland asserted that she "deserves the admiration of the whole universe." Though she rarely had a good word for any other member of her sex, Mme Roland had nothing but praise for that "heroine worthy of a better century."[40]

Her respect for Charlotte Corday for ridding the country of a notorious scourge is tinged with a modicum of wistful envy. Mme Roland's own role would be more modest: she would become the chronicler of the Revolution, an author in spite of her reservations about women authors. As her most recent biographer Guy Chaussinand-Nogaret has written, "her whole life strained in that direction."[41] Prison had, ironically, provided the opportunity for her to realize her writerly self. At thirty-nine, from her cell, she sent for her favorite books, acquired pen and paper, and unshackled the creative force within.

Her verbal explosion was surely overdetermined and lends itself to more than one interpretation. For the historian Dorinda Outram, Mme Roland is a classical case of Freudian sublimation, with sexuality finding release in literary expression.[42] Certainly, too, the prospect of a shortened lifespan produced in Mme Roland a sense of existential urgency, impelling her to fashion for future generations an exemplary self-image. Imminent death could be conquered symbolically through a literary monument that would represent her as she wished to appear for all eternity. Both of these interpretations could apply to men in similar situations. Yet gender-specific factors surely intensified the force of Manon Roland's output. For the first time in thirteen years she was freed from the daily demands of marriage and motherhood. In prison she found that room of her own which Virginia Woolf, in a later century, would posit as the prerequisite of the woman author. Nothing was to prevent her from wedding herself, as in her youth, to the written word. She could finally aspire to full citizenship in that republic of letters which she had renounced at twenty-two because of her sex. The analogy with citizenship is apt here, for the early Revolution had designated all women as "passive citizens" and men who met certain criteria as "active citizens," granting the vote only to the latter. In the republic of letters, the words "passive" and "active" distinguish readers from writers. For the first time Mme Roland claimed for herself a literary status, not merely as the writer of personal letters and circulars under her husband's name, but as an author in her own right. And indeed after her death she would become, on the basis of her five-month prison output, the most celebrated memoirist of the French Revolution, blurring that separation between the public and the private self she had taken pains to establish.

It is intriguing to speculate upon her fate had she been, like Dostoevsky, suddenly reprieved. Perhaps she would have returned to her earlier opinion that a woman loses more than she gains by authorship, and retreated into needlework. Perhaps, on the other hand, she would have pursued her desire to write the annals of her century.[43] Her imprisonment may well have provided a boundary experience, which shattered internalized gender-based constraints and from which there was no turning back.

Since her death, the persona of Mme Roland in her memoirs has inspired radically different reactions. One of her younger republican contemporaries, Mme Cavaignac, could not forgive her for being more concerned with posthumous glory than with the daughter she was leaving behind. In her memoirs, Mme Cavaignac wrote that the loss of her own daughter had been the "most terrible misfortune that can strike us in this world."

From this maternal frame of mind, she castigated Mme Roland for priorities different from her own:

> The woman on the verge of death, leaving a daughter of a few years practically without asylum, who affects not to regret life and who is concerned only with posterity and the name she will leave behind; the mother who . . . does not cry in despair over the child she is going to abandon . . . playing the statesman until the last moment . . . that mother will never be my heroine.[44]

But the eminent critic Sainte-Beuve—free from such maternal concerns—took a very different stance. He praised Mme Roland's "grave, simple, and historic" character and eulogized her "as one of the most perfect representatives . . . of that political generation which had desired 1789 and which 1789 neither exhausted nor satisfied."[45]

Sainte-Beuve's younger contemporary, the poet Louise Colet, honored Roland with a dramatic scene in verse, paralleled by a similar homage to Charlotte Corday. Colet published the two poems together in the book *Charlotte Corday et Madame Roland.* Her tribute to those two representatives of the Girondin spirit was intended to counter the female image of the "sinister `tricoteusee' and furies of the guillotine" associated with the extremist Montagnard faction.[46]

The writer and statesman Alphonse de Lamartine, fascinated with Mme Roland while he was composing his History of the Girondins (1847), portrayed her as the soul, not only of the Girondin party, but of the entire Revolution. "There is a woman," he wrote, "at the origin of all great things. The Revolution found this woman in Mme Roland." But for all his poetic evocation of her enchanting beauty and passionate soul, for all the ennobling virtues and political influence he granted her, Lamartine did not remain faithful to this idealized image. In the antifeminism of his old age, he joined the ranks of such historians as Adolphe Thiers and Pierre Joseph Proudhon, who believed that nature and society have assigned to the two sexes fundamentally different roles which should not be violated, even by women as remarkable as Mme Roland and Mme de Staël. "The public role belongs essentially to man; the domestic role to women," Lamartine concluded in this later appraisal.[47]

At the time of the centennial of the Revolution, Mme Roland's glory—due in part to Lamartine's *History of the Girondins*—had reached its zenith. An oversized commemorative album compared her to France's greatest heroine: "Thus died the most noble woman who has appeared in history since Joan of Arc. She was the strongest and truest character in our Revolution." And two hundred years after her death, on the occasion of the bicentennial of the Revolution, she would be recognized by the notable French scholar Elisabeth Badinter as the only woman besides Marie-Antoinette to have exerted an undeniable influence on revolutionary politics.[48]

Her resurrection by contemporary feminists would have surprised and probably vexed Mme Roland. She who disdained the company of women, who wanted posterity to know that women never constituted a significant part of her small circle of friends, would certainly object to being segregated from her male contemporaries and placed (as in this book) among the females, most of whom—it must be admitted—were inferior to her in education and literary talent. Yet her life and writing prove that though she played the queen bee to her sister creatures, her fate cannot be fully understood without attention to the politics of gender.

No better indication of the sexual politics affecting her destiny exists than the reproachful statement found in the newspaper *Le Moniteur* several days after she was guillotined. It lumped together three women who had stepped out of the "natural sphere" of their sex and been rewarded, within a span of three weeks, with public execution: Marie-Antoinette, Olympe de Gouges, and Mme Roland. From the perspective of the official press, these three offered useful negative examples. "Women," Le Moniteur admonished, "never attend popular assemblies with the desire to speak out." Remain within the silent domain assigned to the fair sex and avoid the fate of Mme Roland, "a monster from every point of view."[49]

From *monstre* to *monstre sacré* (sacred cow)—that has been the posthumous itinerary of Mme Roland. From the antiheroine of a cautionary tale to secular sainthood one hundred years after her death, Mme Roland has indeed commanded the attention of posterity. Today she is recognized as a complex and indomitable woman, a creature of her time and a precursor of our own. In her struggle to comply with eighteenth-century mores and to fulfill her unique potential, we recognize the gender shackles that did not drop off with the Revolution. Mme Roland dealt with being female in contradictory ways. She held her tongue in public and wrote political documents in private. She refused the company of other women, aside from a few mental equals like Sophie Grandchamp. She mothered a daughter who turned out to be a disappointment because she did not have her own exceptional gifts. She served soup to Danton and wrote admiring letters to Robespierre; later she turned against both of them with venomous words that neither she nor they lived to see in print. She was the devoted wife of a man old enough to be her father and the platonic mistress of a man six years her junior. Immediately following her execution in November 1793, her husband committed suicide, and Buzot chose the same path eight months later.

Her friend Sophie Grandchamp bore witness to Mme Roland's fortitude on the last day of her life. While still in prison, Manon had asked Sophie to observe her on the way to the guillotine: "Your presence will diminish the fear that this odious journey inspires. I shall at least be sure that a being worthy of me will render homage to the firmness which will not abandon me in such a dreadful ordeal." Sophie followed her friend's instructions. She went out an hour before Mme Roland's departure from the Conciergerie and stationed herself at the end of the Pont-Neuf, wearing the same clothes she had worn when they had last met. As soon as she was able to make out Manon's face, Sophie stared directly at her. "She was fresh, calm, and smiling. . . . Approaching the bridge, her eyes looked for me. I read the satisfaction that she experienced in seeing me at this last, unforgettable rendezvous."[50]

Hundreds of other French women are known to have conducted themselves bravely on the way to the guillotine; they left behind a heroinic legacy that grew to legendary proportions during the nineteenth century. Most often they were portrayed as political and religious martyrs, proclaiming their loyalty to the monarchy with a final cry of "*Vive le roi.*" Yet no one was truer to her principles than Mme Roland, a patrician republican to the end. And no one took greater care to ensure that the spectacle of her death would add to her posthumous glory.

Mme Roland's behavior on her last day has evoked different reactions: empathy for the woman who felt less alone knowing she was being watched by a sisterly eye, amazement at her stoical calm, and admiration for her desire to die bravely in public so as to give added meaning to her death. Yet some, like Mme Cavaignac and Lamartine, have criticized her need for applause and her overriding concern with posterity. Without falling into that judgmental stance, it is possible to recognize Mme Roland's acute theatrical sense—a sense shared by many revolutionary players—and her ostensible belief that the unobserved life is not worth living. Would Mme Roland have been content with Sophie Grandchamp written testimony? Though Grandchamp succeeded in conveying her friend's tragic dignity, her account is not as eloquent as Mme Roland's own words surely would have been, had she been given the paper and pen she requested at the foot of the scaffold to write down what she had experienced on her journey from the Conciergerie to the Place de la Révolution.

Just before she met her death, Mme Roland is reputed to have cried out, "Liberty! How many crimes are committed in your name!"

Charlotte Robespierre. From her Mémoires sur ses Deux Frères (*Paris: Au Dépôt Central,* *1835*)

6

THE OTHER ROBESPIERRE

BEFORE THE REVOLUTION, MAXIMILIEN ROBESPIERRE was a provincial lawyer living peacefully in Arras with his sister. Elected to the Estates General in 1789 as a representative from the Third Estate, he quickly became known as the "Incorruptible" for his honesty and stalwart adherence to democratic principles. His fierce rhetoric dominated the Assembly where he championed the cause of liberty, fraternity, equality, and turned the gallery—especially the women—into an audience of adulators. But this great orator and patriot was also, when the time came, the apostle of Terror, as Mme Roland and many of his early admirers learned to their detriment. No one wedded his life more intimately to the Revolution than Robespierre, and when he himself was destroyed by the Terror he had orchestrated, its worst excesses came to an end.

Thirty-four years after the execution of Maximilien and his younger brother Augustin, their surviving sister Charlotte was asked to write a memoir about them. Almost seventy, living in obscure poverty, she was warmed by the friendship of a young man named Albert Laponneraye and by his determination to restore Maximilien's greatly tarnished image. Charlotte's 1828 encounter with the twenty-one-year-old Laponneraye eventuated in the production of a curious autobiographical document, published in 1835, a year after her death. Historians, political scientists, biographers, novelists, and specialists in the French Revolution have seized upon its one hundred pages, ravenous for every factual tidbit concerning the public and private lives of the two male Robespierres. And a few have even professed interest in the sister as well.

Robespierre biographers and historical novelists tend to mold her into the stock character of "the spinster sister.[1] A more nuanced treatment recently appeared in a two-person play based on Charlotte's relationship with Laponneraye, brought to the stage by

Reine Bartève and Jean-Marie Lehec at La Vieille Grille Theater in Paris during the fall of 1989. But the only serious scholarly attempt to present her life is found in the 1910 edition of her memoirs, meticulously annotated and introduced by the eminent French historian Hector Fleischmann. Still, despite the exhaustive accumulation of documentary evidence, Fleischmann makes little effort to understand Charlotte Robespierre, much less to portray her sympathetically; he judges her as he judges all women: "She is a woman, and as such, no exception to the average nature characteristic of her sex."[2]

Today, with our interest in "average" women at an all-time high, Charlotte Robespierre's story takes on special meaning. What can be learned about the life of an obscure woman who has come down in history as a footnote to her brothers' lives? From her memoirs, which focus largely on her two brothers and their involvement in revolutionary politics, we are able to glean the historical facts of her existence and a sense of her temperament. Supplementing her memoirs with a few of her letters and several other texts written by her contemporaries, it is possible to piece together this life, so profoundly allied to the Revolution and so deeply harrowed by its course.

Charlotte Robespierre was born in Arras in 1760, twenty months after her brother Maximilien. Within the next three years, her mother gave birth to another daughter, Henriette, and another son, Augustin. At age four Charlotte lost her mother; shortly thereafter, her father, while traveling to forget his grief, also died. The children were then parcelled out to relatives, the girls taken in by paternal aunts, the boys by their maternal grandparents.

In 1768 Charlotte was sent to a convent school in Tournay, where she and twenty other boarders received the education considered suitable for young ladies from the provinces. In light of subsequent history, it is often forgotten that the Robespierres could claim noble status. The young ladies learned writing, religion, lace making, and home economics. Charlotte was to remain in this cloistered setting for nine years, with her sister joining her there in 1773.

In the meantime, Maximilien had been sent, not to a second-rate provincial school, but to the prestigious Collège Louis Le Grand in Paris. While Charlotte's references to her own studies are skimpy at best, she lavishes upon Maximilien's school years copious adulation. He is presented as a brilliant student—a fact borne out by other accounts—with "a sweet and fair disposition that made him loved by all."[3] Here and elsewhere Charlotte's attempts to promote her brother to sainthood fail through their excess. Her obvious idolatry, coupled with a desire to rehabilitate Maximilien in the eyes of history, colors all aspects of her account of their early life, retrospectively casting Maximilien the child into the role of family hero and savior. For example,

> Each year he came back to us for the holidays. We always saw him with transports of joy. How quickly the days we spent together passed, after the absence of a whole year! When the moment for him to return to school arrived, it seemed as if we had possessed him for only a few minutes. It was while Maximilien was studying in Paris that we had the misfortune of losing our little sister. It was thus decreed that our childhood would be bathed in tears and that each of our early years would be marked by the death of a cherished object. This fatal destiny had a greater influence than one can imagine on Maximilien's character; it made him sad and melancholy.[4]

And what of the influence of these events on Charlotte's character? Has she possibly projected upon Maximilien part of her own "sad and melancholy" nature? The death of her younger sister when Charlotte was twenty must have seemed like another form of orphanage. The most consistent companion of her youth, the one who had lived with her in her aunts' home and followed her to the convent school, was now gone. With both her brothers away in Paris, Charlotte must have felt more isolated than ever.

But a year later, in 1781, her life was to take a more fortuitous turn. Having finished his legal studies, Maximilien returned to Arras to practice law and took up residence with his sister. She became, for the first time, the mistress of a household, responsible for every detail in her brother's domestic life.

Imagine a young woman, orphaned in her fifth year, placed in a convent school from age eight to seventeen, mourning the loss of her only sister, and suddenly, at twenty-one, mistress of the lodgings she shared with an adored older brother, one of the most eligible bachelors of Arras. How she enjoyed her cozy family life and her new place in provincial society! Those were to be the happiest years of her life, a life structured around Maximilien's needs:

> He worked a great deal, and spent long hours in his study when he wasn't at the hall of justice. He got up at six or seven, worked till eight. Then his wigmaker came to dress his hair. He had a light breakfast . . . and went back to work till ten, when he got dressed and went to the court. After the session, he came home for lunch; he ate little and drank only watered-down wine. . . . After lunch he went out for an hour's walk or a visit. Then he came back, closed himself once more in his study until seven or eight, and spent the rest of the evening either with friends or at home.[5]

Her portrait of Maximilien could be that of any hard-working, honest, sober member of the bourgeoisie. In his relationship with his sister and aunts, Charlotte portrays him as frequently preoccupied, uninterested in their light talk and card playing, yet "naturally gay" and capable of "laughing till the tears flowed." As for the fair sex, Maximilien definitely had his conquests, including a certain Mlle Deshorties whom he courted for two or three years. Charlotte assumes that he probably would have married her "if the voice of his co-citizens had not snatched him from the sweetness of private life and launched him upon a political career."[6] Politics were to be his deepest passion.

What were Charlotte's reactions when her revered brother was called to Paris by his election to the Estates General in 1789? Clearly very proud of his political ascendancy, proud too that they remained in close contact through the mail, she quotes from his correspondence: "You are what I love the most after 'la patrie' [the fatherland]." She obviously included this fervent declaration in her memoirs to suggest both her value as his favorite person and his worth as a patriot.[7]

A document left by Pierre Villiers, Maximilien's secretary in 1790, confirms his attachment to his sister, but also reveals a hidden facet of the deputy known for his austerity. "I knew of only one woman, aged twenty-six, whom he treated rather badly and who idolized him. Very often he wouldn't let her in when she came around. He gave her a fourth of his salary; I sent the remainder . . . to the address of a sister living in Arras of whom he was very fond." It seems likely from this letter that Robespierre paid a woman regularly, probably for sexual services, while in the eyes of the world the "Incorruptible" lived the life of an ascetic. The myth of the virtuous Robespierre, "chaste by choice," has not disappeared from even our most recent assessments.[8]

While the older brother was making history in Paris, the younger one, Augustin, succeeded Maximilien as a fledgling lawyer in Arras and as his sister's joint tenant. Both followed their brother's dramatic rise to power in the National Assembly; they adopted his revolutionary ideas and tried to promote them among their fellow citizens in Arras.

We get a glimpse of Charlotte's interests and activities from a letter to Maximilien dated April 9, 1790. She reports that the good citizens of Arras are "pleased with the patriotic contribution," referring to a decree issued by the revolutionary government requesting all citizens to contribute a fourth of their income to the nation. She also notes that the municipal authorities have begun a campaign to raise money for the poor, but that "many people do not want to pay anything additional. They give as their reason that we shouldn't feed the poor to do nothing, that we should make them work." This letter also contains more personal information on Charlotte in her dealings with a certain Mme Marchand.

> We've had a falling-out. I allowed myself to tell her what all good patriots ought to think about her newspaper, what you thought about it. I reproached her for always putting in odious remarks about the People. She got angry. She maintains there are no aristocrats in Arras, that she knows them all to be patriots, that it's only hotheads who find her gazette aristocratic; she told me a heap of nonsense and since then she hasn't been sending us her paper any longer.[9]

Whatever her ideological justifications, Charlotte does not appear in a very favorable light. She comes across as officious, self righteous, even arrogant. It is the first of several fallings-out to take place in the next few years. As for the letter's style, it is considerably more colloquial than her memoirs and filled with spelling errors. This and a few other letters written in her hand preserved in the National Archives in Paris suggest that her memoirs were substantially corrected by Laponneraye.

This same Mme Marchand, editor of the *Affiches d'Artois*, published two ironic articles on the "patriots" of her city, including Charlotte and Augustin, on the occasion of Maximilien's visit to Arras in October 1791. In the first she describes a missed meeting in a neighboring town:

> M. et Mlle de Robespierre went to meet him . . . at the head of a delegation composed of a number of their friends. . . . A wreath was carried in a basket by two of the ladies. What a pity for the group! Robespierre did not arrive. . . . Well, the group decided to dance. They were right to dance; one shouldn't go so far for no reason. . . . They came back to the city: the wreath was still at the head of the parade.

In the second article, published a week later, she reports Maximilien's belated arrival and the visit of several members of his entourage to her house.

> They wanted me to speak more respectfully of M. Robespierre. They wouldn't put up with any joking on that score. I asked for permission to laugh from time to time: so many people are crying! . . .
>
> Their tone was that of a conqueror of the Bastille . . . mine was that of a woman who knows one should respect women. . . . I reminded them of my sex and they shaped up.[10]

This unknown woman, publisher and editor of her own newspaper, portrays herself as resisting masculine intimidation. Her articles suggest the mettle of a bold woman, whose outspoken political views contrast markedly with the more dependent nature of her contemporary, Charlotte Robespierre.

IN SEPTEMBER 1792, both Maximilien and Augustin were elected to the Legislative Assembly. Charlotte and Augustin left Arras for Paris where they found Maximilien lodged with the Duplays, a family of ardent republicans. For a time, Charlotte lodged with the Duplays as well. In recounting the story of Maximilien's involvement with the Duplay family and her own difficult relations with them, Charlotte finally assumes a leading role in her memoirs. The reader is presented with the situation of a woman in her early thirties, who had kept house for her older brother for almost a decade and for her younger brother for three more years. She had come to Paris in the hope of establishing a household in which the three siblings could finally be together, but what did she find?

> When I arrived from Arras in 1792, I stayed with the Duplays, and I noticed right away the strong influence they had on him. . . . This influence had as its source my brother's good nature, on the one hand, . . . and Madame Duplay's incessant and often tiresome endearments, on the other.
>
> I resolved to extricate my brother from her hands, and in order to do so, I tried to make him understand that in his position, occupying such an elevated political rank, he should have his own place. . . .
>
> Madame Duplay was very angry with me. I think she bore me ill will for the rest of her life. We thus lived together alone, my brother and I, for a short period of time, whereupon he fell ill. His sickness was not dangerous. He needed much attention, and I certainly saw to it that he wanted for nothing. I didn't leave him for a moment. I looked after him constantly. When he was better, Madame Duplay came to see him. . . . She started saying very disagreeable things to me. She told me that my brother did not have all the care he needed, that he would be better off in her family . . . and she pressed Maximilien to return to her home. . . . Robespierre, in spite of my protests, finally decided to follow her. "They love me so much," he said, ". . . they have shown me such great kindness, it would be ungrateful for me to reject them."

For once, Charlotte is critical of Maximilien; she reproaches him for not putting her interests above those of another. "But after all, should he not have thought that his preference for Madame Duplay would distress me at least as much as his refusal could have distressed that lady? Between Madame Duplay and me, should he have hesitated? Should he have sacrificed me for her?"[11]

This is perhaps the truest personal moment in Charlotte's memoirs, the moment of release from sisterly obedience when the voice crying for love, recognition, and justice refuses to be stifled. For one passionate moment, Charlotte drops the veil of the hagiographic biographer and bares her own anguish, decades after her brother's defection. Sounding like a wife abandoned for another woman, she calls upon the reader to empathize with her past injury: she, who had been briefly restored to what she considered as her rightful place as mistress of her brother's home, was abruptly replaced. It is understandable that she felt bitter, even against her revered brother, and especially against the woman whose maneuvers had caused his desertion. The rivalry between Charlotte and Mme Duplay was complicated by the fact that the latter had four daughters, one of whom—Eléonore—was reputed to have been either Maximilien's mistress or his fiancée. Charlotte insists that both opinions were equally untrue. Whatever his involvement with Eléonore Duplay, a gulf between Charlotte and Maximilien gradually developed, one so large that Charlotte, like many who came to call upon the great patriot at the Duplay residence, often found him sequestered behind closed doors.

Charlotte did have an ally in one of the Duplay daughters, Elisabeth. "She was not," Charlotte wrote, "like her eldest sister, set against me. Several times she came to wipe away my tears when Mme Duplay's indignities made me cry."[12] This friendship is supported by Elisabeth Duplay Le Bas's own autobiographical account, presented in the following chapter. In her short memoirs, the younger Duplay daughter described her life in Paris during the early years of the Revolution and her close relationship with Maximilien and Charlotte Robespierre, who introduced her to her future husband, the deputy Philippe Le Bas.

During the winter of 1792-93, Charlotte's first in Paris, she did her best to maintain the family bonds. With Elisabeth Duplay she frequented the Legislative Assembly and occasionally dined out with her brothers. A letter dated February 17, 1793, from Rosalie Jullien, the wife of a substitute deputy from the Dauphiny, offers a picture of the three Robespierres invited to dinner by another Jacobin family:

> I was delighted with the Robespierres. The sister is naive and natural . . . she came two hours before her brothers, and we had a chance to talk together as women. I got her to talk about their domestic habits; they're just as we are—unsophisticated and sincere. Her brother . . . is abstract, like a thinker, dry like a minister. . . . He doesn't have our tender sensibility, but I believe he wants the best for the human race, more through a sense of justice than through love. . . . The younger Robespierre is more animated, more open, an excellent patriot, but common in his thoughts and petulant in disposition.[13]

This rare close-up portrait of the three Robespierres zeroes in on their most pronounced features: Charlotte's simplicity, Maximilien's abstraction, Augustin's temper. These personal characteristics are to play their part in the final falling-out between Charlotte and her brothers. Charlotte records the circumstances of that unhappy break in a chapter describing a trip to the south of France in the company of Augustin and M. and Mme Ricord. Jean-François Ricord and Augustin Robespierre, both Convention deputies, were sent on an investigatory mission to Nice. In Charlotte's account, Augustin welcomed her proposal to accompany him "with joy."[14]

Their descent by carriage into the provinces during the summer of 1793, when the south of France from Lyons to Marseilles was studded with counterrevolutionary uprisings, brought them close to peril on several occasions. Finding Lyons in full insurrection, the deputies made haste to move on. In order to make their presence less conspicuous, they took back roads, stopping in small towns such as Manosque, but even here their stay was "not without danger," given the menacing attitude of the population. In their next stop at Forcalquier, the local patriots of that city offered their services, staying with them through the dinner hour, which was interrupted by an express message from the mayor of Manosque warning them that counterrevolutionary soldiers from Marseilles were on their trail. The foursome quickly made their way on horseback into the mountains, leaving their carriage behind. Accompanied by "a dozen patriots" serving as their guides, they traveled all night "on terrible paths, descending very rough hills" on horses that had difficulty finding their footing.[15] After numerous adventures worthy of a picaresque novel, they arrived in Nice, where a division of French troops promised a less hazardous sojourn.

At first Charlotte enjoyed the company of Mme Ricord. While the men were engaged in official business, the two women occupied themselves with making shirts for the soldiers. In the evening, they explored the outskirts of Nice, either on foot or on horseback, but when their equestrian outings were criticized as "aristocratic" and word of this criticism reached Maximilien in Paris, Charlotte bowed to her brothers' demand that she give up "the pleasure of riding." From Charlotte's perspective, it was the machinations of Mme Ricord, intent on seducing Augustin, that caused the rupture between the two siblings. She characterized Mme Ricord as a wicked coquette, who wanted to destroy the relationship between Charlotte and Augustin so as to rid herself of "a severe and rigorous witness."[16] And she succeeded.

It is not difficult to imagine Charlotte's feelings in this situation, dismissed as Maximilien's housekeeper and now alienated from Augustin as well. She had cared for her younger brother in Arras, promoted his career in every possible way, come with him to Paris with the highest of hopes, accompanied him on his mission to the south, only to find herself an importunate intruder in his liaison with Mme Ricord. According to Charlotte, Mme Ricord engineered her dismissal through a letter from Augustin commanding her to return to Paris: "Imagine my astonishment! My brother, without seeing me, without saying good-bye, sends me away like an outcast."[17] The brother and sister were never to see one another again.

Was Charlotte simply perceived as a spoilsport by her younger brother? Was she indeed the victim of another woman's coquetry and wiles? Did her own "chaste" habits as a respectable single woman come into conflict with those of Augustin and his mistress and the French tradition that allowed a married woman more sexual freedom outside the conjugal situation than an unmarried woman? Charlotte's convent school upbringing, without the benefit of a mother; her lack of marital experience; her adherence to the prescriptive behavior for unmarried women, especially in the provinces; and her uncompromising ideals did not lend themselves to the looser private morality of a revolutionary milieu. She could not condone the boldness of some of her female contemporaries, particularly when it impinged upon her brothers' lives. She felt profoundly threatened by them and deeply betrayed by Augustin's preference for one such woman.

A letter from Augustin to Maximilien preserved in the National Archives in Paris throws some light on the increasingly strained relations between Charlotte and her brothers.

> My sister has not a single drop of blood which resembles ours. I have learned and seen so many things about her that I consider her our greatest enemy. . . .We must take a stand against her. We must make her leave for Arras and thus distance ourselves from a woman who contributes to our mutual despair.[18]

This letter, written in early 1794, was to condemn Charlotte to a temporary exile, of less than a month. She was sent back to Arras, accompanied on her voyage by an old curate named Le Bon. Her memoirs are silent on this disgrace; other sources reveal that Charlotte was brought back to Paris by the Convention member Florent Guyot. Here (and elsewhere) it is impossible to ignore the patriarchal aspects of her situation; dependent on her brothers for financial and social support, she was moved about like a child, always under the surveillance of male authority figures. Her memoirs indicate that, unlike a few more daring women (for example, Mme Marchand or the feminist Olympe de Gouges), she never questioned the right of men to tell women what to do.

The last chapter of her memoirs focuses on the last months of her brothers' lives, and mainly on Maximilien's. The author is anxious to place him firmly at the summit of the pantheon, above such figures as Danton and Louis Saint-Just, all good revolutionaries but lacking—she averred—some of the virtues that made her brother superior to his contemporaries. It is possible that Laponneraye, himself the author of several treatises on the revolutionary years, expanded her notes for this chapter into a more substantial historical document.[19] We are in the presence of unabashed political hagiography, designed to counter the ignominy visited upon Robespierre's reputation after his death.

The very last pages revert to the story of Charlotte as she herself experienced the dreadful Thermidor days. Portraying herself as a hapless victim of a revolution gone mad, Charlotte's account is oddly similar to those written by female aristocrats with opposite political loyalties:

> The next day, the tenth of Thermidor, I rush into the streets, my head full of anxiety, my heart full of despair. I look for my brothers. I learn that they have been taken to the Conciergerie. I run there, ask to see them, plead with folded hands, get down on my knees in front of the soldiers. They push me away, laugh at my tears, insult me, strike me. Several people, moved by pity, drag me away. My reason became clouded. I no longer knew what was happening, what would become of me. Or rather, I found out several days later; when I came to myself, I was in prison. [20]

This passage reminds us not only of other contemporary memoirs, but also of numerous preromantic and romantic works of fiction in which the heroine is buffeted about by a relentless fate. She is all trepidation and sensibility, prey to the cruelties of masculine power. The conventional "black-out," often occasioned in novels by an attempted rape, ends when she wakes to the reality of imprisonment.

This account of how she came to be a prisoner is followed by an account of how she extricated herself from that situation. Her tale of a letter written from her cell at the urging of an unnamed coprisoner has a fictional ring: "Profiting from my horrible situation, my dejection, my despair, and my distraught spirits, she made me sign a statement containing things that were unworthy of me."[21] Charlotte fears that this letter, the exact contents of which she has forgotten, was used by Maximilien's detractors to further blacken his name.

Whether such a letter ever existed (thus far it has not been found) or whether, as Fleischmann surmises, Charlotte confused it with another document, this last entry in her memoirs reveals an uneasy conscience. But even though she expresses concern for the consequences of her letter, she refuses to take responsibility for it. Her destiny is always presented as determined by the diabolical machinations of someone else. This sense that fate was against her from the start is more than a romantic pose. Orphaned in childhood, Charlotte Robespierre began early in life to see herself as a victim of outside forces. Whatever the circumstances, she projected the blame on others—frequently women: Mme Marchand, Mme Duplay, Mme Ricord, or the mysterious woman in prison. The memoirs do not offer a single instance in which Charlotte tries to understand the ways in which she herself may have contributed to her personal tragedies (except for one incident in childhood centered around her laxity in caring for Maximilien's pet pigeons, the neglect of which led to their death). We are in the presence of a self-righteous old lady intent upon justifying herself to posterity.

Her self-justification is, of course, minor in comparison to the vindication she constructs for Maximilien. He is always portrayed as being in the right, except in the matter of Mme Duplay. It is always the others—the other members of the Committee of Public Safety, for example, who were responsible for the Terror. It was Danton, with his dissolute habits and lapsed hostility toward the nobility who brought about his own execution, not Robespierre who led the Convention against the Dantonists. And it was Robespierre's jealous enemies who engineered the coup against her brothers, "against all the good Montagnards [the deputies on the extreme left] or rather against the people, of whom they were the purest representatives."[22] Her memoirs stand as a monolithic apology for a formidable public figure who continues to inspire controversy two centuries after the Revolution.

The memoirs end with Maximilien's death, although Charlotte was to live on for forty more years. She considered her own life worthy of documentation only to the extent that it was coterminous with her brothers' lives. The later period of her life was marked by a strange quirk of history: Charlotte Robespierre was to receive a pension from the French government that lasted, under various regimes, for at least fifteen years and probably longer.[23] Issued by Napoleon, whom she had known through Augustin, and renewed by the restored Bourbon monarch Louis XVIII, a pension was granted to the sister of the regicide Maximilien Robespierre, whose speeches at the trial of Louis XVI had hastened the king's death and the destruction of the Old Regime. And Charlotte Robespierre, fervent republican, was willing to accept support from the kings of France.

Elisabeth Duplay Le Bas, for one, condemned Charlotte for accepting this pension. In a note ringing with indignation, Mme Le Bas wrote that she preferred being a washerwoman to asking for help from her husband's enemies, whereas Mlle Robespierre—it pained her to report—had not refused their assistance. Laponneraye, on the other hand, defended Charlotte on the grounds of her advanced age, ill health, and material destitution: "To have rejected the pension . . . would have condemned her to die of hunger and extreme poverty, since her brothers had not left her anything."[24]

She lived very modestly on this pension, her last years spent in a tiny apartment in the rue de la Pitié, with the companionship of a young woman named Victoire Mathon, who was named as Charlotte's inheritor in her testament of 1828. In that same year, her meeting with Laponneraye was to transform her few remaining years. Laponneraye was to become not only a collaborator, but also a financial and moral helpmeet, the son she had never had.

In accepting a small sum of money from him, she wrote a gracious note to express her maternal gratitude. "I accept then [this gift] from one who has for me the sentiments of a son, whom I consider as such, and for whom I have so much affection. . . . I accept with pleasure! That word says it all. I think you will be pleased with me."[25] There is something quite touching about the kindness bestowed upon a seventy-year-old woman by a twenty-one-year-old man and her almost childlike desire to please him. One might say that she found in Laponneraye not only the son or grandson she never had, but the affection ultimately denied her by her brothers.

She was, of course, undoubtedly of interest to Laponneraye primarily as the Robespierre sister. Her memoirs are mainly a testimonial to Maximilien, yet they allowed her to write her own story, at least obliquely. The format of a memoir provided a means for Charlotte Robespierre—as it did for many other women in the past—to enter into recorded history through the life of a famous male relative, and thus, ironically, to have the last word. [26]

Madame Elisabeth Le Bas, née Duplay, widow of the deputy Philippe Le Bas. From Paul Coutant, Le Conventionnel Le Bas (*Paris: Flammarion, 1901*)

7

<hr>

THE WIDOW LE BAS

THE POET PAUL VALÉRY TELLS A STORY he heard from the painter Edgar Degas. When Degas was a boy, he used to accompany his mother on visits to an elderly lady known as the Widow Le Bas. One day his mother noticed hanging in her hallway several portraits of revolutionary leaders, Robespierre, Saint-Just, and Georges Couthon. In response to Mme Degas's amazement that her friend should continue to display "the heads of those monsters," Mme Le Bas replied: "Hold your tongue, Célestine, they were saints.[1] Valéry was still alive during my childhood. I was thus only two lives away from that of Mme Le Bas, the widow of a deputy to the Convention, one of the men who had been condemned with Robespierre on the ninth of Thermidor!

The circumstances under which I first discovered the memoirs of Elisabeth Duplay Le Bas are indicative of the cavalier treatment traditionally accorded such texts. Having glimpsed her as an old woman through the eyes of Degas and as a young woman in Charlotte Robespierre's memoirs, I set out to find her. For a long time she was nowhere to be found. Then one day, in a book titled *Le Conventionnel Le Bas* published in a series called *Autour de Robespierre*, I came across the picture of a refreshingly beautiful young woman and forty-nine autobiographical pages recounting her life from 1792 to 1794.[2] No name on the book cover indicated that she and her writing had been cannibalized whole into the life stories of Philippe Le Bas and Maximilien Robespierre.[3]

Elisabeth Le Bas's memoirs reenact the romance of a young bourgeois woman with one of the Convention deputies. Played out against the backdrop of the National Assembly and the Jacobin Club, nourished with republican sentiments and patriotic phrases, her love for Le Bas nonetheless resembles every first love, with its transports, hesitations, and misunderstandings.

Scarcely twenty years old in 1792 when she met Le Bas for the first time, married the thirteenth of August 1793, and a mother and widow one year later, Elisabeth was imprisoned with her baby and ostracized after her liberation. Poverty and the loss of several family members added to her misfortunes. Yet she never renounced her republican principles, as she passionately proclaimed in 1842: "I love liberty; the blood that flows in my veins, at the age of seventy, is the blood of a republican."[4] Until her death in 1859, the revolutionary portraits seen by the young Degas hung on her walls.

Her memoirs begin *in medias res:*

> It was on the day that Marat was, carried in triumph to the Assembly that I saw my darling, Philippe Le Bas, for the first time.
>
> I found myself, on that day, at the National Convention with Charlotte Robespierre. Le Bas came to greet her. He stayed with us a long time and asked who I was. Charlotte told him I was one of the daughters of her elder brother's host. . . . He asked Charlotte if we came to the Assembly often and said that on a certain day there would be a very interesting session. He invited her pressingly to attend.[5]

From the outset her voice has the ring of authenticity. She writes as she speaks and she speaks as she is—direct, lively, and ingenuous.

She recreates the charged atmosphere of the Assembly, with the popular triumphs of such demagogues as Marat and the personal exchanges between speakers and spectators, drawing readers into the scene as if we were sitting beside them.

The narrator knows how to make the most of the historical moment; the beginning of her romance is linked to the legendary day (April 24, 1793) on which Marat, overcoming his adversaries, was carried on the shoulders of a jubilant crowd back to the Assembly. Such intoxicating circumstances were decidedly favorable to the flowering of love.

Charlotte Robespierre played the role of friend, confidante, and mediator for the young woman and her future spouse. This was before the quarrel between the Duplay family and Charlotte, alluded to in Elisabeth's memoirs without any explanation: "At that time, my mother loved her very much; she had not yet had reason to complain about her." At another point she adds that Mme Duplay treated Charlotte like a daughter and mistakenly believed her to be "as pure and as sincere as her brothers."[6] Yet there is nothing in Elisabeth's account to support these slurs on Charlotte's character.

The Robespierre sister chaperoned Elisabeth at the Convention sessions, introduced her to the deputy Le Bas, witnessed their first exchange of words and trinkets, and counseled the younger woman on the early flutterings of love. At one session, the two women came with sweets and fruit to offer to Le Bas and to Charlotte's younger brother Augustin, also a deputy.

The author in old age delights in the recollection of every minute detail. Totally identifying with the impressionable young woman she once was, she captures in writing the freshness of her former feelings. Her entire memoirs gravitate around the period of her courtship and the one great love of her life, as recorded in a series of small, even trivial events. At the next Convention session, the stakes rise from oranges to jewelry. Le Bas takes Elisabeth's ring passed to Charlotte for the latter's inspection, and lends the women a lorgnette. Elisabeth remembers:

I wanted to give him back his lorgnette. . . . He begged me to keep it . . . I asked Charlotte to ask him again for my ring; she promised she would, but we did not see Le Bas again.

He had asked the younger Robespierre to make his excuses and to tell us he was not feeling well and that, regretfully, he had been obliged to leave. And I too, I had my regrets not to have my ring and not to have been able to give him back his lorgnette. I was afraid of displeasing my mother and of being scolded.

Charlotte said, to console me: "If your mother asks for the ring, I shall tell her how it came about." All of that made me very unhappy: it was the first time such a thing had happened to me.[7]

Budding love, as Elisabeth depicts it, is a comedy of errors, the mishaps contributing to its intensity and leading in a roundabout way to love's ultimate victory. This is not a play by Diderot or Sedaine, but the very stuff from which such comedies were fashioned. Or was it the other way around? With life and art, it is proverbially difficult to know which comes first. What is certain is that the affective and moral atmosphere pervading this memoir is similar to that found in eighteenth-century bourgeois drama, as well as in the paintings of Greuze, which have become touchstones for the prevailing sensibility.

The would-be lovers are presented as chaste and above reproach, the purity of their actions guaranteed by the watchful eye of a respectable chaperone and the ever-present fear of a stern mother. Their love, consecrated within hallowed halls, must write itself according to a republican script. Yet how far are we from many other love stories, from the first glimpse of the beloved in medieval romance to the *coup de foudre* of the nineteenth-century novel? Forever there is a first time. Forever there are obstacles to be overcome. Elisabeth's story is still moving today because, despite its historical packing, it springs from that emotional reservoir common to all who have read even minimally or lived long enough.

After the suggestive exchange of objects initiated by Le Bas—a ploy that produces anxiety in a young woman new to the game of love—a serious obstacle presents itself. Le Bas falls sick and cannot return to the Convention. Elisabeth responds to his illness with signs of sorrow that perplex her friends. "Everyone noted my sadness, even Robespierre, who asked me if I had some secret sorrow. . . . He spoke to me with kindness: 'Little Elisabeth, think of me as your best friend, as a kind brother; I shall give you all the advice you need at your age.' "[8]

Now the great Robespierre enters into the story, replacing his sister as Elisabeth's friend and confidant. Since he lived with the Duplays as a boarder and honorary family member, Elisabeth calls him "brother" and shares his biological sister Charlotte's worshipful attitude. In the language of recall she slips back into the form of an adoring girl: "He was so good! He was our protector when my mother scolded us. That happened to me sometimes: I was very young, a little hare-brained. He gave me such good advice that, young as I was, I listened to it with pleasure."[9]

Both Elisabeth and Charlotte's memoirs present Robespierre in this light. These two who knew him in a family context attest to his goodness, whereas others who judged him as a political player—Mme Roland, Mme de Staël, and, of course, the royalist memoirists—portray him as a heartless monster. It is possible, as we have since learned from the lives of Nazi prison guards, to be both a good family man and a cruel executioner.

Elisabeth's gilded picture of Robespierre serves to light up her own modest life with reflected glory. There is no doubt that the crucial events of her history were triggered by his presence in her parent's home. Because of him, she had come to know Charlotte Robespierre; because of her, she had met Philippe Le Bas, Maximilien's friend and colleague. Robespierre's triumphs had been shared by her beloved, and Robespierre's fall carried with it her husband's death sentence. Robespierre plays a major role as marriage broker in Elisabeth's memoirs, but never the leading role. Unlike most other women memoirists, this author occupies center stage from the start and rarely relinquishes the limelight. Even Le Bas, the ostensible source of her autobiographical worth, is given only a secondary part.

Another legendary figure appears briefly in her story: Danton, cast as a villain. Elisabeth met him through a mutual friend, Mme Panis, who took her to his country house at Sèvres. At their first meeting, Elisabeth was repelled by his ugliness and even more so by his forthright sexual advances.

> He said I appeared to be unwell, that I needed a good [boy] friend—that would bring back my health! . . . He approached, wanted to put his arm about my waist and kiss me. I pushed him away with force. . . .

> I immediately begged Madame Panis never to bring me back to that house. I told her that man had made vile propositions to me, such as I had never heard before. He had no respect whatsoever for women, and even less for young ones.[10]

The memory of a wanton Danton is not out of keeping with his reputation. During his lifetime and after his death, weaknesses of the flesh dogged his public image, just as Robespierre's austerity colored his. Depending on the historical moment, those contrasting attributes have been downgraded or applauded. In our own permissive age, Robespierre's abstinence has been seen as coldly inhuman, and Danton's carnality viewed as a positive expression of vitality.[11]

For Elisabeth Duplay Le Bas, Danton's advances were despicable. Casting back into a well of sexual fears, she dredged up a number of would-be seducers—no less a figure than Danton would have drawn her into an abyss of vice; others crop up regularly throughout her story. In the eighteenth-century imagination that produced Richardson's novel *Clarissa Harlow* and Laclos's *Liaisons dangeureuses*, not to mention the pornography of Crébillon-fils and the Marquis de Sade, an unmarried young woman's first duty was to protect her virginity and her reputation.

After two months of illness, Philippe Le Bas returned to public life. Elisabeth ran into him by chance at the Jacobin meeting hall where she had gone to reserve seats for the evening session. It had been announced that Robespierre was to speak and on such occasions "there was always such a large attendance that one was obliged to reserve seats in advance." As she tells the story, it is clear that her encounter with Le Bas at the Jacobin Club occupied a choice niche in her store of memories.

> Imagine my surprise and my joy when I saw my beloved! His absence had caused me to spill many tears. Imagine my happiness when I recognized him!

> I found him very changed. He recognized me right away and approached me with respect. He asked for

news of myself and all my family. . . . Finally, after a few minutes of silence, which he was the first to break, he asked me many questions and tried to test me.

He asked if I was not going to be married soon, if I loved someone, if clothes and frivolous pleasures were to my taste, and, when married and a mother, whether I would like to nurse my children.

I answered that I would follow the example of my excellent mother and always ask her advice.

Then he said that . . . he wanted to ask me to find him a very lively woman, who loved frivolous pleasures and did not plan to nurse her children herself—that would make her too much of a slave and deprive her of the pleasures a young woman should care for.[12]

Was the trap laid by M. Le Bas for Mlle Duplay fact or fiction? It has the sound of those convoluted trials of love found on the stage from Shakespeare to Molière and Marivaux. Yet the exchange does evoke the tenor of the times: Elisabeth is asked whether she intends to breast-feed her children. Although this ultimate eighteenth-century criterion for female worth appears in other women's memoirs, it is never presented so baldly as a premarital test of character. In fact, in other memoirs like those of Mme Roland, the question is reversed: will the prospective husband allow his wife to nurse their children? In Elisabeth's account, she, of course, turns the test to her own advantage. When he requests that she find him a "lively woman," she responds that he should "charge another person with that task" and starts to leave, whereupon he is completely won over by her virtue and charm.

He said: "Dear Elisabeth, I have caused you a lot of pain, but please excuse me. Yes, I admit it, I wanted to know your way of thinking. Well then, the one I asked you to find for me, my dear Elisabeth, is you yourself. Yes, my friend, it is you I have cherished since the day I saw you for the first time."[13]

Here as elsewhere the author follows the conventional use of dialogue permitted to memoirists. She places on Le Bas's lips the words she wants to remember, even if they are probably not the exact words said in real life. Memoirs, close cousin to the novel, had not yet been subjected to the more rigorous methodology of twentieth-century oral history and the tape recorder.

The lovers continue to reveal their true feelings, their anxieties during their absence from one another, the frustrated desire to obtain information about each other from mutual friends. Le Bas had thought ten times a day of writing her, but refrained for fear she would be compromised by his letters. A visit from Maximilien Robespierre had assured him that the Duplays were pure people, "devoted to liberty." Philippe was also visited by Augustin, who was his same age: "He praised you, said he had for you the friendship of a brother," that "you [and your sisters] had been brought up by an excellent mother who had trained you to be good housekeepers, that the interior of your house was immaculate and brought back the golden age, that everything there breathed virtue and pure patriotism, that your excellent father was the most worthy and most generous of men."[14] Here the words put into Le Bas's mouth depict the Duplays as an ideal republican family with strong civic and domestic virtues. This utopian vision of her family transmitted through an imaginative memory and projected into her lover's speech contributed to the mythology of righteous republicanism decades after its demise. It enhanced, too, Elisabeth Duplay Le Bas's self-image as the daughter of that honorable tradition.

Once the lovers had plighted their troth, it remained for Elisabeth's family to give their approval. The author made the most of that episode, turning it into another emotion-laden trial. She remembers an evening stroll in the Tuileries Gardens with her mother, during which Philippe formally asked for Elisabeth's hand. Her mother, "surprised by that request, answered that she did not intend to marry the youngest of her daughters before the older ones."

> A rather heated conversation then took place between my mother and M. Le Bas; he told her that he was not in love with my sisters Eléonore and Victoire. "It is," he said "Elisabeth whom I have loved for a long time." . . .
>
> My mother . . . said to Philippe that I was still too young and a little flighty.
>
> "I love her like that," he responded. "I shall be her friend and mentor."[15]

Because Le Bas was ten years older than Elisabeth, well educated and well placed, he was able to speak to her mother as an equal, while Elisabeth remained mutely on the sidelines. And the next day, when he addressed both parents together, Elisabeth was not even allowed to be present. Excluded from the marriage discourse, then subjected to her father's mock-earnest reproaches, she was thoroughly infantilized before her parents admitted that they had consented to Le Bas's request.

> Imagine my happiness! I could not believe it. . . . We flew into my father's and mother's arms. They were moved to tears.
>
> Robespierre came to share our joy. That good friend said to me: "Be happy, Babet, you deserve it; you were made for each other."
>
> Then my father, Robespierre, Le Bas and my mother drank chocolate together.[16]

With Elisabeth's parents' blessings and those of the great Robespierre, the engagement period was officially under way. According to tradition, it should be looked back upon as a time of rapture, but it, too, had its ordeals, deriving from both personal misunderstandings and national turmoil. Elisabeth recalls one incident that once again resembles a stock episode from comedy or fiction—that of the wicked calumniator who slanders the prospective bride, incites her fiancé's jealousy, and sows temporary discord between the two lovers. Once again Elisabeth demonstrates how her forthright innocence overcame more sophisticated antagonists and reassured her intended of her worth, after one of Philippe's acquaintances "had said many nasty things about me and had vigorously advised him not to marry me, trying to make him believe that I had had lovers and that one of them should have been obliged to marry me, adding that there was no fortune in my father's house and that I had, moreover, received no education."

> I was profoundly distressed and said to him: "As far as learning is concerned, if I have not received very wide instruction, nature has given me the gift of a pure heart and good and tender parents, who have brought us up wisely and given us an education capable of making us virtuous wives." As for the infamies that had been debited to my account, I told him I was very hurt to see that my Philippe had believed them.[17]

Ultimately, of course, after further investigation and the advice of Mme Duplay and Robespierre, Philippe realized he should never have given credence to the lies of a scoundrel, who had probably wanted the deputy to wed his own daughter. Here as elsewhere, Elisabeth's story presents Le Bas only in his role as her lover; he is alternately the gallant suitor, the jealous fiancé, the tender husband, and the concerned father, always framed within the circle of her private vision. We hear little of his political life until national events came crashing down on both of them.

The wedding date was set. Elisabeth had twenty days (two *décades* according to the new revolutionary calendar) to prepare her trousseau. Her father, the owner of several houses, placed a vacant one at their disposal. And then, the first of several national intrusions into Elisabeth's private life occurred. "Good God! What sorrow came to strike us again! At the moment of being united, we were separated. My friend was obliged to present himself promptly to the army. The Committee of Public Safety had just named him [for a special mission] and enjoined him to leave the same day." Robespierre's sober counsel, with his concern for the nation in danger and the necessity of doing one's patriotic duty, went unheeded by Elisabeth, who readily admits: "I was having so much pain that I did not want to be a patriot any longer. . . . I was inconsolable. . . . My health suffered considerably." Between the needs of the nation and her need for Philippe, there was no contest. Philippe, too, according to Elisabeth, wrote from his garrison that it was impossible to endure the separation, that if he was not brought back to Paris for their marriage, he "would fall sick."[18] Love-sickness had not yet lost its literal meaning.

Elisabeth played her trump card. She bombarded Robespierre with entreaties, beseiged him so unrelentingly that he had Philippe brought home to Paris. They were married at City Hall on the tenth of Fructidor (August 26, 1793). "What joy for us! How happy I was! I thought I should never be separated from my husband; but alas, it was to be otherwise."[19]

Within a few months, Philippe was sent off again. Elisabeth asked her father to find her another house so she could be closer to her mother. She was pregnant. The news of her pregnancy was greeted with joy by all—including Robespierre—but her health began to decline and Robespierre was called upon once more to bring back her soldier husband. They were happy and tranquil in Paris for awhile until Le Bas was designated with Saint-Just to be sent to the Army of the Rhine. With Robespierre's prompting, Elisabeth and her sister-in-law Henriette were allowed to accompany them. The story of their journey to the front bears certain resemblances to that of Charlotte and Augustin Robespierre and the Ricords on their mission to the provinces. Long carriage journeys afforded uncommon sallies into the unknown and worked themselves into literature as a quintessentially eighteenth-century topos. Elisabeth's first experience in a relay carriage was remembered as a marvelous interlude during which she and her eighteen-year-old sister-in-law were constantly entertained; the two men read aloud plays by Molière and passages from Rabelais and sang Italian songs, all of which made a strong impression on two young women who had never ventured far from their parents' home before; "Everything seemed extraordinary to us, and especially to me, being Parisian and having gone only very rarely to the country."[20]

Elisabeth's particular brand of naïveté, in contrast to her more sophisticated male companions, is apparent in numerous episodes, and never more so than in the "foolish thing" she said upon seeing the countryside in winter for the first time. "We won't have any wheat this year; the snow is going to destroy the whole harvest!"[21] Even as she tells the story in her old age, there is a sense of embarrassment at having shown so much ignorance of seasonal change.

Arriving finally at their destination, Elisabeth and Henriette were given as their protector the venerable mayor of Saverne and as their personal maid a charming young woman who spoke only German. The latter became so attached to her mistresses that they wanted to take her back to Paris when they left, but Philippe, conscious of the dangers lurking in Paris for a pretty, unmarried young woman, vetoed the plan.

The narrative breaks off at this point and is picked up again abruptly under the heading "Catastrophe of the Ninth of Thermidor." The tone changes dramatically from the follies and foibles of youthful love to tragic disaster on a national and personal scale. Elisabeth remembers her husband's premonitions of catastrophe several days before the coup that destroyed Robespierre and his close associates. Le Bas is reported as having exclaimed to her: "If it weren't a crime, I'd blow your brains out and kill myself; at least then we would die together. But no! There is that poor child!"[22] The child, a boy, was five weeks old. In her account of the ninth of Thermidor, we witness revolutionary trauma invading the household. As soon as her husband was arrested, government officials came to put the seals on their apartment. "They took all our personal correspondence, our family papers. . . . The guardian [of the seals] cost us five francs a day. Le Bas was brought by agents of the Committee of Public Safety to witness this operation, and then was conducted to the Prison de la Force."[23]

Le Bas sent a message from prison requesting a folding bed, a mattress, and a blanket. Elisabeth and her sister-in-law, carrying these items, hired a coach and drove to the prison where they found a delegation from the Paris Commune, which had come to protect Le Bas and the other Thermidorians. Momentarily granted freedom, Le Bas went to face his destiny at the Hôtel de Ville. Elisabeth records his last, patriotically inspired, words, intended for the edification of their son: "Nourish him with your own milk . . . inspire in him the love of his country; tell him that his father has died for her; adieu, my Elisabeth, adieu! . . . Live for our dear son; inspire him with noble sentiments, you are worthy of them. Adieu, Adieu!"[24]

Elisabeth writes that she never saw him again. She does not say that he shot himself several hours later at the Hôtel de Ville in the same room where Maximilien was gravely wounded by his enemies and from which Augustin threw himself out of the window. Instead, she paints her own despair.

> I went home distraught, almost crazy. Imagine what I felt when our dear infant stretched out his little arms to me . . . strength and reason abandoned me; I could not hold out. From the ninth to the eleventh [of Thermidor] I remained on the floor. I no longer had strength nor consciousness. I did not go to bed. Good God! And one does not die from suffering.[25]

This dark moment of the soul was never forgotten. Her astonishment fifty years later that she did not die of anguish speaks for almost all the women in this book. As Elisabeth lay unconscious on the floor, the mob carried Robespierre and his associates past the Duplay house on their way to the guillotine; that terrifying procession was witnessed furtively through the shutters by Eléonore, Elisabeth's sister and Robespierre's reputed fiancée.

Shortly thereafter, members of the Committee for Public Safety led Elisabeth and her infant son to the Talarue prison. Her sister-in-law Henriette joined her voluntarily in a dark cell where there was "scarcely space for two folding beds, two chairs and a very little table." The only light came through a tiny skylight. This is how Elisabeth sums up her life situation: "I had been a mother for five weeks; I was nursing my son; I was less than twenty-one years old; I had been deprived of almost everything."[26]

Before long she was deprived of her sister-in-law's company as well, for it was deemed too risky for a pretty, single woman to remain to help the prisoner and her baby. Elisabeth accuses "miserable types, like Ricord" (whom we last saw in Charlotte Robespierre's memoirs) of trying to seduce Henriette and of even promising Elisabeth her liberty in return for Henriette's favors.[27] Elisabeth's sister Eléonore replaced Henriette. Remembering El& onore's devotion, Elisabeth at seventy voiced eternal gratitude. The two women led a grim existence, their daily routine described in the following manner:

> Obliged to wash my son's diapers, I descended at ten o'clock at night with a lantern. There was a water trough in the courtyard; I went down when all the prisoners had retired. I had to obtain from the jailer permission to wash my child's diapers; then I went back to my attic (because I was above the stables; there were stinking odors). As it was necessary to dry them, I put them between my mattresses and those of my good sister, who had sacrificed herself to come to share my weariness and my hardships.[28]

The tribulations of Elisabeth, Henriette, and Elenore undoubtedly match the stories of countless women, though few have written them down. Women's heroics in surviving so as to nurture their dependents have not been the subject of national epics; we must look to the personal literature of memoirs, diaries, and letters for such unsung history.

The prison ordeal bred in Elisabeth Le Bas a wild rage. In her interactions with her captors, there was none of the dignified silence of the Queen of France. She spoke her mind with an impassioned ferocity that grew to reckless proportions. When propositioned by government agents to marry one of the deputies and thus "abandon the infamous name" of her husband, she cried out, "Tell those monsters that the Widow Le Bas will never abandon that sacred name except on the scaffold." To their threats that she would then remain much longer in prison, she retorted, "I'm not afraid of your threats; I'm no longer afraid of death."[29] Such defiance in the face of prolonged incarceration and even death derived from an intractable belief in the righteousness of her husband's cause. Clinging to her married name, she emerged from prison after nine months as a force to be reckoned with. When the government, through the intervention of one of her husband's former friends, sent her the papers that would grant her a pension, she was furious. In the man's office, she dramatically rejected all official assistance: "There, with a pin and a quill, I pierced my skin and wrote with my blood . . . that if a claim had been made for what was due to my husband, I was not asking for help from his assassins. I signed: 'The Widow Le Bas.'"[30]

Can this be the same woman who, not so long ago, had been terrified of her mother's discovery that Le Bas had taken her ring? In less than two years and fifty pages, the narrator journeyed from flighty maidenhood to widowhood with a vengeance. The persona of the Widow Le Bas is that which Elisabeth chose to maintain throughout the rest of her very long life. Proud of the Le Bas name and its revolutionary reputation, proud too of her own independence, the Widow Le Bas became what the French call *un personnage*—a character. If at seventy she was able to pen such a rousing manuscript, if at eighty she still defended the revolutionary heroes whose portraits hung on her walls, what a formidable woman she must have been!

As a memoirist, Elisabeth Le Bas left behind precious documentation on private life amid the ruins of revolution, and one of the rare records of romantic love. Oranges and sweets, rings and lorgnettes, folding beds and diapers become evocative symbols of the human struggle for happiness, or mere survival. The revolutionary moment explodes into the passionate sentences of long-dead heroes. Her own words catch fire as she speaks the phrases enshrined in memory, phrases now amplified and reformulated, so as to capture the thoughts and feelings she *might* have expressed, *should* have expressed, as well as those she probably *did* express. The incidents she recalls borrow from or refute other eyewitness accounts, especially that of Charlotte Robespierre. Or they merge with scenes remembered from drama and fiction, producing *romanesque* encounters between ideal lovers and confrontations with base villains. Elisabeth Le Bas remembered the revolution as her own domestic tragedy. That she should focus so narrowly on her private relationship with Philippe Le Bas, ignoring the larger political scene except for its intrusions into her conjugal life, may derive from the fact that she wrote her memoirs for her son and not for publication—indeed, they would not find their way into print until 1901.

Yet there are more fundamental psychological reasons for this narrow personal focus; Elisabeth chose to remember only her prelapsarian happiness with Le Bas because it represented the flowering of her affective existence, an experience rendered even more precious by its short duration and tragic sequellae. The Revolution had nourished and then destroyed the one great romance of her life; Elisabeth clung to that memory in old age as to a life raft.

Wars, revolutions, catastrophes intersect individual lives at different points in the life cycle. The French Revolution began in 1789 when Elisabeth was sixteen; it ended in 1794 when she was barely twenty-one. Those years of her life were traditionally the time when women in the Western world were expected to become open to heterosexual love and, above all, to make a good match. Elisabeth fulfilled those expectations to her own and her family's great satisfaction. The internal and external pressures impelling her toward love were not deterred by the forces of revolution. Her passage into adulthood, her initiation into sexuality, would not wait until the Revolution was over. In the French language, the word *femme* means both "woman" and "wife," with the implication that in order to become a mature woman, one must also become a wife.

Elisabeth made the transition from childhood to womanhood in the proper time sequence. She also became a mother during the first year of marriage, following a common demographic pattern. And then, unexpectedly, she became a widow far ahead of her time. For the rest of her life—a full sixty-five years of widowhood—she would look back nostalgically to the period from the fall of 1792 to the summer of 1794 as the paradise from which she had been violently ejected.

The experience of romantic love often holds a central place in women's imagination. Byron's well-known distinction that "man's love is of man's life a thing apart; t'is women's whole existence" may offend our contemporary feminist sensibilities, but there is certainly much truth in this saying when applied to women in the past.[31] Women's "overvaluing" of love, as the psychoanalyst Karen Horney phrased it, was an understandable consequence of the few outlets available to them.[32] Especially in France, female worth was conceived by men, and internalized by women themselves, as dependent upon their erotic attractiveness. Elisabeth could not afford to lose the memory of her one great love.

That this memory helped sustain her in the bitter years after her husband's death, that it helped her resist the advances of suitors deemed less worthy than Philippe Le Bas, that she was inspired to transmit her husband's revolutionary ideals to their son— all these psychodynamic forces are evident in her memoirs. The preservation of her husband's place in the shrine of memory alongside the picture of herself as a desirable young woman became the psychic work of widowhood. The scenario of their romance playing endlessly on the stage of her imagination was not affected by the peripeteia of her later years. Although the formidable Widow Le Bas makes only a brief but unforgettable appearance at the end of her memoirs, Elisabeth never relinquished her internal image of a youthful self. When memory spoke, it spoke in the verdant voice of an ingenue, belying the weathered body it inhabited.

Madame de Staël. Engraving by C. H. Muller. Reproduced from Oeuvres Complètes de Mme la Baronne de Staël (*Paris, Treuttel et Wurtz, 1820*)

8

GERMAINE DE STAËL'S
CONSIDERATIONS OF THE
FRENCH REVOLUTION

GERMAINE NECKER DE STAËL OCCUPIES A PLACE in French letters shared by few women. Like George Sand in the nineteenth century and Simone de Beauvoir in the twentieth, she was famous during her lifetime for novels and essays, as well as for flamboyant love affairs and a dramatic lifestyle. She commanded the attention of both admirers and detractors, including, among the latter, Napoleon, who sent her into the "ten years of exile" that constituted the title for one of her books.[1] With seventeen volumes of collected works published immediately after her death, she was recognized posthumously as the earliest French theoretician of Romanticism and as the foremost French spokesperson for the political liberalism that would shape modern Europe.[2]

At the end of a relatively short life—she died in 1817 at the age of fifty-one—she composed her *Considerations of the Principal Events of the French Revolution* in which she set out to justify the Revolution without minimizing its costs.[3] However flawed and however brutal, the Revolution provided the cornerstone for Staël's vision of progress.

Other women of her class (though few of her wealth, for she was heiress to one of the large fortunes of Europe) may have flirted with the Revolution, or even espoused its cause, only to divorce themselves from its claims once its face had become bloodied. Staël remained married to the Revolution's highest ideals throughout its frenzied course and precarious aftermath. Indeed, she was far more faithful to them than to her long-suffering husband, the Swedish Baron de Staël-Holstein, who fathered only the first of her four children and from whom she was legally separated after fifteen years of mutual incompatibility.

In a very real sense, she was born into the Revolution. Daughter of the Swiss banker Jacques Necker, Louis XVI's influential minister from 1777 to 1781 and 1788 to 1790, she grew up in the company of Diderot, Georges-Louis Buffon, and the other celebrated philosophes whose discourse at her mother's Friday night salons promulgated the early Revolution's vision of social justice. She studied Latin and English, philosophy and dance, and above all the art of conversation that was to be the obsessive glory of her life, seducing men and women alike. She was twelve years old before she had a playmate her own age.

For most of her childhood, the three Neckers constituted a kingdom of their own, with the financier father designated as the savior who would restore prosperity to the French. In this triumvirate, Mme Necker played a not inconsiderable role, especially when it concerned feminine virtue. Her Swiss Protestant morality has become, like her daughter's later flamboyant sexual freedom, part of the Necker family lore.

Incontestably, Jacques Necker was the great love of Germaine's girlhood, the emotional nucleus around which numerous other passions would subsequently collect, yet never eclipse. He was also the formative influence of her most cherished political principles, among them the paradigm of the English system of bicameral government. It was to vindicate his reputation, inextricably bound up in his daughter's mind with the Revolutic.i itself, that she embarked upon her *Considerations of the French Revolution.*

Staël's *Considerations* differs significantly from other women's memoirs of the Revolution. It is primarily a politico-historical analysis abounding in comparisons with other nations, namely England and sometimes America. It takes the long view of history, beginning with a general overview of European politics that reaches back into feudal society, and ending with the period between the Revolution and the Restoration; indeed, less than half of the 600-page opus deals directly with the years 1789-95. The author sets for herself the goals of rising "to the height of impartiality" and of viewing the revolutionary past "as if it were already far from us."[4]

Yet for all its lofty aspirations toward objectivity, the *Considerations* is largely testimonial, the memoirs of a witness to revolutionary turmoil. The author's elevated stance and broad view of history did not preclude the numerous personal close-ups that give this work its special stamp of authenticity. Jacques Godechot, in his introduction to the latest edition of the *Considerations*, writes that "Madame de Staël does not strive to be objective."[5] I would say that she could not be objective in spite of her best efforts, but that the emotional undercurrent in her work should not necessarily be judged as a shortcoming. It may, indeed, have sharpened her vision.

The *Considerations* can be read simultaneously as subjective history, political theory, autobiography, biography—most notably that of her father—and even as travel literature. The work itself is as distinctive from the other women's memoirs considered in this book as Mme de Staël's life was from their lives. No other woman memoirist had lived more intimately with the workings of public office during her childhood; none, with the exception of Mme de Genlis and Mme Roland, had been so personally embroiled in backstage politics; and none had attained through her writing the respect of the greatest minds and monarchs of her age. Thus, when she set out to compose her history of the Revolution, she knew it would be read by the elite of Europe and that it held the possibility of influencing future history.

In all these ways Mme de Staël's life was more like a man's than a woman's. She never questioned her right to assume male prerogatives, and, consequently, her account of the

Revolution is less "feminized" than those of her sister writers. She tells us nothing about domestic matters because that was not her sphere. Hers was the public or semipublic realm that stopped short of the Assembly and the tribunal only because of gender barriers. Otherwise she would undoubtedly have rivaled the deputies Mirabeau in eloquence and Condorcet in prefeminist proposals. And yet, for all that, Mme de Staël often observed from a female stance, as her novels Corinne and Delphine demonstrate, and as the *Considerations* reveals, if one looks closely enough.

This chapter will not overlook those places, however rare, where Mme de Staël's sex and gender make themselves felt. Her attention to what other women do and say, as if their behavior had some relevance to her own, is one marker of a female sensibility. Her descriptions of Marie-Antoinette triumphing over her fears in public, and of lower-class women ensnared by violence, resonate with her own innermost anxieties. Her reproving comments on the power of women under the Old Regime are almost comical in light of the enormous power she herself exercised throughout her life. And however liberated she was from the constraints of a female body, the fact that she was pregnant at one of the most dramatic moments in her life was deemed integral to her narrative.

I shall limit this chapter to the first half of the *Considerations*—the half ending with Staël's retreat from Paris in 1792—and pay equal attention to what she chose to remember and how she transposed that memory into memoir. A supreme stylist can be observed molding national history around her father's political career and marking it with her own theatrical temperament.

THE *CONSIDERATIONS* BEGINS WITH AN EXAMINATION of the historical antecedents of revolution. The author outlines a trajectory of moral and political degeneration inaugurated in the seventeenth century with Cardinal Richelieu's policy of drawing the nobility to Paris and changing them from provincial seigneurs into servile courtiers. With the development of absolute power under Louis XIV, the fate of the nation was sealed for a hundred years. Mme de Staël judges Louis XIV as despotic and Louis XV as debilitated. Louis XVI comes off much better. Indeed she portrays both Louis XVI and Marie-Antoinette as personally sympathetic:

> Marie-Antoinette was one of the most likable and most gracious persons ever seen on the throne, and nothing prevented her from preserving the love of the French, because she had done nothing to lose it. The personal character of the Queen and King was thus completely worthy of attachment. But the arbitrary nature of French government, as developed over centuries, harmonized little with the spirit of the times. . . . When the people feel the need for political reform, the private qualities of the monarch are scarcely sufficient to halt the force of that impulse.[6]

Louis XVI simply had the misfortune of being the king at a time when absolute monarchy was no longer a tenable form of government in France. Despite his personal virtues and a desire to do the best for his people, he could not fully comprehend the change in mentality that had taken place during the Age of Enlightenment, which was no longer compatible with the hierarchical nature of Old Regime society. His primary failing was an inability to dispense entirely with the doctrine of divine right—"a fatal prejudice, unfortunately, for France and for him."[7]

But the major figure around whom the first section, indeed the first half, of the book is structured is not the king, but Staël's father. Whole chapters are devoted to Necker's character as a public figure, his plans for finance and administration, as well as his times in and out of office. In his daughter's psyche, he was the spiritual father of the Revolution, its principal actor during the hopeful years, its missing player when the Revolution turned sour. In presenting her father's life, Mme de Staël initially tried to maintain the distant stance and objective tone she had set as her goals. She referred to him, along with his wife, in the third person, as if she, the author, were unrelated to them.

> Monsieur Necker, citizen of the Republic of Geneva, had since his childhood cultivated literature with great care, and . . . always blended elevated feelings and philosophical considerations with the practical aspects of life. Mme Necker, who was certainly one of the most learned women of her day, constantly brought together in her home all the best that the eighteenth century, so fecund in distinguished men, could offer by way of illustrious talents.[8]

While it is true that Necker wrote numerous works, among them a treatise crowned by the French Academy, it is hardly for his literary achievements that he would be remembered by historians other than his daughter. Her exaggeration of his importance as a man of letters and the glorification of his personal character are the book's most glaring biases.

Staël's emotionless third-person voice cannot maintain itself once she becomes involved in the story of her father's public career. Suddenly the tone changes and the author speaks in the first person. She recounts her parents' visit to the Parisian hospice they had founded, a visit saddened by the knowledge that Necker was about to resign from his first ministry:

> The Sisters of Charity . . . offered them flowers and sang verses drawn from the psalms. . . . I still remember that he had never been so deeply moved. . . . Alas! Who at that time would have believed that such a man would one day be accused of being hard, arrogant, and factious! Ah! Never has a purer soul crossed through the storms, and his enemies, in slandering him, committed an impiety.[9]

An attack on the father is perceived as an attack on all that is sacred. The insult to Necker, when he was forced in 1781 to resign from office, and the insults following his second resignation nine years later, come together in the mind of his fifty-year-old daughter to be vented in a belated cry of pain. In the world of memory, time follows its own associative sequence; the adult narrator still wounded by paternal loss (Necker had died in 1804) circles back to the mind of the teenager she once had been and the naive pleasure she had experienced at the thought of returning to their country house at Saint Ouen: "I was too much of a child not to be delighted by some sort of change in the situation. However, when I saw the ministry secretaries and clerks at dinner, all in gloomy sadness, I began to fear that my joy was not very well founded."[10]

Here at last is the young Germaine Necker mediated only through the memory of her adult incarnation, the author Mme de Staël. This Necker—de Staël persona will continue to reappear throughout the 600-page treatise whenever her personal story can be made to converge with national history.

Before leaving Staël's account of her father's first ministry, it is worth noting her observations on the role played by women. "Women of a certain rank," she wrote, "meddled in everything before the Revolution. Their husbands or their brothers always enlisted them to go to the ministers: they could plead their case without impropriety."[11] Though her father was obliged to listen to their pleas and to suffer their name dropping, he was, according his daughter, immune to their wiles. Justice and sound finance were his only guides.

Mediation and lobbying have always been women's work, and never more so than in the eighteenth century. Mme de Staël's depiction of the meddling ladies turns a blind eye to her own similar campaigns on behalf of her favorites—Louis de Narbonne who became minister of war through her determined efforts, the writer Benjamin Constant whose political ascendancy she masterminded, Talleyrand whose appointment as minister of foreign affairs after the Revolution was obtained thanks to her intercession, and Lafayette whose release from the prison of Olmütz was largely her doing. Such activities by women did not cease with the Old Regime. Unable to exercise power directly and for themselves, many women intrigued endlessly for their husbands, fathers, sons, brothers, nephews, and, as exemplified by Germaine de Staël, for their friends and lovers. It is interesting to hear her chide her sisters for activities she performed more successfully than any of them.

From her mother she had acquired a taste for social gatherings and the ability to surround herself with distinguished men—this would grow to courtly proportions during her adulthood. She had learned the roles of hostess and patron in her mother's salon, but whereas Mme Necker had been happy to share the stage with others, Germaine de Staël always commanded the limelight. Most of the men in her life had a hard time shining equally in her company, despite the presence of some of the choice minds of the age—for example, the French statesman and diplomat Talleyrand, the German critic and translator Auguste Wilhelm Schlegel, and the Franco-Swiss writer Constant. Among the women, those who had both talent and wit, like the consummately cultivated Julie Récamier or the painter Elisabeth Vigée-Lebrun, were welcome in her inner circle. She was typically generous with her women friends when they were her cultural equals, as the affectionate memoirs of Mme Vigée-Lebrun demonstrate.

Aside from political intrigue and the patronage of her salons, other traditionally female activities held little interest for her. There is no evidence that she took up those charitable programs that provided an altruistic outlet for other privileged ladies. Her mother, for example, was the benefactress of a hospice she founded in 1778, which still bears the family name, and, according to her daughter, she consecrated much of her time, during her husband's first ministry, to the betterment of several other hospitals and prisons. Mme Necker also appears in the memoirs of Mme de Ménerville and Angélique de Maussion as one of the great ladies sponsoring the work of La Charité Maternelle, an organization founded on the eve of the Revolution to support poor women and their babies.[12]

Nor did Germaine de Staël, when the time came, pay much attention to the care of her children. They were left in the hands of wet-nurses (despite the politically correct emphasis, then as now, on maternal breast-feeding) and male tutors, and scarcely saw their highly peripatetic mother. She was nothing if not unconventional regarding the traditional mandates for women. She outstripped all her female contemporaries—before, during, and after the Revolution—in her passionate quest for self-determination.

STAËL's ACCOUNT of her father's public career recommences in about 1787 with the story of his rivalry with Charles de Calonne, the minister of finances between 1783 and 1787. Mme de Staël rarely had a good word for any of her father's rivals, and, in the case of Calonne, she undermined his character with one of those ironic jabs for which she was famous: "The frivolity of his character dogged him, and he wasn't skillful in practicing evil, even when he intended to do so."[13]

She criticized Calonne for encouraging the court in its taste for luxury and for distributing money too liberally. Even after the French-supported American War of Independence was over, he continued contracting loans, which her father considered suitable only for wartime. The rivalry between Necker and Calonne ultimately brought Necker the king's disfavor. To defend himself against some of Calonne's accusations, Necker published his 1787 records of the national finances. Since this publication was explicitly prohibited, Necker became the recipient of a *lettre de cachet* ordering him to go into exile forty leagues from Paris.

Once again Mme de Staël projects herself into the narrative with an indignant outburst: "I cannot describe the state I was in at that news; that exile seemed to me to be an unparalleled act of despotism; it was a question of my father whose noble and pure sentiments were intimately known to me." But she blames this act not so much on the king as on a system of government that allowed for such abuses of power. This would be a constant theme in her analysis: the *lettres de cachet* by which the king could arbitrarily call for the imprisonment or exile of any of his subjects were among the first royal prerogatives to fall with the Bastille. Mme de Staël, writing in 1816 when fears about new forms of repression under the Restoration ran high, reminds us that "the *lettres de cachet,* like many other illegalities, were then very much in use."[14] By pointing to the abuses of power under Louis XVI, she undoubtedly hoped to curtail them under Louis XVIII.

The news of Necker's exile served only to increase his popularity. "All of Paris came to visit M. Necker during the twenty-four hours he had to prepare his departure. . . . all the châteaux forty leagues from Paris were put at his disposal."[15] Such behavior was common, according to the writer Mme de Genlis, who noted in her own memoirs the fashionable antagonism to the court in the years immediately preceding the Revolution: "A disgraced minister was sure to find favor with the public, and, if he had been exiled, everyone hurried to go to see him."[16]

It was only through the intercession of Marie-Antoinette that the king's first impulse to banish Necker from France was changed into a milder form of exile. Despite this example of the queen's protection, Mme de Staël calls her "one of the great obstacles that M. Necker encountered in his political career," especially during his second ministry.

Finally public opinion forced the court to recall Necker. His daughter remembers that when she happily announced his renomination to her father, he responded: "At present it is too late." She depicts Necker as accepting the new appointment out of a sense of responsibility, but with little hope, sensing that the cards had already been stacked against adequate reform. He is reported as uttering another of those lofty reflections intended to convey the character of a sublime sage: "The daughter of a minister has only pleasure, she enjoys the reflection of her father's power; but power itself, especially now, is a terrible responsibility."[17]

There is no doubt that Jacques Necker was a remarkable man. Few French ministers have been as popular with the people, and no other can claim to have incited by his dismissal from office an insurrection that gave birth to a national holiday. Mme de Staël's account of the momentous days between the convocation of the Estates General in May 1789, and the storming of the Bastille in July make for colorful reading. But when we recall the author's portrayal (quoted in chapter 2) of the procession of deputies marching to church the night before the opening of the Estates General, with Mme de Staël observing from a window alongside Mme de Montmorin, we cannot help noticing that this widely cited passage is followed by a much less memorable description of the first session of the Estates General the next day. Try as she may, Mme de Staël cannot undo the boring impression produced by the speakers, and principally by her father who declaimed for two hours on the subject of the national debt and the measures needed to rectify it. One of her contemporaries, Mme de La Tour du Pin, recalled Necker's speech as "unbearably dull" and asserted in her memoirs that she had never felt "so weary as during that speech, though M. Necker's supporters praised it to the skies."[18]

In those first weeks of national deliberations, Necker is portrayed as steering a prudent course between the Scylla of arbitrary royal power and the Charybdis of unfettered republicanism. Acknowledging her father's typical moderation, his daughter remarks, "In this circumstance, as in almost all others, he walked between two extremes."[19] Eventually, however, the center could not hold against the extremist forces that would find their expression in incidents of mounting violence.

Necker's quarrel with the nobles who wanted to turn back the clock, his refusal to countenance the presence of foreign troops intended by the court to put an end to the newly formed National Assembly, his immense popularity with the people—all the events precipitating Necker's dismissal as minister and his subsequent glorious reinstatement are deftly related. The novelist's skills are turned to the purposes of history, which was conceived, at this stage, as a suspenseful family drama. On "the eleventh of July, at three in the afternoon, M. Necker received a letter from the King ordering him to leave Paris and France. . . . Two days after his departure, as soon as his disgrace had been made known, the theaters were closed as if a public calamity had taken place. All of Paris took up arms."[20]

Jacques Necker's person takes on mythic proportions as he alone is credited with having triggered the July 14 uprising. To say the least, the exile decreed by the king boomeranged. Without excusing the "bloody assassinations" committed at the Bastille, Mme de Staël chooses to highlight its "grandeur." She reminds us that no internal or external faction was necessary to produce the insurrection. For a devotee of Rousseau, the spontaneity of the Revolution guaranteed its purity.

Necker's triumphant return to Paris provided Germaine de Staël with her happiest memory, constituting "the last day of prosperity of my life which had, nevertheless, scarcely opened before me."[21] Twenty-three years old, wife of the Swedish ambassador, already a formidable mistress of society and a budding writer, Mme de Staël had an unbelievably eventful life before her. Her father, however, had indeed reached the apogee of his career.

WHEREAS NECKER DOMINATES THE STAGE during the years leading to the fall of the Bastille as recounted in Part 1 of the Considerations, in Part 2, which traces the history of the Assembly from the summer of 1789 to June 1791, he is obliged to share the spotlight with his archantagonist, the Comte de Mirabeau. Mme de Staël compares them to two Roman leaders of vastly different moral worth: "In every historical period there are great persons one can consider as the representatives of the principles of good and evil. Such were Cicero and Catiline in ancient Rome; such were M. Necker and Mirabeau in France."[22]

She castigates Mirabeau for his notorious amorality, for vanity regarding his noble birth, for expensive tastes, and especially for political arrogance: "Mirabeau . . believed himself strong enough to overthrow the government, and establish on its ruins any order of things that would be the work of his hands. This gigantic project led to the ruin of France and to his own ruin." She grants him the one attribute that cannot be denied—a great gift for oratory—and in this respect she appears as entranced as any of his countless admirers. Indeed, her descriptions of his magnetic performances add luster to his formidable reputation. On one occasion at the Assembly, painting the horrors of bankruptcy, "he made himself heard with such refulgence" that he won her admiration for a full two hours, despite her disbelief in his good intentions. She attributes Mirabeau's astonishing eloquence to his voice, as well as to the caustic words and gestures that seemed to flow from his soul like the "force of life." Earlier, however, she had asserted that her father "would have triumphed over Mirabeau" in a verbal duel had they been permitted one.[23] But since Necker, as the king's minister, was reduced to sending memorandums and could not enter into the Assembly debates, Mirabeau won an uncontested victory at the podium. Staël seems to have forgotten her father's conspicuous oratory failure at the opening of the Estates General.

She makes an interesting observation about the French custom of allowing public figures to read their speeches, in contrast to the British practice forbidding prepared statements and requiring improvisation. With her usual preference for the British, she lauds the advantages of a system that eliminates all but the most agile thinkers or at least encourages orators to perfect their faculties. The French are depicted as wanting to obtain the applause of the gallery by any means; hence the number of demagogues who engaged a stable of hack writers. She quite rightly points out that Mirabeau, who "improvised with difficulty," kept an atelier of employees to help write his works.[24]

The only public figure Mme de Staël wholeheartedly admired, aside from her father, was the Marquis de Lafayette. She praised him for his republican virtues learned firsthand as a soldier during the American Revolution and compared him favorably to his mentor George Washington: "He had the same lack of self-interest, the same enthusiasm, the same perseverance in his beliefs." By contrast, in Mme de Tourzel's memoirs, Lafayette suffered by this same comparison, for, in her view, he had not calculated "the difference between France and America, nor the lack of resemblance that existed between himself and the person he had the pretension of imitating."[25] Of course, Mme de Tourzel, an ultraroyalist, had no sympathy with the ideal of constitutional government shared by both Lafayette and Mme de Staël. Yet all three were defenders of the king, and in the case of Lafayette, at the risk of his own life. Time and again, during the turbulent first years of the Revolution, Lafayette as head of the National Guard personally defended the royal family against mob violence.

The pinnacle of Lafayette's career occurred on July 14, 1790, when he officiated at the Festival of the Federation, to which the eighty-three departments had sent representatives from all the National Guards. Mme de Staël notes that "all of Paris crowded to the Federation of 1790, as they had the preceding year to the destruction of the Bastille." Her description of the patriotic zeal generated by this event concurs with that of Mme de La Tour du Pin and Mme de Tourzel, but without the latter's irony. Staël writes enthusiastically of the highborn ladies who joined in the voluntary labor that prepared the ground for the ceremony. She remembers the benches arranged under a tent to serve as shelter for the king and the court, and the eighty-three banners representing the departments of France. Across from the amphitheater where the royal family was seated, an altar had been erected for the mass celebrated by Talleyrand, who was the bishop of Autun (and probably Mme de Staël's first lover). "Lafayette approached this altar to swear fidelity to the nation, the law, and the king. . . . The spectators were ecstatic."[26]

There were, however, undercurrents of anxiety among those "capable of reflection," including Jacques Necker. Mme de Staël explains away her father's diminished popularity as compared to Lafayette's. "Since M. Necker had sacrificed his entire popularity to the defense of the principles of a free and limited monarchy, it was left to M. de Lafayette to be the principal object of the people's affection on that day; . . . but whatever his political opinion might have been, if he had wanted to oppose the spirit of the times, his power would have been broken." Staël is determined to insinuate her father into the picture, suggesting that Necker, had he not been so thoroughly principled, would have been the hero of the day, as he had been the year before. Lafayette's more opportunistic behavior is excused on the grounds that neither he nor any other man could have opposed the prevailing ideological currents. "Ideas reigned at that time and not individuals. Even the terrible will of Bonaparte himself could have done nothing against the direction of their minds." History, as Staël conceived it, had its own impetus. The Revolution, engendered by the abuses of the Old Regime, was driven by an egalitarian vision of the future for which the people themselves were not yet prepared. Squeezed between the sage minister and the formidable First Consul, Lafayette was certainly not the man to oppose that force.

On the whole, Mme de Staël remembers the first three or four years of the Revolution as a brilliant time in French history. She attributes much of that brilliance to the fact that "political affairs were still in the hands of the first class" defined as "those gentlemen who were more proud of their own merit than the privileges of their class." These liberal aristocrats were joined with "men of the third estate, distinguished by their enlightened ideas and their talents."

Clearly Mme de Staël was no populist. Whatever her liberal political ideas, she never abandoned a certain elitism in her judgment of who should exercise power. Her ideal remained that of a meritocracy modeled upon the society of the early Revolution when "all the vigor of liberty and all the grace of the old politeness were united in the same people." Liberty, in Mme de Staël's book, did not disdain civility.

And in this best of all historical moments, French women had a special role, in contradistinction to their English counterparts: "Women in England are accustomed to being silent in the presence of men when it is a question of politics. Women in France directed almost all the conversations in their homes, and their minds had been honed at an early age to the smoothness that such talent requires."[27] This national difference in conversational patterns is borne out by contemporary manuals of decorum: English women were enjoined to become good listeners, whereas French women were encouraged to become good speakers as well.

As many including Mme de Staël have observed, this was the last, autumnal flowering of women's reign. The Revolution would turn against its vocal women, destroying upper-class salons and middle-and working-class women's clubs, along with any notion that women had a claim to political rights. In November 1793, the Convention would explicitly forbid women's gatherings and attendance in any political assembly. But before women had been demoted to mute domesticity, Mme de Staël could still bring together at her dinner parties the most intelligent men and women of both royalist and liberal camps, in the belief that "at a certain lofty height people can always understand each other." As she looked back to that last tableau of Enlightenment civilization in Paris before the Terror, she praised the ideal of verbal communication—in her view "the most noble pleasure of which human nature is capable." Compared to other periods in her life—her time at the Court of Versailles, her many years at Coppet in Switzerland, her season at Juniper Hall in England—Parisian society from 1788 to 1792 offered a golden age. "Those who lived at that time cannot prevent themselves from admitting that one has never seen both so much life and so much intellect anywhere else."[28]

Nostalgia informed Mme de Staël's memories in a manner distinct from most of her contemporaries. For her, the losses of the Revolution were less material or social than aesthetic and philosophical. What had been lost was the eighteenth-century ideal of a common culture, of ideas and values that could be communicated and shared by superior minds. There is no doubt that this vision was elitist by today's standards. Yet it was at the same time universal in that the qualifying attribute for communal membership was "mind" or "reason," the property of all human beings regardless of gender, class, race, or religion. This humanist ideal inspirited the early Revolution.

Those were the years when the Constituent Assembly wrote into law the many liberties already taken for granted in 1816 when Staël was completing her opus. And as if to remind her readers that those liberties could be lost with the restored Bourbons, she enumerated them at length. Torture, which was still practiced in 1789, was abolished shortly thereafter. Freedom of religion was proclaimed. The English system of criminal jurisprudence providing greater protection for the accused was introduced into France. Religious vows previously forced upon women and men, and especially upon the youngest sons, were suspended. Positions as military officers, previously restricted to the aristocracy, were opened to all. A uniform system of taxes was established. The sale of church properties "lifted from poverty a very large class of society."[29]

And above all, the liberty of press proclaimed in 1789 was not suspended until August 11, 1792. She remembered seeing at the door of the Assembly "the most mordant insults directed at the members of the majority, their friends, and their principles." And those who were in the minority at least had the satisfaction, in their own newspapers, of making fun of the majority party. Retrospectively, Mme de Staël had nothing but praise for the proliferation of political journalism, though at the time she was less sanguine, especially when she herself was attacked by the press. As the historian Anne Soprani has pointed out, she bemoaned "the fierce animosity against women" manifest in infamous libels written by aristocrats as well as democrats.[30] A quarter-century later, in the *Considerations*, all was forgiven. She whose life had been devoted to conversation and writing, who had known the social privations wrought by exile and the censorship of her works under Napoleon, remembered only the benefits associated with the free exchange of ideas possible during the early Revolution. "One breathed more easily, there was more air in one's chest, and an unlimited hope for unfettered happiness had forcefully taken hold of the nation, as it takes hold of men in their youth, with illusion and without caution."[31]

Jacques Necker, however, was no longer a young man. During this same period he progressively lost the last of his illusions and became increasingly versed in caution. He did not wait around until his association with monarchy would have led him to the same fate as his king. On September 8, 1790, he slipped away to Switzerland where he was to spend the rest of his life. He left behind, on loan to the nation, two million pounds—half his fortune. That money would become a source of trouble for his daughter, who tried to recoup it from Napoleon and would not succeed until she was at death's door.

MME DE STAËL STAYED ON IN PARIS. Her father's departure did not put an end to his daughter's social and political ascendancy, which reached its peak in 1791 with her intrigues on behalf of her various friends and lovers. Indeed a comedy circulated early in 1791 called *The Intrigues of Madame de Staël* portrayed her as a nymphomaniac stirring up riots to benefit her lovers. She succeeded by the end of that year in having her lover Louis de Narbonne appointed minister of war. The queen, in a note to her own reputed lover Axel de Fersen, wrote, "At last Comte Louis de Narbonne is minister of war. . . . What glory for Madame de Staël, what joy for her to have the whole army at her disposal."[32]

Of these personal triumphs, not a word appears in the *Considerations*. It was certainly not the time, in 1816, to remind the restored monarch of the role she had played in making and breaking political careers, and for a woman, such activities were always suspect. Instead, she recollected the major public events of 1791; namely, the death of Mirabeau, the king's flight to Varennes, and the acceptance of the Constitution.

Mme de Staël's eloquent tribute to Mirabeau is worthy both of him and of her. "I admit that, in spite of Mirabeau's horrible wrongs," she wrote, "his death struck me painfully, and all of Paris experienced the same feeling. During his sickness, an immense crowd gathered every day and every hour in front of his door."

All the parties then regretted Mirabeau. . . . He died at the most brilliant moment of his career, and the tears of the people who accompanied his funeral rendered the ceremony very touching. It was the first time in France that a man famous for his writing and his eloquence received the honors that were previously accorded only to great seigneurs or to warriors. The day after his death, no one in the Constituent Assembly could look without sadness at the place where Mirabeau had the custom of sitting. The great oak had fallen.[33]

Such belated admiration for Mirabeau was not shared by royalist memorialists such as Mme de Tourzel, Mme Campan, and Mme de Chastenay. Of the funereal pomp accorded Mirabeau, Mme de Tourzel wrote disdainfully, "Nothing was greater proof of the demoralization of the French people than to see it render such honors to a man to whom one could reproach the greatest of crimes, and who had drawn his country into an abyss of misfortune."[34]

Still another view of Mirabeau is found in the memoirs of Mme Roland. With her republican sentiments and enthusiasm for the heroic, she praised him as "the only man in the Revolution whose genius could direct men and impel an assembly; great by his faculties, little by his vices, but always superior to the vulgar mass." While she knew that Mirabeau had begun to come to terms with the monarchy—a grave failing in the eyes of that intransigent republican—she missed him all the same, especially as she contemplated the fate in store for her husband and herself at the hands of Robespierre and company. Then Mme Roland allowed that Mirabeau had provided a necessary counterforce to the "ruffians" and "mongrels" unleashed after his death.[35]

On the whole, women memoirists did not treat the leaders of the Revolution kindly. Mme Roland called them "pygmies" and concluded that France had exhausted its manpower. Mme de Staël was more generous in her appraisal of certain men—her father, Lafayette, and even Mirabeau—but she too recognized the lack of worthy men after 1791. Her memories of Robespierre, for example, were consonant with the ubiquitous negative campaign conducted against him after his death. She caustically recorded their first face-to-face encounter at her father's house in 1789 when Robespierre "was known as a lawyer from the Artois with very exaggerated democratic principles. His features were ignoble, his skin pale, his veins of a greenish color; he supported the most absurd theses with a sangfroid that had an air of conviction." She granted that at the beginning of the Revolution he had sincerely adopted ideas promoting equality of fortune and rank, but claimed that he soon lost whatever virtues he possessed because his character was fundamentally "envious and spiteful." She compared him sardonically with his "rival in demagogy, Danton, the Mirabeau of the populace": Danton was "more witty than Robespierre, more accessible to pity; but one suspected him, rightly, of being able to be corrupted by money. . . . Danton was a factionist, Robespierre a hypocrite; Danton wanted pleasure, Robespierre only power." Yet she conceded that "no name will remain from that period [1792-94] except for that of Robespierre. He was, however, not more clever nor more eloquent than the others; but his political fanaticism had a character of calm and austerity that made him feared by all his colleagues."[36]

Fanaticism, the source of Robespierre's power, was for Mme de Staël the greatest of political evils. It was the generating principle behind the crimes of the terror perpetrated by citizens convinced of their own uncontestable virtue. "*Ecrasez l'infâme!*"— Voltaire's battle cry in the face of religious intolerance—became Staël's unspoken axiom whenever she confronted extremist forms of one-party or one-man rule, be it absolute monarchy, Robespierre, or Napoleon.

STAËL'S ACCOUNT OF THE FLIGHT of the royal family to Varennes in June 1791 reveals great indulgence toward the king. She claims that he had certainly experienced "sufficient grievances at that time to have had the right to leave France." She even suggests that he might have been rendering a great service to the Constitutionalists by putting an end to a hypocritical situation since everyone knew that the king's political acts were not voluntary, despite public pretense to the contrary. Remembering a conversation she had had in England in 1793 with Charles Fox, head of the Whig party, she records his wish that the king had been allowed to leave the country; then the Constituent Assembly could have proclaimed a republic, and France "would not have been soiled by the crimes committed afterwards toward the royal family." Mme de Staël wistfully imagined that a reasonable constitution would have emerged from the struggle between the two parties had the king escaped. And in that conciliatory spirit, she reflected, "What one must avoid above all in France is the complete triumph of one party."[37] It would take many more decades before that liberal creed, already flourishing in English soil, became rooted in France.

Of 1791, the one event remembered with relative enthusiasm is the completion of the Constitution, which received high marks for "the abuses it destroyed" and poor ones for "the institutions it founded." In accepting the Constitution of 1791, the king was able to put an end to his captivity, profiting from the general amnesty accorded to all who had taken part in his flight to Varennes or committed any other political offence. "Festivities took place, as if one believed oneself happy; rejoicing was ordered so as to persuade oneself that the dangers had passed." The king and queen were greeted by genuine applause at their first return to the Opera.

> They were doing the ballet of Psyche. At the moment when the furies were dancing and waving their torches, and when that burst of flame illuminated the whole hall, I saw the King and Queen's faces in the pale light of that imitation of hell, and a fatal foreboding of the future seized me. The Queen forced herself to be courteous, but one felt a profound sadness behind her obliging smile.[38]

Ah! the past! How poignant, how gratifying it must have been to look back to the last moment when a different fate for the royal couple and the nation was still possible. How satisfying for the writer to suggest a tacit analogy between the fury-ridden Hades created on stage and the mob-directed inferno that would soon overtake the king and queen and all of France. And how consoling to depict oneself, with the backward projection of hindsight, as one of the few prescient souls who perceived in a flash the future destruction of everything that august assemblage held dear.

The new constitution lacked the support of the conservatives. Whereas Mme de Tourzel had presented that fact as an inevitable and justifiable consequence of their attachment to the Crown, Mme de Staël blamed the aristocrats for the failure of the new constitutional monarchy: "The prejudices of French gentlemen were such that they rejected any form of free government; it is to this major difficulty that one must attribute the most serious flaws of the Constitution of 1791."[39]

The elimination of the conservative force in government was linked to the massive emigration of the nobility, a subject discussed at length in Part 3 of Staël's *Considerations*. Here the author distinguished between voluntary emigration and forced emigration. All emigration prior to the fall of 1792, before the monarchy was overthrown and the reign of terror had begun, was placed in the first category and condemned, whereas the latter emigration, including her own, was condoned. "We all emigrated to protect ourselves from the perils of which each was menaced." "All" refers, of course, to the members of her class and political stripe. Whatever their grievances, Mme de Staël criticizes the earlier "unthreatened" emigrants on the grounds that they had swerved from the essential principles of society that forbid an alliance with the enemy against one's own people. She fashioned that principle into a forceful aphorism: "There are inflexible duties in politics as in morality, and the very first is never to deliver one's country to foreigners."

Staël's analysis of the emigration of the French aristocracy has distinct pre-Marxist parameters, for she understood that the international links between members of the same class took precedence over their loyalty to the nation: "Unfortunately, the nobles of France considered themselves to be the compatriots of nobles of every country rather than the fellow citizens of Frenchmen." She recognized the circumstances peculiar to French history that had created in France "two nations in one" and a group of émigré noblemen who treated "the French people as insurgent vassals."

And for all that, the aristocrats who went into exile did not lose their love of the mother country. The idea of attachment to the land of one's birth, with its distinct language, culture, and social institutions, provided a key thesis for de Staël's mature works. In conjuring up the vision of the hapless émigrés, she allows for an elegiac interjection: "Ah! One cannot transport one's household gods to the hearth of foreigners!" The love of country is presented as indestructible, and the emotion of homesickness proffered as a basis for ethical behavior. "Often," she remarked, "after a long absence or partisan quarrels have destroyed all your relations, you no longer know anyone in that country which is your own; but at the sound of its name, the sight of its outline, your whole heart is moved; and rather than fight against such impressions as chimera, they should serve as a guide for the virtuous person." This emotional rhetoric, inherited directly from Rousseau, situates moral authority in one's feelings: the voice of the heart and the voice of conscience are conflated into one unfailing law for personal behavior.[40]

Like her father who spent the last fourteen years of his life in Switzerland writing to justify his past ministry and offering unheeded advice to the French, Mme de Staël always linked politics to a morality of sentiment. She quotes at length Necker's *Executive Power of Great Nations*, a work that underwent five editions in 1792, to support the contention that he had predicted many of the evils that eventuated from the Jacobin domination of the Legislative Assembly and its erosion of "truly republican sentiments." The latter are defined as "generosity toward the weak, the horror of arbitrary measures, respect for justice, indeed all the virtues which the friends of liberty deemed it an honor to possess."[41] Clearly the author placed herself among those with "republican" sentiments, using the term broadly to denote universal liberal values. She used the substantive "republic" more narrowly to denote a specific form of representative government.

In recalling the events that led to the proclamation of the Republic on September 21, 1792, Mme de Staël finds herself caught between her later preference for "a republic over all other forms of government" and her earlier commitment to constitutional monarchy. Since, in 1792, the Republic could be established only by destroying an already existing monarchy, Staël argues that those with "truly republican sentiments" favored the gradual evolution of republican ideals under the king. "When Louis XVI was still alive, when the nation had received his pledges, and when it in return had freely pledged its own," it was a mistake, she concludes, to have risked the benefits one already possessed for the sake of a word.[42] Staël's fluctuation on this matter stems from her belief that the people were not ready for a republic; after so many centuries of feudal hierarchy, they were scarcely ready for a constitutional monarchy. The republic, born prematurely, would initially feed on many of its potential allies.

As Staël describes the events of 1792, the pace accelerates and action overtakes analysis. The author paints vast historical frescoes with an eye for the colorful detail. Her description of the anniversary festivities of July 14 is one of her most powerful. She juxtaposes the mob's boisterous demonstrations in favor of Pétion, the Jacobin mayor of Paris, against the king and queen's pathetic efforts to retain some measure of public dignity, as "the men from Marseilles . . . passed in front of the makeshift platform on which the royal family was placed, crying out: Long live Pétion! . . . Scarcely a few feeble voices could be heard saying: Long live the king! like a last cry, like a last prayer."

> The look on the queen's face will never be erased from my memory; her eyes were overwhelmed with tears; the splendor of her attire, the dignity of her bearing contrasted with the troops that surrounded her. . . . The king went by foot from the pavilion where he had been seated to the elevated altar at the other end of the Champ-de-Mars. There he was to pledge allegiance for a second time to the constitution. . . .
>
> One had to have the character of Louis XVI—that martyr's character he never betrayed—to have been able to endure such a situation. His manner of walking, his countenance had something very particular; in other circumstances, one might have wanted more grandeur from him; but it was enough at that moment for him to remain exactly the same in order to appear sublime. I followed from a distance his powdered head in the middle of all those heads with black hair; his full dress, still embroidered as in the past, stood out alongside the clothes of the people who pressed around him. When he mounted the steps of the altar, it could have been a holy victim offering himself voluntarily as a sacrifice. . . . From that day forth, the people did not see him again until he was on the scaffold.[43]

Louis XVI as martyr to the Revolution was a legend Mme de Staël helped to perpetuate. Her eyewitness depiction of his last public appearance before his execution carries the graphic intensity of a motion picture. She follows his slow, dignified walk across the field, his white head contrasting with the black ones around him as if to symbolize his moral worth. The king's acquiescent ascent to the altar calls forth the image of a voluntary sacrificial offering and leads to the reflection, following the ideas of René Girard, that Louis XVI filled the necessary role of religious scapegoat.[44] Mme de Staël might have added: Had only his sacrifice sufficed to quench the thirst for blood so many other deaths would have to satisfy!

Although she was not, like certain other memoirists, present at the invasion of the Tuileries on August 10, 1792, nor imprisoned during the September massacres, Mme de Staël's accounts of those days convey the horror that swiftly enveloped Paris. She evokes the "monotonous, lugubrious, and rapid" sound of the forty-eight alarm bells from each of the Parisian sections that began to ring before midnight on August 9 and continued throughout the night. Standing at her window with several of her friends, she listened apprehensively to the news relayed every quarter-hour by a voluntary patrol of Constitutionists. Rumors circulated that the suburbs had risen up under Santerre, the former brewer who had led the Tuileries invasion, or François Westermann, the military officer who was to play a decisive role in the Vendean Wars. "No one expected to live more than another day."

> All of a sudden, at seven o'clock, the frightful sound of the cannon from the suburbs was heard; and in the first attack, the Swiss guards were the winners. . . . It must be said that the king should have put himself at the head of his troops and opposed the enemy. The queen was of that opinion, and the courageous advice she gave her husband in that circumstance does her honor.[45]

The king's decision to give up without a fight is not viewed kindly. Without specifically condemning him for lack of courage, Mme de Staël implies that courage, in this instance, was on the distaff side.

Her account of the terrible August and September days centers around her attempts to save the lives of several endangered friends. As the wife of the Swedish ambassador and a citizen of Switzerland, she was in a better situation than most. When she heard that many of her friends among the Swiss guards protecting the king had been massacred, she rode out in her carriage in quest of further news, undeterred by the men in the streets who silently gestured to her coachman that throats were being cut across the Seine. Later she went out by foot to visit some of her friends in modest houses where they had been able to find shelter, finding "armed men sleeping in front of the doors, stilled by drunkenness, and only half waking so as to pronounce a few execrable curses. Several women of the people were also in the same state, and their vociferations were even more odious."

Here as in other firsthand accounts of the Revolution, the behavior of lower-class women is judged severely. Mme de Staël, for all her personal refusal to accept gender-based restrictions, was not above such prejudices when applied to others. She contributed her share of unflattering portraits to the composite picture of drunken, lowerclass women viewed as traitors to their sex. Like many others of a philosophic bent, she supported generosity to the needy in the abstract, but was repulsed by the poor when encountered in the flesh.

It was undoubtedly difficult to remain objective while describing the most dreadful days of French history; the very process of narrating such scenes gave her pause. Like other memorialists, she expressed reluctance to recall the gory details of the September massacres, yet resolved to recount her own experiences.

With the invasion of Austrian and Prussian troops, it was rumored that all "decent people" would be killed by the sans-culottes. Among her aristocratic friends, Messieurs de

Narbonne, Montmorenci, and Baumets were personally menaced, and each was in hiding. She persuaded two of her friends to come to the Swedish embassy where she locked them in the most inaccessible room. Her account of this event and of her own narrow escape from Paris makes for spellbinding reading:

> One morning, one of my servants . . . came to tell me they had posted at the corner of my street the description and the denunciation of M. de Narbonne: he was one of the persons hidden in my house. . . . Shortly thereafter, the formidable domiciliary visit [house search] took place in my house. M. de Narbonne, having been declared an outlaw, would perish the same day if he were discovered; and whatever precautions I had taken, I knew very well that if the search were carefully undertaken, he could not escape. I mustered all my forces and I felt, in that circumstance, that one can always dominate one's emotions, however intense they may be, when one knows that one is exposing another person's life.

Will M. de Narbonne be discovered? Will Mme de Staël be able to outwit her antagonists? The besieged protagonist dipped into the received wisdom of her class in responding to her interrogators; she decided to make fun of them. "Nothing," she contends, "is more agreeable to men of that class than wit and humor, because, in the excess of their rage against aristocrats, they take pleasure in being treated as their equals." The strategy succeeded, and Mme de Staël reconducted her interrogators to the door, silently blessing God for the "extraordinary strength" He had lent her at that moment. Thus Mme de Staël emerged from this episode as the worthy heroine of the man whose life she had just saved—a man known to have been her lover.

Granted a passport that allowed her to go to Switzerland, she might have left Paris immediately, but she remained to help some noble deputies incarcerated in the Abbaye prison. It occurred to her that Louis Pierre Manuel, the procurator of Paris, had an interest in literature—indeed, he had recently published Mirabeau's letters preceded by his own preface (parenthetically judged "very bad" by Mme de Staël, without skipping a beat of her story). Assuming that Manuel might be susceptible to the solicitations of a woman of letters, she wrote to request an interview. Their meeting, set for the "democratic" hour of seven in the morning, is described with attention to such psychologically revealing details as Manuel's self-portrait on his desk and his vulnerability to her emotionally charged words.

> I painted to him the terrifying vicissitudes of popularity, of which one could cite examples every day. "In six months," I said to him, "you will perhaps no longer have any power (within six months he had perished on the scaffold). Save M. de Lally and M. de Jaucourt [captive deputies]; reserve for yourself a sweet and consoling memory for the time when it will perhaps be your turn to be outlawed." . . . [Manuel later] wrote me . . . that M. de Condorcet had obtained M. de Lally's freedom and that, responding to my prayer, he had just granted M. de Jaucourt his liberty. Happy to have saved the life of such an estimable man, I made up my mind to leave the next day, but I committed myself to take the [deputy] abbé de Montesquiou from outside the [Parisian] gate and conduct him, disguised as a servant, as far as Switzerland.

Mme de Staël's prose may be more elegant, her intellect more keen, and her narrative talents more sophisticated than those of her sister memoirists, but she is no different from them in portraying herself as self-sacrificing and courageous when put to the test. Like the heroines of her novels, she demonstrates the requisite virtues of altruism and bravery, all the more necessary when the protagonist represents the author, and the author, understandably, wants the world to think well of her.

The account of her long-delayed departure from Paris and her close encounter with death crowns the entire work. It is a tale told against the backdrop of invading troops and mob uprisings, with the narrator threatened at every point of the way. One senses her determination, and fear, as she attempted to push forcefully or tread cautiously in her path toward freedom. Her first decision was to depart in a six-horse carriage with her servants in full livery. That "very badly conceived" decision could have been fatal, as Mme de Staël realized after the fact, because "what one should not do is stir up the imagination of the people, and the worst post-chaise would have conducted me with greater safety." Her story continues with the appearance of a frenzied female mob:

> My carriage had scarcely gone four paces when, at the sound of the postillion whips, a swarm of old ladies, emerging from hell, threw themselves on my horses, and cried that I should be arrested, that I was taking with me the nation's gold, that I was going to join the enemies. . . . Those women attracted a crowd in an instant, and common people with savage faces seized my postillions and ordered them to take me to the assembly of the neighborhood section where I lived.

Using a vocabulary common to many revolutionary narratives, Staël portrays the women as hellish furies and the mob as a tribe of savages. Having barely escaped from this ordeal, she confronted another one at the section offices; there she was denounced as planning to take outlaws with her into exile, and dispatched with a guard to City Hall.

The prospect of crossing Paris and descending at the Place de Grève in front of the Hôtel de Ville was terrifying, since, as Staël reminds us, it was on that building's stairway that several people had been massacred on the tenth of August. She points out that "no woman had yet perished," though the following day the Princesse de Lamballe would be massacred by the crowd. In retrospect, Staël had good reason to believe that she herself might have been the first of her sex chosen to mark the end of the ban against the killing of women.

For women, it can be argued that the Terror officially began in September 1792, when they began to be assassinated along with the men. It took Mme de Staël three hours to cross Paris through a crowd that assailed her with death threats. Reflecting on her situation, she wrote: "It wasn't I they were cursing, they scarcely knew me; but a big carriage and clothes trimmed with braid represented in the eyes of the people all they should destroy." With that characteristic combination of action-laden description and retrospective reflection, Staël portrays herself as naively seeking aid from several gendarmes, who "responded with the most scornful and menacing gestures." Incidentally, she tells us that she was visibly pregnant, which only worsened the situation because instead of feeling more sympathetic toward her, the gendarmes were more irritated because they felt more guilty. Nonetheless, the one who had been placed in her carriage became touched by her situation, and promised to defend her at the risk of his own life. He would be called upon to do so at the Place de Grève, as Mme de Staël dramatically recalls. "I got out of my carriage in the middle of an armed multitude, and I advanced under a vault of spears. As

I was going up the stairway, equally bristling with lances, a man directed against me the one he held in his hand. My gendarme defended me with his sword; if I had fallen at that instant, it would have been my life."

Her activities of September 2, despite the many life-threatening hazards to which she was subject, form a picture of a determined, strong-willed woman. Each of five long paragraphs filling two pages begins with the first-person pronoun: "I had," "I entered," "I spent," "I got out," "I arrived"—all suggesting an intelligence in the midst of chaos. Fully in the limelight, she plays to a crowd of readers, who share her perilous adventures and applaud her ultimate victory.

There remained the ordeal of confronting the authorities and the mob gathered inside the Hôtel de Ville. In order to render that encounter more awesome, Mme de Staël invokes the name of the archdemon Robespierre, although it is unlikely she even saw him on that day. As she awaited her turn to convince the bureaucracy of her right to leave Paris, an unexpected stroke of luck came her way in the figure of the procurator of Paris, Manuel. Astonished to find her there, he sequestered Mme de Staël and her chambermaid into his own office. It was to be a long wait.

> We remained there for six hours . . . dying of hunger, thirst, and fear. The window of Manuel's apartment overlooked the Place de Grève, and we saw the assassins coming from the prisons, with their arms bare and bloody, and shouting horrible cries. . . .
>
> As soon as Manuel saw me again, he cried out with much emotion: *Ah! I am so glad I freed your two friends yesterday!* In reality, he suffered bitterly from the assassinations that had just been committed, but he no longer had the power to oppose them.

Manuel's situation as a revolutionary unable to control the Revolution is encapsulated in a brilliant metaphor: "An abyss opened up behind the steps of each man who acquired authority, and as soon as he went backwards, he fell into it."

That night Manuel took her in his own carriage back to the Swedish embassy. He promised to send her a new passport the next day that would allow her and her chambermaid to cross the border. Thus, Mme de Staël was indebted to Manuel not only for her two friends' lives, but for her own as well. In her account he comes off much better than he does in those of Mme de Fars Fausselandry and the Princesse de Tarente.

The deputy Jean Tallien, too, known for his victory over Robespierre twenty months later, also appears as helping several aristocrats in their time of need. Both Mme de Staël and Mme de La Tour du Pin attest to his assistance. In Staël's account, it was Tallien who brought her the promised passport and accompanied her to the gate of Paris. Moreover, he kept secret the knowledge of several heavily compromised persons remaining in her house.

It was the third of September, 1792, an infamous day in French history. Half of the prisoners in Paris—about 1,300 people—were being slaughtered. As she drove away from the city, "the tempest seemed to abate, and in the Jura mountains nothing recalled the appalling agitation that was being played out on the Paris stage."

The threat of foreign invaders was less terrifying than the scene she had left behind. Mme de Staël concluded her hair-raising tale by stating, "At that moment, the only foreigners I saw were the assassins under whose daggers I had left my friends, the royal kingdom, and all the decent people of France."

FOR THE NEXT TWO AND A HALF YEARS, Mme de Staël remained abroad; she would not return to Paris until May 1795. As presented in the *Considerations*, the revolutionary events occurring during her absence lack the verve of her earlier eyewitness accounts. To describe the victory of the French over their foreign enemies, the trial and death of Louis XVI, the Terror, the Vendean Wars, and the fall of Robespierre, she had to rely on her memories of news conveyed to her in Switzerland or England and the numerous records accumulated since 1795, including her father's two-volume history of the Revolution.

Try as she may to resurrect Necker in the second half of the book through lengthy quotations from his writing, his presence no longer animates history. As Linda Orr has written in a fascinating interpretation of the *Considerations* as a form of Freudian family romance, the Swiss father of the French Revolution eventually gives way to the formidable Corsican, Mme de Staël's "sibling" antagonist. Napoleon is presented as the "illegitimate heir" to the Revolution of which Staël considered herself the "rightful daughter."[46] Between the beneficent father eulogized in Parts 1 and 2 and the malevolent emperor castigated in Parts 4 and 5, Germaine de Staël had briefly enjoyed an act of her own. Like many other women memoirists, she had ridden on the coattails of a powerful male relative, screening herself behind his glory until she was able to declare, like Mme de Fars Fausselandry, that it was her moment to command center stage. The events of September 2 and 3, 1792, drew her into the political vortex from which she escaped only by chance, courage, and cunning. Retrospectively she fashioned her story into a self-dramatizing triumph over revolutionary atrocity. Borrowing techniques from her novels and plays, she placed her personal story at the apogee of the national epic in a plot of ascending and descending action. The message is unmistakable: when she was forced to retreat from Paris, Revolution and Terror had become synonymous. Henceforth, revolutionary politics would become permanently tainted by its justification of massacre and summary executions.

In concluding her prodigious memoirs, the author was not above flattering the reigning monarch, Louis XVIII, in the hope that flattery would serve the cause of liberty and promote some of the early Revolution's lost ideals. Recognizing the long shadow of crime cast by the Revolution during the Terror, she considered the situation of many former victims, steadfast in memory and implacable in their desire for revenge, who were now convinced that "the arbitrary power of a single person" was their only sure preservation. She feared that those injured parties crying for reparation "could turn Louis XVIII into a despot, if his lofty wisdom did not prevent him from becoming one."[47] It was to Louis XVIII's personal good sense, and to his desire for the approbation of such as herself, that she appealed.

The Revolution's noblest aspirations had not been destroyed for Mme de Staël, even with the Terror, Napoleon, and the restoration of monarchy in France. She wrote her last work in the hope that the goals of political and social justice espoused by the enlightened community of 1789 would yet be realized. She wrote it, too, as an enduring monument to her father, and to herself.

Louis-Ferdinand Aubry, *Woman with Her Basket Before a Prison Door.* The letter in her hand reads: To the Citizen Aubry in La Force. *Musée de la Révolution Française, Vizille*

9

PLIGHTS AND PLOYS IN THE PROVINCES: MADAME VALLON AND ALEXANDRINE DES ECHEROLLES

WHEN MME DE STAEL SLIPPED OUT OF PARIS in September 1792, she felt she was leaving the tempest behind her: the further she advanced toward the Swiss border, the calmer the scene before her eyes. Yet the Revolution was by no means confined to Paris. Throughout France, in regions far from the capital, millions of lives were being shaken by revolutionary upheaval.

Each of the eighty-three departments newly formed in 1790 responded in its own way to the prodigious production of decrees handed down from Paris. Some were extremely rigorous in following the letter of the law, while others had to be whipped into compliance by representatives on mission. Women's accounts of life in provincial departments bear witness to the toll extracted from them and their families, often at the hands of zealous men in positions of local authority. Since all the memoirists were, in some sense, at odds with the new regime, it should not surprise us to find the Revolution painted in its worst light. The metanarrative was that of the hunter and the hunted, with the narrator, in every case, linked to the latter. Either she feared for a close relative or she herself was the object of the hunt. Setting aside those memoirs that recount the Vendean Wars, which will be considered separately in the following chapter, we shall encounter several women scattered across France, from Brittany and Normandy to the south and southeast, with special attention to two teenaged girls from Blois and Lyons.

Typically, the women recorded suspenseful dramas in which the lives of family members, or their own lives, were at stake. From the center of France, Mme Carra de Vaux, aunt of the future poet Alphonse de Lamartine, described in one nervous breath her overlapping anxieties during the month of October 1793: "We were hiding my brother-in-law. . . . I had just given birth to a son; I was nursing him; my sister de Lamartine was at

Mâcon in the same situation, her husband had been put in prison, but as she was nursing, they let her go free."[1] Nursing offered one of the few loopholes to the imprisonment of women, just as pregnancy could be usually be counted on to stay the executioner's hand.[2]

Similarly, in Nîmes, Mme Juillerat-Chasseur was hiding her brother, a lapsed commander of the National Guard, who had lost his patriotic enthusiasm after the Paris massacres and the execution of the Girondin deputies. He hid out in the family home, refusing to leave despite the danger of arrest because his wife was sick and despondent after the death of an infant son. Even when the local sheriff came to warn Mme Juillerat-Chasseur of her brother's imminent arrest, allowing him time to escape, he would not budge.

At eleven o'clock at night, she went to call on a friend with a minor government position. She asked him and his wife for advice regarding her brother's predicament.

"Don't turn him in," they said.

"But where can he hide?" she asked.

"Let him come here," they answered. "The house is small; we don't see anyone, and the position my husband occupies spares us from domiciliary visits."[3]

Despite the refuge offered by these republican friends, the brother stayed at his wife's side, where he was eventually arrested. While he was in prison, his indefatigable sister continued to work behind the scenes on his behalf and ultimately obtained the prized certificate declaring that he had never left the country as an émigré; otherwise he would have been subject to execution and the confiscation of his possessions.

Hiding a relative, friend, or oneself became a way of life for a great number of individuals, many of whom found it easier to remain inconspicuous in remote parts of the countryside or in provincial cities rather than in Paris. Mme de Chastenay and Mme de La Tour du Pin outwitted their pursuers by withdrawing from Paris to the provinces; the former kept a low profile with her family in Rouen during the Terror, while the latter went underground with her husband and children in the Bordeaux region until they managed to escape to America. The families of the future Mme Delahante and the future Baronne Lambert, both small children when the Revolution began, retreated to Normandy with the police at their heels. In their new provincial settings, each discovered greater gender segregation and differences in the treatment of girls and boys than they had known in their sophisticated, upper-class, Parisian milieux.

The Baronne Lambert's family was the powerful Pannelier d'Arsonval clan related to the queen's first lady-in-waiting, Mme Campan. Alexandrine Pannelier d'Arsonval's father, who had been responsible for having the carriage made in which the king had fled to Varennes, sought asylum in the town of Valognes where they then lived "as peacefully as the circumstances would permit."[4] Some of their furniture, servants, horses from Paris, and even a music teacher for the young Alexandrine accompanied them. But in time, the political climate made it inadvisable to display the slightest traces of rank: even "a fork on which one might have seen our coat of arms could have put my parents in prison."[5] Indeed, Alexandrine's father was ultimately arrested and imprisoned in the local jail; for many months his small daughter visited him there carrying secret messages to and fro in a bandage wrapped around her finger.

The atmosphere in the town of Valognes was decidedly democratic. "Whoever did not use the familiar 'tu' form of speech was suspect; I was seven years old and had to have not only the tricolored ribbon on my head, but a certificate of public-spiritedness." In the primary school attended by her brother, the boys were taught to recite the new Declaration of the Rights of Man. From her aristocratic and gendered stance, Alexandrine did not appreciate the fact that state-run schools were one of the Revolution's greatest contributions to society. As of December 1793, free primary school education, both for boys and for girls, became compulsory, though, in fact, it would take decades before that mandate was put into practice throughout the land. Her own education would take place after the Revolution in a private school for upper-class young ladies established on the outskirts of Paris by her aunt Mme Campan.

But during the Revolution in Normandy, she and the other members of her family lived a much less elitist life. Her mother did not dare miss the local celebration of the Festival of the Republic, which took place in a church. What remained in Alexandrine's memory was the image of a man in a red cap standing on a chair shouting "Long live the Nation! Long live the Republic! Down with the priests!" A mass of people with short jackets known as "carmagnoles" rushed to the main altar and side chapels, and "In an instant, everything was broken: statues, paintings, ornaments, reliquary shrines." This scene was repeated in many churches throughout France as part of a dechristianisation process that closed churches or turned them into revolutionary temples, outlawed both men's and women's monastic orders, substituted revolutionary festivals for religious holidays, and sent refractory priests into prison, exile, or hiding.

With her father and two of her uncles in prison and one of her aunts hiding out in the country, little Alexandrine became adept at dissimulating in order to protect endangered family members. Like the future Mme Delahante in the same circumstances, at six and seven they were "no longer children."

To read these works one would think that every lodging had a suspect hiding in the attic or cellar. The willingness of individuals to offer shelter to those running from the police, and the ingenious strategies devised to avoid detection, often read like masterful spy or detective stories. The hunt quickened its pace after the national decrees of July 1792 that allowed local authorities great latitude in searching out "suspects," defined broadly as "bad citizens."[6] As of August 1792, "domiciliary visits" were inaugurated with the ostensible purpose of determining the number of arms possessed by the populace. Suspects were to be disarmed and their weapons given to citizens departing for the recently declared war against Austria and Prussia.

Local police authorities took advantage of these domiciliary visits to ferret out aristocrats, priests, and other counterrevolutionary suspects. Prisoners would then remain for indeterminate periods in jail under the label "suspect"; indeed, since a trial was often the gateway to the guillotine, most inmates preferred prison to appearance before a judge, especially if it meant transfer from the provinces to Paris, where the accused lost whatever influence they might still have in their home community.

Life inside provincial prisons provided the subject matter for a number of memoirists: Mesdames de Bohm, de Duras, and de Pons, who were inmates of the château de Chantilly just north of Paris; Mme du Peloux still further north in Pas de Calais near the Belgian border; Mme de La Villirouët and Mlle de Saint-Luc in Brittany; Sister Besnard in Angers; Mme Vallon in Blois; and Mme Ranfer de Bretenières in Dijon. These accounts tell us a good deal about the treatment of prisoners, which varied enormously from region to region and from prison to prison. In some, the men and women were separated; in others, sexes, ages, and classes intermingled. In many of the old prisons, individuals were locked in their cells at night, whereas in the new ones converted from former monasteries, convents, colleges, and even châteaux, inmates often had the free run of the building and courtyard. Some wardens allowed inmates to gather for various forms of entertainment—dancing, singing, playing cards; others limited gatherings to three or four people and only at certain hours. Changes in regulations were often arbitrary, depending on the policies or temperament of the authorities in charge.

A fairly typical prison for women, in this case the mothers, wives, and daughters of émigrés, was created in March 1793, in Dijon. Once a religious establishment, this prison housed up to one hundred women, including Mme Ranfer de Bretenières, who left this picture of the internal conditions.

> The house was ugly but vast. . . . Half of it was closed; they preferred to make twelve people sleep in one room. . . . The only place the prisoners could walk was in a courtyard surrounded by a thirty-foot wall where a sewer, privies, and a dunghill were located and where one smelled a foul odor. . . .
>
> Children younger than six had permission to enter three times a week to be with their mothers. Not having any of that age, I went nine months without seeing my daughter. Everything that was brought to the prisoners was searched with the most scrupulous exactitude, the linen unfolded, the bread cut up, the pastries broken. . . . At nine o'clock the doors of the house were closed and the prisoners could no longer go into the courtyard.[7]

From the sexually integrated prison of Carhaix in Brittany, Mlle de Saint-Luc wrote a satirical account of her detention there, including the following description of a change in regulations announced by the prison commissioner.

> "From now on," he said, "you are going to have your meals in common: the poor, the rich will eat together and will be served very frugally—a soup and boiled beef at lunch, a roast and salad for dinner, and all the provisions which arrive for you individually will be shared."

Whereas earlier each prisoner had purchased his or her separate provisions, allowing four or five rich citizens to dine sumptuously on "suckling pig, excellent stews, turkey, duck, partridge, ham, cold and hot pâtés, without mentioning all the meat and fish pies, creams, and other delicacies," after the communal meals became mandatory, everyone at the prison of Carhaix went hungry. "Even the most moderate people were beside themselves; they threatened to force the prison doors if they were kept locked up without food."[8]

Food provided a common theme for the prison memoirists, who tended to remember the specifics of what they ate with a typically French passion. Inmates were expected to pay for their food according to their financial circumstances, and those with means sometimes shared their provisions with the less fortunate. Mme Vallon, née Puzela, remembered the largesse of a certain gentleman in the prison of Blois, who spared no expense keeping an open table every night for fifteen to twenty people. As a teenager from a poor family, she was dazzled by the aristocratic lifestyle discovered within prison walls: "The dinner was very splendid, very gay. They spoke about very interesting things, literature and history. I didn't speak at all, but I listened with the kind of interest that showed how very much this conversation pleased me."[9]

Mme Vallon's testimonial, related in the following pages, is unusual in that it concerns a family struggling to gain a foothold in the middle class. It is also a highly personal story of a young girl coming of age in a time of revolution under the watchful tutelage of a somewhat bizarre father. A highly conservative Catholic and staunch royalist given to political collisions with the local authorities, he was considered a fanatical counterrevolutionary in the region around Blois, where he made his living as a notary. As Mme Vallon noted at the beginning of her memoirs, her early history was so intertwined with that of her father that both lives had to be told simultaneously. "Their" story is in many ways representative of provincial life during the Revolution, despite the idiosyncrasies of the father's character.

The first effect of the Revolution on the Puzela family was that the father's income as a notary was considerably reduced due to the elimination of the seigniorial courts of justice. Mlle Puzela's mother, with a family background in trade, decided to open a store to supplement their dwindling resources. She borrowed money from her own mother to get started, "and suddenly," in the narrator's words, "we were merchants."[10] The "we" definitely included Marie-Catherine Puzela, aged thirteen, who spent the next four years as a provisioner for her mother's store. This entailed scouring the countryside for supplies, she on her donkey accompanied by her father on foot. Since it was beneath him to do anything more than chaperone his daughter, she did all the negotiating and handling of items. Some of her worst memories concerned requests for delays from their creditors, a task she was always delegated to perform. The narrative of her involvement in her mother's business gives us a rare entry into the lives of millions of working-class women and children who helped support their families during the troubled revolutionary period, when husbands and fathers were often deprived of former forms of employment or sent to the wars.

In 1792, when all priests were required to swear allegiance to the Constitution of the Clergy, her father openly opposed the installation of the constitutional priests in his parish church. He became a member of the Society of Non-Conformist Catholics, and was for a short time mayor of the town of Saint-Cyr-du-Gault, until he was suspended from his functions. Denounced to the Committee of Surveillance of the District of Blois for his "opinionated character" and for wearing the mayor's scarf after he had been deprived of office, he was placed under arrest and declared incapable of continuing his profession as a notary. Not only did they affix seals on all his papers, but they also affixed them on the armoires containing the family linens and on the merchandise in the store, which prevented Mme Puzela from continuing her business. She requested that the seals be lifted on the grounds that it would be unjust to punish her for her husband's crimes, and eventually this was done. She also initiated the first of many petitions for her husband's release from the state of arrest.

He, in the meantime, having been informed that he was about to be incarcerated, had fled with his daughter. Prearrest warnings seem to have occurred with relative frequency in the provinces, where close interpersonal relations offered some counterforce against the police. Hiding out in one place or another, changing residence frequently so as to escape detection, wandering from the home of one friend or relative to another, Puzela disguised himself as a gardener, as a servant, as anyone other than himself. Often his daughter had "to go to warn him, to be witness to his complaints, to wipe his tears and shed some bitter ones herself." After several months in hiding, her father was denounced, discovered, and imprisoned in a former Carmelite convent. Mlle Puzela, now seventeen, asked that she be allowed to join her sick father in prison. "I rejoiced in secret at the idea of sharing my father's shackles. . . . My preparations were not difficult: two little cotton dresses, six morning caps, and some linen composed my entire wardrobe."[11] By sheer force of determination, and a few bribes, she schemed her way into prison, though she did not have official permission to remain there.

The stories of women who chose to share the fate of their fathers in prison constitute a sentimental chapter in the history of the Revolution. The most notable model was Mlle de Sombreuil, remembered for having saved her father from the Paris prison massacres of September 1792. Throwing her arms around her father, she told his would-be assassins that they would have to murder her as well. Mlle Cazotte was similarly effective in defending her father, only to lose him to the public executioner several days later. Mme de Fausselandry asked to be imprisoned with her uncle, the Abbot Chapt de Rastignac, but though she survived the massacres at the Abbaye prison, he did not.

Mlle Puzela was already familiar with these models when she came to share her father's prison cell. In her memoirs she presents her actions as "natural," though others are reputed to have made much of them and to have called her "courageous." The committee members to whom she applied for permission to join her father would give her only temporary passes. They tried to dissuade her by saying she would no longer be marriageable by the time of her father's release. In a society where it was common for women of her age to be married, the seventeen-year-old Marie-Catherine was putting her future in danger by committing to a long imprisonment. But she was not to be dissuaded. "There I was," she wrote, "installed at the head of his bed, dividing my time between work, reading, and the cares I gave him."[12] She did needlework that earned fifteen sous a day—enough to pay for half their expenses. Earlier she had arranged for a townsperson to furnish a simple lunchtime meal at a modest fee, while small packages sent from Saint-Cyr sufficed for their breakfasts and suppers.

After a month in prison (though her pass was officially valid for only two weeks), her father's health improved sufficiently so that they began to make visits to the other prisoners. At this point she discovered the group of aristocrats whose lifestyle so impressed her. "That house was filled with prisoners from a very distinguished class. . . . The airs of high society were unknown to me; but I remarked very quickly that candor and innocence captivate everyone's heart."[13]

The first time she and her father were invited to the open table in the large refectory, she was astonished by the elegant appearance of the people gathered there. Her host, a gentleman poet, sang a few songs composed in prison, and after dinner, "one went to take a walk in the garden." From her description, they might have been at the château of Blois, instead of its prison. As she put it: "I could not get over my astonishment. How did they preserve in the midst of misfortune and the uncertainty of events that sense of security, that taste for luxury, in short, that lightness of spirit!"[14]

Several months passed in this fashion without any memorable events other than the arrival of new prisoners, including the former nuns from the Hôtel Dieu hospital, who brought their own beds with them. When Mme Puzela came to visit, gaining entry by bribing the warden, she was able to appropriate the bed of a very sick nun who had been sent home to her family. The warden clearly was flexible in his treatment of the prisoners and their families, especially when softened up with money and gifts, such as the chiffon offered by Mme Puzela as fabric for his wife's caps. But the members of the prison commission were a different matter; whenever they came to inspect, regulations were tightened, and social events for inmates became less numerous.

Around this time, in December 1793, there were rumors that a revolutionary army would assassinate all t he prisoners in the region to keep them from being liberated by counterrevolutionary armies from the Vendée. Within the prison walls, the inmates heard the detonations that destroyed the bridge of Blois in an effort to prevent the Vendeans from crossing the Loire. The narrator remembered waiting "with resignation, but in a state of anxiety difficult to describe."[15]

They heard the horrible story of the 900 or 1,000 prisoners taken from Saumur under the command of Petit, who had 700 or 800 of them shot before they reached Amboise. By the time this convoy reached Blois, there were 200 prisoners left, half of them women. This account differs markedly from the version given by R. Levasseur, the deputy on mission responsible for sending the convoy off from Saumur in the first place. In his memoirs, he states that there were 300 prisoners, all dangerous Vendeans apt to rebel if the Vendean troops attacked Saumur. He gave Citizen Petit the authority to bind the prisoners "two by two and to shoot them in case of revolt." Several prisoners were indeed "sacrificed, but it was a small number."[16] Which version are we to believe?

Inside the prison of Blois, Mlle Puzela heard the cries of the mob calling for the assassination of all the prisoners: "Give us the enemies of the state! Give us the traitors to the nation!"[17] In contrast to the behavior of the Parisian municipality during the massacres of September 1792, the local Blois authorities quickly responded to the threat of mob assassination; they removed their prisoners from the monastery by a back exit, piled them into a row of straw-filled carts, and transported them to another location.

Mlle Puzela's name was not on the list of prisoners read out loud in the courtyard, yet she managed to persuade one of the guards to let her accompany her father. As they were led out of town, the convoy of carts stopped in front of the guillotine. She was certain that this was the end for all of them. But the carts started to move again and, followed by a mob that shouted threats and curses, they took the road to Orléans.

Their pace was so slow that it took eight hours to get to Beaugency only 30 kilometers away. There they were deposited at an inn called La Fora, where prisoners were expected to pay for their lodgings. In the case of the priests, who had no money, they were parceled out to the churches. As the prisoners entered the inn, they were greeted with a gruesome scene: the prison convoy originally from Saumur under the command of Petit had preceded them, and "they had just shot some of the prisoners in the courtyard . . . they were carrying them away when we entered." The narrator had the honesty to add: "We had no more tears to give to the suffering of others, we felt only our own; and, who would believe it, after such a spectacle, we demanded loudly that they serve us supper."[18]

At six in the morning, the drums announced departure. En route, the prisoners encountered a troop of revolutionary soldiers who threatened to assassinate them, but they were miraculously saved by the arrival of another group of republican soldiers, the Hussards, who placed them under their protection and guarded each cart with unsheathed swords. By now Mlle Puzela was in shock: "I had seen death without fear, I had seen my life saved without experiencing any feeling, I was in a state of paralysis."

Finally they arrived in Orléans where they were conducted to an old Franciscan convent transformed into a state prison. The difference from their former prison setting was immediately apparent in the person of "the jail-keeper with an atrocious mien and four stout dogs." Each tiny cell had a mattress on the floor, two little chairs, and a little table. At nine o'clock at night all the prison doors were closed, and a guard locked each cell until eight the next morning. During the day the prisoners were free to walk about the corridors and the little courtyard.

Inmates were given only bread and water, but as in most other prisons they were allowed to purchase their meals. The prison itself operated a thriving canteen; for forty sous (four francs) one could have a substantial lunch. Even this, however, was more money than the Puzelas could afford if they were to order two meals. They went down to the kitchen and found it had a wide variety of possibilities, including one lunch that was so copious as to be enough for two: "a piece of boiled beef . . . a bottle of wine," with the bread thrown in gratis. At six francs, it was a bargain.

The deeply embedded French concern for food persisted in the prisons of Orléans and Blois, as in numerous prisons throughout the land. So too, French habits of sociability along hierarchical lines did not disappear within prison walls. At Orléans, Mlle Puzela found a new protector in the form of a retired general, who introduced her to a second group of inmates richer than herself. In the evening they would gather in a room with a fire and manage, through good conversation, to pass the time agreeably. After the first of these evenings, Mlle Puzela was astonished to realize that she had had a good time: "In good company there is a tone that fills the simplest things with interest." The next day the general came to her cell with jams and candies and "so much goodness" that he appeared to the young girl like "an angelic creature."

Marie-Catherine Puzela made her social "debut" in prison within a class she would not have been able to frequent under normal circumstances. She was taken up by an old marquise, imprisoned on the charge of having fired a few patriotic servants. This seventy-yearold woman maintained her aristocratic airs and clothes in prison, and insisted on sending her servant to fetch linens for her new protégée, since the latter had left the prison of Blois in such a hurry as to have nothing with her but a single dress and cap.

On the subject of the cap, the marquise advised Mlle Puzela to take it off—it was definitely seen as a mark of the unfashionable moral rigor of her class—but her father insisted she retain it. He was not about to change his standards of morality, even in the face of favors offered by members of the nobility. Moreover, he was not at ease in their company, as was apparent from his awkward efforts to participate in their conversations. When they spoke of literature, he confused the authors and the centuries, and uttered anachronisms that brought smiles to their lips. Such interactions were extremely painful to his daughter: "I suffered cruelly from them, because my father was my glory, just as I was his consolation."

Shortly thereafter, rumors flew that the prisoners would be sent to their death in Paris, following the fate of other groups of prisoners from Orléans. Instead, the local officials protected them by having them transferred to the prison of Pontlevoy near Montrichard. Marie-Catherine was allowed to ride with three elderly prisoners in a large Berlin carriage that preceded the convoy of two or three vehicles and fifteen carts. If one could pay for a better mode of transportation, one was obviously allowed to do so.

The new prison was a former *collège* (the equivalent of a private, Catholic grammar school) where "one was not really a prisoner except by one's word . . . we played, danced, and made music." There were ninety-one prisoners, including nuns and priests. But by now Mlle Puzela was eager to give up her role as her father's companion because she felt pressured by the attentions of a certain undesirable gentleman from whom her father had accepted a sizable loan. When her mother arrived with a petition requesting her husband's liberty, Mlle Puzela decided to return to Saint-Cyr.

Marie-Catherine Puzela had spent the winter of 1793-94 in prison attending her father. She and her mother then did battle with the local authorities to obtain his release. Their manipulations on his behalf are so typical of women's role during this period, and so well told in the memoirs, that they are worth recounting in detail.

On the way home from prison, the two women heard the grievous news of the death of Mme Puzela's son and Marie Catherine's half-brother, killed in battle in the republican army after three years of service. Mother and daughter immediately went into a store to buy black material for mourning clothes. There they heard that a representative on mission was in Blois for the express purpose of granting liberty to a few prisoners. Through a complicated chain of events, they went to see a certain Mme Renard, a woman "of equivocal virtue," and a friend of the representative

Jean Guimberteau. Promising to plead their cause, Mme Renard arranged a meeting that very day. When the Puzela women arrived, they were distressed to find Guimberteau with three members of the local revolutionary committee, who knew their case and were already predisposed against them. Yet Marie-Catherine had the presence of mind to write on the petition that her father was "charged with the care of three children, and had just lost a son in the service of the Republic," which was not quite accurate since the dead soldier was from his wife's first marriage. The case was adjourned to the next day. By way of thanks, Mme Puzela had a chicken sent to Mme Renard from Saint-Cyr.

With high hopes, they went the next morning to Guimberteau's lodgings, only to be greeted reproachfully: they had not told him that Puzela's prison term was for the duration of the war because he was such a dangerous enemy of the nation. "You are mistaken," the young girl cried out, defending her father with a boldness she had not suspected in herself. But in spite of her pleas, her father was not released.

Further consultation with Mme Renard indicated that Guimberteau would be unable to do anything for Puzela while the local committee members were present. After three anxious days, the women heard that he was about to leave for Tours. They hurried to Mme Renard, who immediately rushed to Guimberteau, throwing herself at his feet and declaring that she was Puzela's relative as well. She begged him to sign a document stating that "the citizen Puzela is crossed off the list of prisoners and returned to the class of citizens." The Puzela women, waiting on a balcony, heard from a distance Mme Renard's jubilant cry of "Victory! Victory!"

But the local officials still had to issue a written release. The women decided to ask an officer of Mme Renard's acquaintance to accompany them, fearing that if they went alone, the committee would seize Guimberteau's paper and take no further action. The officer agreed that "everything being arbitrary, that could happen to women," but, as Mme Renard remarked, "With a sword and epaulettes, you can impress those people."

Evidently their strategy for combating municipal sexism with masculine military presence was effective, because before long Mlle Puzela was on her donkey, trotting to the prison to announce her father's release. "They cried out, 'Monsieur Puzela is free. His daughter has obtained his freedom!' " Here as elsewhere, Marie-Catherine presents herself as her father's protector and savior. In this saga of filial devotion—a not uncommon literary phenomenon in women's autobiographies from this period—she comes across as a father-identified daughter, whose personality had been molded to his needs and whose thoughts mirrored his prescriptions for female virtue. Her acts and utterances never challenged the patriarchal order.

Release from prison did not put an end to Puzela's conflicts with the authorities. He managed to get himself imprisoned again for using an outdated passport marked with the royal fleur-de-lis, and his daughter was once again required to make several journeys to the commissioners to obtain his freedom. At eighteen years old, Marie-Catherine was the major emotional support of a father considered "a crazy person . . . mixed up with the quarrel of the kings," in the blunt language of her aunt.[19] To make matters worse, he was without employment and his wife's business was practically nonexistent.

At this point, Puzela decided to try to acquire another notary position. This necessitated at least twenty trips to Blois, the father on foot, the daughter once again on her donkey. By October 1794, Puzela had been named the notary of Saint Dye, a small town where many royalists had gathered, especially from Paris and Nantes. Both father and daughter were shocked by the luxury and "epicurean life that one led in Saint Dye," as if to defy all the recent calamities. Very soon, the father's intransigent personality again made life difficult for the Puzelas. He refused to attend the services of the new constitutional priests, and he openly expressed disdain for the lifestyle around him. His daughter often had to shield him from other members of the community, who looked at them "as if they belonged to a different world."

Moreover, in her nineteenth year, she was obliged to become her father's clerk, a job she disliked for several reasons, not the least being her poor handwriting. She was not comfortable in dealing with anyone above the station of a peasant, and would have preferred some form of education in reading, writing, history, and poetry. When she went out, always wearing a cap and unfashionable clothes, it was always under very strict conditions. Still, she recalled: "I would have been almost happy if my father had not always been in conflict with the spirit of the inhabitants of the region."

Finally she became very sick and experienced what we would probably diagnose today as some sort of psychosomatic collapse.

Fortunately her parents were alert enough to bring in an excellent, psychologically perceptive doctor. He told them that her illness had been caused by a "style of life scarcely suitable" for one of her sex, age, and character.

Accepting this verdict out of love for his daughter, Puzela did what he thought best: he decided to marry her off at once. He chose her future husband, Paul Léonard Vallon, a royalist like himself, who had earlier been imprisoned in Paris at Sainte Pélagie and who was still under police surveillance. As victims of the Revolution, the father and future son-in-law were linked by "their misfortunes." These bonds provided sufficient reason for Puzela to transfer his daughter to the care of another man, without even asking for her approval.

As Mme Vallon related this episode to her children many years later, she accepted his judgment without the slightest reservation. "In his mind, there was no necessity to have the assent of his daughter; they arranged everything and presented your father to me as the one who would soon be my husband, before I was even a convalescent. . . . I consented to everything with a feeling of joy. . . . Three weeks later I married your father."

One might say that the transfer of the young woman from father to son-in-law was complete two years later when Puzela died and Vallon took over his post as a notary. The brave young woman who had shown so much courage and even boldness in protecting her father during the Revolution was completely submissive in marriage. She embraced the role of wife, perhaps, though she does not say so, because the role of daughter had been so oppressive. Later she embraced the role of mother with equal enthusiasm. Her total acceptance of the domestic sphere and opposition to any other role for women are explicitly expressed in a final statement addressed to her daughter: "I hope my daughter will never endanger herself by leaving her sphere! And that all her cares are limited to the interior of her house." To this conservative credo, she added the further hope that the existence of her children would give her reason to be "reconciled with the past."

Mme Vallon's story has considerable documentary value both as personal autobiography and as historic memoir. Growing up in her father's orbit and in the larger matrix of revolution tested her mettle almost to the breaking point. Coming from what we might today call a dysfunctional family, she had been obliged to bend to the will of a tyrannical father who would not alter his behavior even though it put his own life in jeopardy and caused his family grave hardship. Marie-Catherine's covert form of protest had been translated into psychological illness, followed, in later life, by wholesale retreat into the domestic sphere. The knowledge that she had survived a "disastrous epoch where all sorts of cruelties had been united" and that, despite her father's peculiarities, she had nonetheless kept faith with him and his values, fed her sense of self-worth and deep conservatism. Revolution was considered "a dreadful word, an execrable word that should be written only in blood."[20] Yet the Revolution had provided her with personal opportunities of which she had taken full advantage—the opportunity to constitute herself as her father's savior, to link her fate intimately with his, and even to have him

solely for herself during her adolescence, when, if we are to believe Freud, a girl may feel
much rivalry with her mother. She took the lead in acting as an intermediary between
her father and the local authorities, following a mode long considered suitable for
women. A female face, especially a young one, had obvious advantages in the process
of softening commissioners, manipulating prison wardens, and enlisting protectors of a
higher social rank. It is also possible that the provincial setting made her task somewhat
easier than it would have been in Paris, since there was none of the anonymity associated
with the capital. Though her father was clearly considered a bad sort, a fanatic, and a
counterrevolutionary, the municipal authorities, familiar with his case, were inclined to
treat him more as a hot-headed lunatic than as a dangerous enemy of the state. Whatever
his "crimes," they were probably going to have to live with him after the war was over. It
also appears that the region around Blois was more moderate in its politics than some of
the other parts of France, such as Lyons, Nîmes, Toulouse, Toulon, and, of course, the
Vendée, where passions flared into bloody confrontation. Although all the departments
were subject to the same national laws, there was enormous variation as to how they were
applied. Much depended on regional political sentiments or merely the idiosyncracies of
the local authorities.

The Lyons uprising of May 1793 provided the key chapter for another autobiography
written by a woman who had been an adolescent during the Revolution. Like Marie-
Catherine Puzela, Alexandrine des Echerolles was the devoted daughter of a father pursued
by the police. A retired military officer, he was originally asked to head the National Guard
of his native Moulins in the Bourbonnais, but his firmness in pursuing law and order, as
well as his noble status, incurred the enmity of the local officials, who put him in prison.
Alexandrine was as resourceful as Marie-Catherine was in gaining entry to her father's cell
and in remaining there. After two months, her father was released due to the intercession
of the president of the tribunal, but he was obliged to leave Moulins, where his presence
was considered "troublesome" to the community. He decided to go to Lyons in the hope
that he and his daughter could lose themselves among its 150,000 inhabitants. What they
found was a city preparing to rise up against the Republic.

As witnessed by a girl who was scarcely fourteen, the Lyonnais were a courageous
people daring to defy the dictatorship of Paris. After they had overthrown the Jacobin
municipality and sent its leader, Joseph Chalier, to the guillotine, the people of Lyons
began to prepare for defense against an imminent siege, which was to last two months.
Men and women of every age contributed their labor, from the digging of trenches to the
building of bastions. "A single heart beat in every breast, a unique sentiment inspired the
men and the women: to resist tyranny. The most delicate women participated in armed
exercises, in the testing of cannons. Nothing seemed to frighten or surprise them."[21]

This idealized version of the revolt, highlighting the enthusiastic participation of
women, recalls their similar role in preparing for the 1790 Festival of the Federation in
Paris. Then it was a communal republican activity, a celebration representing the best
fraternal moment of the Revolution. Here it was a group effort born from disillusionment
and the full knowledge of inevitable bloodshed.

The young Alexandrine shared in the general fervor. Under her father's tutelage, she
followed lessons in military defense with the zeal of an impassioned student preparing

for an exam. "So intense was the interest animating me that the slightest word became engraved in my memory." Through the eyes of an alert, intelligent girl, we experience the bombardment of the city that began in August 1793. We relive her excitement and fears as she spent the night at her window watching the bombs explode. "If death did not fall with them, the bombs offered an agreeable spectacle. . . . It was beautiful and terrible."[22]

She descended into the streets to join the bucket brigades of women putting out fires. When her sixty-six-year-old father was given the post of commander in defense of the city door at Saint-Irénée, she and her aunt took up lodgings nearby. Since the suburb of Saint-Irénée was built on a mountainside more defensible than other sections of Lyons, flocks of citizens sought refuge there, filling the houses from attic to cellar, and even the underground level of the church. As the city was not encircled at that point, peasants from the countryside were able to bring in their produce, providing "a kind of abundance unknown in the center of Lyons." But in time, given the number of people congregating in a small area, food became rare and expensive.

In the face of growing hunger, especially among the poor, the local priest began to solicit donations from the many new residents in his parish. He asked Alexandrine's father if she could accompany him on his rounds. Alexandrine's reaction to her father's consent was typical of women's attitudes when enlisted for some public activity: "I joyfully saw myself called to play an active role in our history, which gave me a great importance in my own eyes." Though she was able to make fun of her sense of self-importance—and that is part of the charm of this particular narrative—Mlle des Echerolles was clearly as eager as any of her female compatriots to participate actively in the great spectacle taking place before her eyes. With resources dwindling, the priest and young girl's efforts produced only enough money to provide for the very poorest and the very sickest parish members.

As the siege continued, many houses were destroyed, food became scarcer and scarcer, and famine was widespread. Many were reduced to "a detestable bread," and slept in rooms filled with mattresses laid out side by side on the floor. When the insurgent troops in retreat began to return to the city, their numbers increased the general want, which was exacerbated, according to Mlle des Echerolles, by traitors signaling to the enemy the location of food warehouses vulnerable to bombs. Soon the enemy was at the city walls, and on September 29, "they attacked from all points. They fought at all the doors. I will not try to paint the noise, the tumult, and the horror of that day."

At the end of the day, Alexandrine's father gave up his post and counseled everyone to flee. "Obeying his will we left Saint-Irénée, too distressed to think about the cannon balls or bullets that were whistling over our heads." They returned to their old lodgings in the center of Lyons with the knowledge that it was the beginning of the end.

General de Précy, the commander of the insurgent troops, decided to lead those who had borne arms out of the city in an effort to spare the lives of the peaceful citizens. Two columns of soldiers slipped out, the first successfully under the protection of a thick fog. The second left after the fog had dissipated, and was detected by the enemy: "It was cut to pieces. There were a great many deaths. . . . Many women, who perhaps contributed to the loss of the column by making it heavy and cumbersome, shared the fate of the husbands they had not wanted to leave." Here as elsewhere in her story, Mlle des Echerolles does not forget the women; unlike many other memoirists of the Revolution, she was acutely sensitive to women's involvement in the struggle, alternately expressing pride in their accomplishments and bemoaning their common misfortune.

Her father, relieved of his post, turned his attention to the fate of his family. First he sought refuge with his daughter and her aunt in a building contiguous to an asylum for orphans and the poor. The sisters running the asylum promised them "poor people's clothes and a place among them in the event of a massacre." Alexandrine was consoled by the goodness of "those pious women" who offered them the hope of escape from annihilation. She was also moved by the sorrowful condition of the wounded patients and the foundling children, the latter all lacking milk since the siege had prevented the wet-nurses from coming to take them to their homes in the country. "A single cow . . . sustained all the rest."

On her return to her apartment, Alexandrine was almost killed by a bomb. Her graphic description of the explosion contains an interesting observation on the wartime mentality of a people under siege: "I heard it whistle, I bent my head; it struck the wall at the spot where I had been leaning; all of that was as rapid as a thought. This kind of peril was renewed at every minute, and ended up by inspiring a kind of insouciance toward danger."

The siege of the city of Lyons lasted from August 14 to October 9. On the morning of October 9, Mlle des Echerolles looked out the window and saw a man pushing a wheelbarrow filled with butter and fowl, indicating that the city had fallen. In an elegiac closure to her chapter on the Lyonnais revolt, she wrote, "Little by little we saw the number of new faces increase, and soon there was no doubt as to the end of that noble struggle. Force had won over justice." She would never forget the sense of community she had known during the siege. Regardless of the personal danger and physical deprivation she had experienced, it was the memory of a city united she most grieved afterward when "every individual found himself alone, detached from that mass of mankind which had been animated by the same spirit only a few days earlier."

> Her physical condition after the siege is best indicated by the following anecdote. Running an errand for her father, she was stopped in the street by a stout man, very red, very gay, very drunk. He took me by the arm and cried out "Good God! what a little arm! how thin you are! I have never seen such a thin arm!" . . . I pulled that little arm in vain, I couldn't get away, he held it firmly. . . . Finally when my fat man lifted his arms to the sky to pity me all the more for having such little ones, I managed to escape.

Such humorous moments are rare in des Echerolles's story, linked as it was to the siege of Lyons and subsequent republican revenge. The Convention decreed that the city would be destroyed, except for the homes of the poor, and that it would henceforth lose the name of Lyons and be called "Ville-Affranchie" (Liberated City). Sixteen hundred houses were quickly demolished and the city fortifications destroyed. Alexandrine observed the destruction of the magnificent eighteenth-century town houses at the Place Bellecourt, dismantled by a human chain "of men, women, and children, who, earning their daily wage very easily, passed a stone, a tile, from hand to hand without hurrying too much, since they wanted to work again the next day."[23] Here the "communal" activities of the citizens of Lyons are viewed less favorably than before.

From October 1793, to the following summer, Lyons underwent a period of devastation and Terror, first under the leadership of the deputy Georges Couthon, and then, when his administration did not prove punitive enough for Paris, at the hands of the even more ferocious deputies, Jean-Marie Collot-d'Herbois and Joseph Fouché. Hundreds of people were sent to the guillotine, and hundreds more shot down en masse in the Plaine des Brotteaux, a field beside the Rhône. In early December, at the time of the inauguration of the Temple of Reason, a petition signed by 10,000 "citizenesses from Ville-Affranchie" begged the authorities to spare further bloodshed. They argued that they had sufficiently expiated their "crimes" in the suffering and executions of the past four months and that further revenge would only incur the negative judgment of posterity.[24] Once again it was the women who pleaded for mercy, and this time collectively, in substantial numbers. But mercy was not the order of the day. In all, 1,905 people were victims of the killings in "VilleAffranchie."[25]

It was impossible for Alexandrine, as for most inhabitants of Lyons, to avoid seeing the executions. Placed permanently in the Place Bellecourt, the guillotine generally received its victims at twelve noon, but however much Alexandrine would delay her passage through the square, she often had the misfortune of finding herself there at the exact moment of an execution. Then, quickening her pace and turning her eyes away, she could still not avoid hearing the cries of "Long live the Republic" striking her ears seven times as seven victims lost their lives.

> Seven heads fell to the acclamation of that mad crowd, which, fortunately for me, was too captivated by this bloody scene to notice my flight and my fear; otherwise, I would have undoubtedly been brought to the foot of the scaffold and been compelled to be its witness, in spite of myself.[26]

During these months, Alexandrine's father was in hiding. In her memoirs, she dramatically evoked his close calls with the commissioners conducting their infamous domiciliary visits, always at night, as well as her own role in negotiating moves to new shelters, a job entrusted to her because her age and small size placed her beyond suspicion. They lived, as she imaged it, with the sword of Damocles hanging over their heads. Ultimately, however, her father escaped to Switzerland, and Alexandrine remained behind in the company of her aunt, a surrogate mother since her own mother's early death.

The story of her aunt's fate dredges up the narrator's most painful memories. Suffice it to say that her aunt was arrested because of her "fanaticism" and reputed "sway over her brother, whom she had encouraged to rebellion." Imprisoned for several months, she was finally taken to the Hôtel de Ville, judged, and condemned. Mlle des Echerolles rushed to the home of the president of the tribunal to plead for her aunt's life. She waited in the courtyard of his building "with a large number of women of all ranks, undoubtedly brought there by the same misfortune." Taking her place among the women whose job it was to plead for their loved ones, she approached anyone with the slightest possibility of staying the executioner's hand. She ran after the commander of the square and barraged him with pleas: " 'She's not guilty. You've taken her for someone else— interrogate her again. Give her back to me. . . . I'm an orphan, she's all I have. What will I become without her?' His only answer was: 'I'll see.'"[27]

Then she ran to the house of one of her aunt's judges. They let her enter while he was being shaved. Although he was reputed to be gentler than his confreres, he too responded, "We'll see." She spent the whole day in the streets, circling around the Hôtel de Ville. Finally she spied the president of the tribunal and handed him the short petition she had written earlier. " 'I'll see' was his only response."

Among the many men she petitioned was a certain Citizen P., who had known her father in happier days. Indeed, because she had seen him at her father's table, Alexandrine thought he would be vulnerable to her tears. He expressed sympathy for her pain, but, "as a public man," said he could do nothing for her.

Despite her relentless efforts to have her aunt reprieved, or at least to be allowed to see her one last time, the only contact came by way of a third party, who transmitted to Alexandrine her aunt's sewing kit and knife on the day of her execution. The distraught young girl remained throughout that "dreadful morning" at the Hôtel de Ville, "prey to an affliction that nothing can describe." She remained fixed by the door out of which her aunt was to exit, crying, frightened, counting the minutes from 11:45 on. At noon the authorities in charge wanted to remove her, and she allowed herself to be taken away. Recalling this bitter moment decades later, Mlle des Echerolles was still asking herself: "Why did I leave? Why did my courage falter? Did she think I had abandoned her?" Survivor guilt would plague her for the rest of her life.

Alexandrine des Echerolles and Marie-Catherine Vallon, born within three years of one another, left behind remarkable eyewitness accounts of the effect of Revolution on young lives in the provinces. Scarcely in their teen years, they were obliged to assume the responsibilities of adults: they strove to protect their elders by pleading and negotiating with the men in power, often placing themselves in humiliating and dangerous positions. One senses, despite obvious efforts at self-dramatization, an authenticity in their accounts that is sometimes questionable in other memoirs. Perhaps their relative youth preserved them from actions of which they would later be ashamed, or simply allowed for the expression of that selfless generosity which is often associated with adolescents when they are motivated by a cause. Cause they had indeed as members of an outcast group. Despite the differences in their rank and social position, their histories contain many psychological resemblances and similar discursive imperatives. Daughters of fathers threatened by the Revolution, they were shaped within a distinct paternal mold and the overarching patriarchal cast of Old Regime society. Theirs was obviously a lost cause, lost to the adherents of a new mentality that would prize fraternity over the rule of the father.[28]

But where are the testimonials of those women representing this new mentality? Where are the memoirs authored by republican women from Lyons or Blois or any of the other provincial cities that harbored groups of women friendly to the Revolution? Where is the story of those who passed stones hand to hand in the demolition of Lyons or cried out "Long live the Nation" at the foot of the guillotine? In 1790, thousands of women throughout France swore the new civic oath on altars erected to the nation. At Orléans, on July 14, a special stand was reserved for "patriotic citizenesses," all dressed in white, decorated with tricolored ribbons and belts, and carrying flowers. The following summer, 600 republican women in Tours and 3,000 to 4,000 in Bordeaux paraded in patriotic processions.[29]

Marie-Victoire Monnardwrote of her near ecstasy during the 1790 Festival of the Federation in her village of Creil in the Oise. "To celebrate the fall of the Bastille," an outdoor meal was organized. Forty guests, including her father, were seated around a table, whose centerpiece was "a kind of château made from pastry in which there were several birds that took flight as soon the first slice was lifted from that edifice symbolizing liberty." The people swore to be faithful "to the nation, to the law, and to the king. A country dance was held after the meal. I found all that superb. My heart was drunk with the joy of seeing that patriotic outburst. I was transported with enthusiasm by those oaths and for the people who made them."[30]

Other evidence of provincial women's positive attitudes to the Revolution come from records of the various Societies of Friends of the Constitution scattered throughout France, from newspaper articles, collections of private letters, and patriotic plays written by women.[31] But as for first-person narratives favorable to the Revolution composed retrospectively by women from the provinces, we must content ourselves with the few patriotic embers that continued to glow in the memories of Mme Monnard, Mme Roland, and Mlle Robespierre as they recalled their youthful fervor in Creil, Lyons, and Arras. Other republican memoirs from the provinces probably died stillborn in the aftermath of Robespierre's downfall or, if they had survived that period, they were probably destroyed during the Restoration when it was not politically correct to express prorevolutionary sentiments.

Failing these testimonials, we face an admittedly one-sided picture of the Revolution painted as a noxious evil emanating from Paris and poisoning provincial life. For the most part, the female narrators of these extant memoirs were not victims themselves, but intermediaries between their family members, whose lives were threatened and sometimes lost, and the local authorities, who pursued them. But in the Vendée region, as described in the next chapter, there were no nonvictims.

Madame de la Rochejaquelein. *By A. Lalouze.* From Mémoires de Mme la Marquise de la Rochejaquelein (*Paris: Bourloton, 1889*)

Renée Bordereau, called Langevin, soldier in the Vendean Wars. *Bibliothèque Nationale*

10

THE WOMEN OF THE VENDÉE

THE VENDÉE IS A VAST, roughly rectangular region in the west of France extending along the Atlantic from the Loire River in the north to the Gironde estuaries in the south, and inland as far as the cities of Angers and Parthenay. Its *bocage* terrain is covered with fields and thickets, scattered hamlets and farmsteads, and more livestock than people. In the eighteenth century, the Vendée was isolated from the rest of France by dint of its undeveloped roads and economic backwardness. From her first trip there in 1790, the Comtesse de La Bouëre remembered an interminable ride in an ox-cart—"the safest way of traveling over very bad and very steep-sided roads." The rural society portrayed in her memoirs was governed by age-old traditions, according to which tenant farmers succeeded their fathers on the same plot of land and ended their days "in the place which had been their cradle."[1] Their wives—the mothers of numerous children—took their meals standing, while the men ate seated on benches around the table. These were the country folk who rose up en masse against the Republic in opposition to the king's execution, the Convention decree authorizing the conscription of 300,000 men, and the expulsion of refractory priests refusing to swear allegiance to the Civil Constitution of the Clergy. Proclaiming their loyalty to monarch and church, Vendean peasants joined with their local nobles in a series of savage counterrevolutionary wars. This violent insurrection lasted from March 1793, when regional peasants first refused to submit to forced military conscription, to May 1795, when the Vendée was obliged to recognize the Republic. In some parts of the Vendée, the fighting lasted until the pacification of July 1796. Pitting the republican "Blues" against the "Whites" of the Royal and Catholic Army, the Vendean Wars constituted the Revolution's longest and bloodiest internal conflict.

For the first months of the revolt, the Vendeans managed to defend themselves against the invading national army. Tens of thousands of peasants, weavers, and country officials formed separate armies under the leadership of a handful of generals: François de Charette, Maurice d'Elbée, Henri de La Rochejaquelein, Louis de Lescure, Charles de Bonchamps, Jacques Cathelineau, and Nicolas Stofflet. Of these, only the last two were not nobles and former officers of the king.

Their surprising victories against the republican troops prompted the national government to take severe repressive measures. On August 1, 1793, the Convention decreed that the Vendée would be destroyed. In the words of the French historian François Furet, "This rhetoric of extermination gave free rein to the soldiers' ferocity and within a few months produced baleful results in the form of deliberate massacres."[2] Henceforth, the republican army not only murdered citizens, raping the women and bayoneting the children to save gun powder, but they also slaughtered livestock, cut down trees, razed villages and towns, sent tens of thousands of people into homeless wandering. It is no wonder that the Vendean Wars inspired numerous chronicles of martyrdom, and that Vendeans are overrepresented among memoirs of the Revolution.

The ten Vendean women whose reminiscences made their way into some form of print were all counterrevolutionaries. Whether they had been raised in two-room huts, ill-heated houses, sumptuous châteaux, or the court of France, they shared an unshakable belief in the righteousness of their cause; and whatever they suffered individually in their unsuccessful defiance of a superior power was seen as part of a collective tragedy. A recent controversial book claims that the national policy of the Republic toward the insurgent Vendeans was nothing less than "genocide" and that women, especially, were targeted for extermination.[3] Certainly these women's stories lend support to the claim that the Vendeans were the victims of revolutionary carnage at its worst, mainly at the hands of republican troops.

Mme de La Bouëre and her husband were luckier than many of the regional aristocrats in that they both survived the insurrection. Other memorialists—Mme de L, Mme de Bonchamps, and Mme de Sapinaud—each a general's wife, saw their husbands killed in battle and their children lost to malnutrition and sickness.[4] Pauline des Chevalleries (later the Baronne de Candé) was forced to flee her home after her father had committed the crime of emigrating in 1793. She, her mother, and sister joined the pack of camp followers that crisscrossed the flat western terrain for almost two years.[5] Another member of the minor provincial nobility—Julienne Goguet de Boishéraud—managed to escape from the notorious Entrepôt prison in Nantes where thousands of prisoners, including her mother, lost their lives.[6] At least ten thousand were summarily executed by firing squad or drowned en masse in barges that were sunk in the Loire by order of the ferocious republican leader, Jean-Baptiste Carrier.

The peasant Renée Bordereau, masquerading as a man, fought fiercely in the royalist army to avenge forty-two members of her family who, according to her story, had been killed by the republicans.[7] In time she became known as the Vendean Joan of Arc.

Françoise Després, a woman of humble origins with an education "beyond her station," served the royal army as messenger, provisioner, and even troop leader. With one eye missing, she was often recognized and imprisoned, and, on more than one occasion, came within a hair's breadth of the guillotine.[8]

Louise Barbier, an innkeeper's daughter, fled her native Cholet with her older sister and younger brother after that large textile town had been burned and its inhabitants expelled.[9] With two brothers conscripted into the republican army and several members of her family massacred by republican troops, hers is a particularly harrowing story of a childhood wracked by civil war.

The Vicomtesse Turpin de would be remembered as a peacemaker. Sent by the republicans in the winter of 1794-95 to offer amnesty to the Vendean chiefs if they would lay down their arms, she arranged the liberation of numerous prisoners in Angers, including many priests and nuns.[10]

These ten women bore witness to their various roles as peacemakers and soldiers, prisoners and camp followers, daughters and mothers, wives and single women, aristocrats and peasants, as each sought to outwit the forces of annihilation. While some wrote copiously with the authority conferred by rank and education, most produced more modest manuscripts intended mainly for family eyes. One—Renée Bordereau—dictated her memoirs because she could not write, and another—Turpin de Crissé—gave her notes and documents to the man who eventually turned them into a book.

Of this group, the memoirs of the Marquise de La Rochejaquelein are the only ones known to a large general public. First published in 1814, they became the touchstone for all other subsequent memorialists of the Vendean Wars, both male and female. When, for example, Mme de La Bouëre's account was finally published in 1890, each of its two justificatory introductions (by the Marquis Costa and a later Comtesse de La Bouëre) begins by linking La Bouëre to her illustrious predecessor in a bid for reflected glory.

Mme de La Rochejaquelein's life did indeed provide epic material. Beginning with the first sentence of her memoirs announcing her birth "at Versailles on the 25th of October 1772," the author proclaimed her relationship to the mighty. The names of major and minor nobility appear and reappear in the early chapters of her work as guarantors of a privileged destiny. Like most members of her class and cohort, she had known nothing in her childhood to suggest that her adulthood would be ravaged by revolution. Ultimately the names of princesses and dukes give way in her story to those of counterrevolutionary military leaders and bloody battle sites.

Mme de La Rochejaquelein had the unique claim of close association to not just one, but to two Vendean generals. Her first husband, Louis de Lescure, was killed early in the wars, and through her later marriage to Louis de La Rochejaquelein, she became posthumously related to her husband's brother, Henri de La Rochejaquelein—the most beloved of the fallen heroes. In the first months of the insurrection, her presence at the side of General de Lescure gave rise to the legend of a superwoman inciting men to battle, nursing the wounded, and escaping with babies under arm from republican troops. The truth, as recounted afterward by the person in question, demanded heroics of a different sort. When her first husband died of battle wounds in November 1793, she was pregnant and in such a debilitated mental and physical state that she almost miscarried. Her description of a doctor's intervention makes medicine, as practiced then, appear as yet another form of torture: "I had been suffering horribly for thirty-six hours; finally the pains were so violent that I started screaming; I was about to have a miscarriage. A doctor was called and said I would have one within a quarter hour, if they didn't bleed me immediately." The doctor himself did not deign to perform such technical operations. He sent a messenger through the streets crying out for the aid of a blood-letter. Presently a military surgeon appeared, a young man almost six feet tall, with four pistols at his belt and a long sword. Responding to Mme de La Rochejaquelein's wild fears, he spoke boldly to assure her of his own sangfroid: "I've killed more than three hundred men in the wars, and just this morning I cut the throat of a gendarme; I'm not afraid of bleeding a woman; give me your arm."[11] The bleeding left her considerably weakened, but she did not miscarry.

In the months that followed, the youthful widow traveled with the army of her new protector, the daring young General Henri de La Rochejaquelein. Sometimes on horseback, sometimes in a carriage, almost always hungry and tired, she experienced the nonstop anxiety of guerilla warfare. She would remember for a lifetime the carnage of dead bodies after one particularly ferocious battle. "My carriage," she wrote, "drove over them. It was night, we felt the bumps, and the wheels crushed the bones of those cadavers. That horrible noise will never leave my head."[12]

Raids, routs, skirmishes, battles, victories, defeats—it is a tale of death on a monumental scale, the women and children surviving " *pêle-mêle* in the meadows," while the men slaughtered each other in combat. Gender distinctions were salient even as armies and camp followers were reduced to the level of beasts. Once, fleeing on horseback from a battle site, the only woman in the middle of a swarm of riders, Mme de La Rochejaquelein was stopped by a fellow Vendean and threatened with his sword: "Chicken-hearted woman, you can't go on." By indicating that she was pregnant, she was able to gain his sympathy and allowed to continue, only to be sworn at by the men in front of her. Her explanation for their hostility attempts to make their sexist behavior understandable as a form of war-induced panic: "In routs, one loses one's head so easily that the soldiers, fleeing for their lives, found it unacceptable for women to do the same."

During another battle, she was taken in by a certain "extremely patriotic and very rich . . . mother of seven children." This kindly republican so impressed Mme de La Rochejaquelein that she begged her to keep her own four-year-old daughter: "I asked her only to . . . raise her as a poor peasant." Her temporary protector, Mme Thore, refused on the grounds that she could not take on an additional permanent charge. Despite the woman's refusal, when Mme de La Rochejaquelein heard the cry of "Raid," she thrust her child into Mme Thore's bed, believing it was impossible to save her daughter herself and that this humanitarian woman "would not be so cruel as to abandon her."

Then fleeing without her daughter, Mme de La Rochejaquelein found herself without the strength to lead her horse through the mobbed streets, and especially through a narrow passage blocked by two other horses. In vain she called out to the fleeing soldiers; no one would stop. Finally she caught the attention of a man with a gentle mien: "Monsieur, take pity on a poor pregnant woman who cannot lead her horse." He took her hand and began to cry alongside her: "I'm a woman myself; we're going to perish together . . . I can't steer my horse any better than you."

Thus buffeted by the winds of war, the Marquise survived one extraordinary adventure after another. Like a picaresque heroine, she assumed various peasant disguises, encountered women dressed as men, abandoned her child in another woman's bed, only to have that child retrieved by her husband's most faithful servant. Were it not embedded in verifiable horror, one would think that her story was largely make-believe. By the end of December 1793, she had once again been obliged to leave her daughter behind, this time because of the child's severe illness. She entrusted her to "honest peasants" who did their best but failed to keep her alive, while the Marquise and her mother crossed into Brittany to hide out. Sympathetic Breton peasants were known to take in all sorts of people—priests, nuns, conscripts, and Vendeans on the run—despite the very real risk of being shot or imprisoned if their hidden charges were found. This was the beginning of a year during which Mme de La Rochejaquelein and her equally highborn mother lived in disguise as Breton peasants, stumbling along in their wooden shoes each morning as they went out to guard the sheep and returning at night to the farm, where they fell into bed with their clothes on. They lived in constant fear of denunciation on the part of zealous republicans, as well as impromptu searches conducted by republican "Blues" on the prowl for outlaws. And throughout the winter Mme de La Rochejaquelein was still pregnant.

Having lost her husband in November and her four-and-a-halfyear-old daughter in January, she gave birth with anxiety to two premature baby girls in April. "What could we do with those children? Counting on only one . . . I hadn't prepared anything to receive them. Everyone looked for rags to cover them as best we could." Within a month the first of the twins was dead. The second survived, far from her mother's eyes, for only sixteen months.

The amnesty of January 1795 allowed Mme de La Rochejaquelein and her mother to travel south to the Bordeaux region, where they had property, and when peace was finally restored, the widowed Marquise went into exile in Spain, where she began to write her memoirs. In 1800, she was permitted by Napoleon to return to France, and in 1802, on her mother's advice, she married Louis de La Rochejaquelein, younger brother of the legendary Henri. "It seemed to me," she asserted with pride, "that by marrying him I would be attaching myself even more to the Vendée, I would be uniting two names which should never be separated." The new Marquise de La Rochejaquelein settled with her husband at family property in the Vendée and gave birth to eight more children. Until her death in 1857 at the age of eighty-five, she was devoted to the care of her progeny and the well-being of those around her. She was, according to all accounts, a tireless protector of the Vendean people, pleading their cause in Paris to those in power and working on their behalf at home. Her funeral eulogy by the Bishop of Poitiers portrayed her busily "preparing with her own hands woolen clothes . . . for the aged, women, and new-born babies." A stained-glass window placed after her death in the chapel of the family château of Clisson depicts her as a venerable old lady surrounded by the local recipients of her charity.

For the greater part of her life, Mme de La Rochejaquelein was a cult figure. The writer George Sand, who had spent her teen years in a convent school with two of the La Rochejaquelein daughters, remembered meeting their mother in Paris when the latter was around fifty and almost blind. Based on her reading of the memoirs, Sand called Mme de La Rochejaquelein the "heroine of a historical novel" and praised her writing for its dramatic, highly moving style. "This book is that of a woman of strong heart and mind. It will remain among the most colorful and most useful documents of the revolutionary epoch."[13]

The life and work of Mme de La Rochejaquelein embody history as conceived and developed within an ultra-aristocratic matrix. Despite her simple manners and egalitarian protestations vis-à-vis her Vendean compatriots, Mme de La Rochejaquelein was—as George Sand reminded us in her own autobiography—inextricably anchored in social hierarchy. The narrative authority of La Rochejaquelein's memoirs derives as much from her class-based self-assurance as from her eyewitness participation in Vendean history. The result is a high-culture phenomenon that compares favorably with the literary productions of her social equals, the Duchesse de Tourzel and the Marquise de La Tour du Pin.

Nothing could be further from the life and work of the Marquise de La Rochejaquelein than the history of Renée Bordereau. The memoirs of this unschooled country woman, published for the first time in 1814 like those of La Rochejaquelein, recount the same Vendean Wars, but instead of 500 pages of highly literate prose, Bordereau's "Military Life in the Vendée" is recorded in a 47-page, poorly printed pamphlet. Her dictated testimonial had been "edited" by the narrator and "given to the Ladies***, who had requested them from her."[14] Thanks to the efforts of these presumably upper-class women, we can today listen to the voice of a semiliterate, eighteenth-century peasant.

Bordereau's brusque and simple language reveals her country origins and long years in the military. As one reads her tales of killing republican soldiers and of carrying wounded comrades on her back, one has to remind oneself that this was indeed a woman. In the original French, sex is inscribed into the language, but in its English translation, without the give-away feminine adjectives and past participles, it is easy to forget Bordereau's gender. For example:

> Arriving near the Loire, I destroyed five of my enemies, and finishing off the day, I broke my sword on the head of the last one. . . . Seeing only one horseman near me, I doubled back to our army. I, alone, killed twenty-one that day. I'm not the one who counted them, but those who followed me; and if they hadn't said so, I wouldn't have spoken about it myself."[15]

As do most memoirs, hers begins with the facts of birth: "I was born in the village of Soulaines, near Angers, in June 1770, of parents who were poor but honest." After this single sentence with its formulaic description of her progenitors, the narrator jumps immediately to the circumstances that determined her career as a soldier.

> The insurrection of the royalists in the Vendée, in 1793, brought to our country armies of republicans who ravaged and massacred without mercy. I saw forty-two of my relatives perish successively; but the murder of my father, committed before my very eyes, filled me with rage and despair. From this moment on, I resolved to sacrifice my body to the King, to offer my soul to God, and I swore to fight until death or victory.

For the most part, the story line follows the daily movements of the army and the personal exploits of its protagonist, all told in a straightforward, virile style. "From Cholet we went to Saint Florent; there we won another victory and took two cannons. . . . Then I found myself at the battle of Thouars on the fifth of May; I abandoned my horse, and for more than two hours fought on foot. It was the abbot Ferré who held it by the reins on those occasions." Twenty years after the events, each battle had become a chapter in the personal mythology of this former warrior.

Among the numerous battles in which she participated, a few obsessed her more than others. At one, she killed four republicans with her hands: "One of them had a child of about six months stuck on his bayonet with two chickens." This horrible image reappears in her narrative, indicating that even though she could kill with her own bare hands, she was haunted by the vision of a child slaughtered like fowl.

She was also clearly sensitive to the situation of women. Pridefully she recalls her exploits as their protector: she saw to it that 1,500 francs were returned to a certain lady after they had been stolen by some of Bordereau's fellow soldiers; she lent her horse and 500 francs to three ladies with a small child; she carried a paralyzed woman in her arms to successive hiding places in the brush. She led a troop to a town, "where the enemy was going to massacre 800 women at 8:00 in the morning; we arrived at 7:30, delivered all of those unfortunate women from destruction, and won a total victory." Recounting this incident, Bordereau gave vent to remembered fury: "I declare that I never fought with such ardor . . . ; the republicans' ferocity had transported me with rage, and I killed two of them at the same time, one with a pistol shot and another with a blow from my sword."

How can we understand this woman who fought like the cruelest of men, without losing her sensitivity toward women and children? Among the scattered examples of women in the military during the eighteenth century, there were few who behaved with so little regard for the conventional attributes of their sex. When Bordereau speaks of her childhood, she never mentions a mother nor any other woman who might have served as a role model, whereas she clearly identified with the men in her family. As she chronicles the wartime, she dons both the costume and the attitudes of the male defender, especially in relation to members of the female sex.

One of her anecdotes suggests a tragicomic aspect of her situation. She was accused of having raped the daughter of a certain brigadier. Brought before the local authorities, she showed her papers and said she had already written to the mayor of the neighboring village to ask him to assure the judge that she was indeed a female. In recounting this incident, she seems somewhat pleased with the idea that another woman might have been attracted to her, though she spells out the impossibility of the charge: "Having the habit of dressing as a man, it might be possible that I pleased that young woman, . . . but I could not have raped her."

Limited to Bordereau's publication, the reader is left with many unsolved questions. Indeed, one might question her entire story were it not for cross-verification from other sources. Two witnesses to her exploits were none other than Mme de La Rochejaquelein and Mme de La Bouère, whose memoirs provide interesting intertextual validation.

In Mme de La Bouère's account, Bordereau appears on the scene when the La Bouère family was hiding in the only building on their property that had not been burned to the ground by republican troops. Mme de La Bouère, her husband, and a group of peasant women had been working on the flax harvest during one of those collective work-days called a grouee in the Vendée. She was occupied with her little girl, while her husband dozed in the corner. All of a sudden the republican "Blues" arrived. All they saw was a group of poor peasants—the count in a spotted old vest, the countess in a faded country dress, both so well disguised that the soldiers did not recognize the aristocrats they were looking for.

While the Blues were searching the house, they heard cries of "Long live the King!" Six armed Vendeans appeared, causing the republican soldiers to take flight. The chief of the detachment was, we are told, "a woman named Renée Bordereau, called Langevin, who, in order to avenge her brothers killed by the Blues, had dressed as a man so as to join the Vendean army. She fought with a courage and audacity that never faltered during the war."[16] Mme de La Bouëre was eventually forced to leave the ruins of her château and to wander with her family from one hiding place to another. She would never forget "the brave lads" who had saved her life and especially their intrepid leader Renée Bordereau.

By contrast, Mme de La Rochejaquelein's account is more explicit in evoking Bordereau's physical traits:

> She was of ordinary height: and very ugly. One day at Cholet, they pointed her out to me: "See that soldier who has sleeves of a color different from his coat. That's a girl who fights like a lion." She was named Renée Bordereau, called l'Angevin, and served in the cavalry. Her unbelievable courage was celebrated throughout the whole army.

In a later supplemental note, La Rochejaquelein added information about Bordereau's postwar fate. Napoleon imprisoned her for a period of six years and she did not gain her liberty until the return of Louis XVIII in 1814. Granted money by the king, she remained in Paris "sometimes as a man, sometimes as a woman; she greatly preferred men's clothes, finding them more convenient."[17]

From the vantage of the twentieth century, Bordereau's preference for male clothing, her adoption of the masculine warrior role, and her possible attraction to other women might suggest a confusion in gender identity or a lesbian identity. But as Marjorie Garber points out in her provocative book on cross-dressing, the concept of sexual orientation as a crucial factor in one's sense of identity is of very recent vintage and probably anachronistiic when applied to someone like Bordereau.[18] We have no accurate picture of her internal experience; her words never suggest that she considered herself sexually deviant because she lived as a man. In her eyes, her acts represented "normal" reactions to an abnormal situation. Frenchmen killing Frenchmen, relatives killing relatives, a father assassinated before the eyes of his daughter—such circumstances were, by their very nature, against nature. Renée Bordereau attributed her decision to become a solder to justified rage, she imputed her courage to the grace of God. She took for granted her unusual strength and her ease in having become an honorary man.

Taking into consideration current theories on atypical gender behavior, and not discounting Bordereau's own understanding of her acts, it is possible to see in her life story a rare example of existential freedom, wrested from society and even biology. The Vendean Wars provided an opportunity, as it were, for her to construct herself as a soldier. Cross-dressing allowed her to blur the distinction between man and woman—to be, at the same time, both man and woman. When the external circumstances of war called for soldierly behavior, something in her rose to meet that call: she seemed to welcome the release from feminine modes for which she felt herself both physically and mentally unsuited. Clearly she was more at home in the guise of a man, though everyone knew she was a woman.

Bordereau's case differs from the few other known women soldiers of the Royal and Catholic Army in that she remained an outcast long after the Vendean Wars had ended, and she continued to wear male clothing until her death. Other female soldiers, such as Mme Bulkeley, Mme Regrenil, Mme du Fief, and the "chevalier" Adam (a woman grocer in peacetime), returned to their feminine lives after the wars.[19]

Another woman soldier, Jeanne Robin, provided a further interesting episode in Mme de La Rochejaquelein's memoirs. Disguised as a man in the troops commanded by La Rochejaquelein's first husband, General Lescure, Jeanne Robin confided her secret to the general's wife because she needed a light-weight regulation jacket, which she did not dare request from the proper authorities for fear that her sex would be discovered. As Mme de La Rochejaquelein recalled, "all the generals, and especially M. de Lescure, had declared several times that they would shave the head of the first woman who followed the army and banish her, disguised or not." Impressed by Jeanne Robin's determination, the narrator promised to keep her secret and to procure the necessary jacket, but she also planned to write to the local vicar to make sure that Robin was "virtuous" and had not followed the army through "dissoluteness." The suspicion of prostitution, or at the least, promiscuity, always hung over the heads of women soldiers. Yet, with the model of Joan of Arc never far from their minds, the general's wife and the church authorities did not vigorously oppose the military campaign of a few women warriors, once convinced of the "purity" of their intentions.

The night before the big battle of Thouars, in September 1793, Jeanne Robin revealed her secret to General Lescure. She begged him to wait till after the battle to send her away, promising: "I shall conduct myself so well that I am sure you will tell me to remain with the army." But she did not live to hear the General's postbattle verdict. A woman's body found among the dead was presumed to be that of Jeanne Robin. Mme de La Rochejaquelein considered it a sacred duty to tell the story of the brave young girl who could not tell it herself.

Despite her eyewitness testimony to both Bordereau's and Robin's exploits, Mme de La Rochejaquelein downplayed women's armed involvement in the Vendean Wars. She stated explicitly that women were seen "rallying, encouraging the soldiers, but not fighting." Contrary to legend, she herself "never had the will nor the courage" to fight. What frequently occurred was that women and children threw stones at republican soldiers, and were taken prisoner and killed. "That," she asserts, "is very different from the rumor spread by the enemy that we marched, like new Amazons, to the war."[20] In her eagerness to reestablish the "feminine" nonviolent nature of her countrywomen, Mme de La Rochejaquelein skirts the fact that some women, most notably in the army of General Charette, did mount horses *en amazone* (astride) or fought on foot with rifles and swords and a variety of makeshift arms. Moreover, they acted as messengers, guards, jailers, and munitions carriers, in addition to playing their traditional roles as nurses and canteen operators.[21]

The carnage experienced in the Vendée remains engraved in the collective memory of the region. Evocations of atrocities committed by the republicans—without reference to counteratrocities committed by marauding bands of Vendeans— are found not only in print but also on local monuments. Numerous churches sprang up in the Vendée during the Restoration, some to replace those razed by republican troops, and still later, in 1894, at the time of the centennial commemoration of the Vendean Wars, many of these regional churches began to commission stained-glass windows depicting the martyrdom of their parishioners.

In the chapel of Saint-Louis-du-Champ-des-Martyrs in the department of Maine-et-Loire, five windows relate the agonizing last moments of the nuns Marie Anne and Odile and the peasants shot with them at Avrillé. At Montilliers, a window commemorates the shooting of several women in the Marchais woods on April 5, 1794. At La Salle-de-Vihiers, another window represents two republican soldiers wounding a little girl and killing her mother. At Chemillé, the stained glass depicts the arrest and death on the scaffold of a regional heroine, Mme de la Sorinière. In the church of Saint-Marsla-Reorthe, one finds the story of two women discovering the body of a little girl, Marie-Anne Chennau. At Ardelay, a window is consecrated to the death of Mme de Hillerin, killed by the swords of two mercenary Hussards.[22]

Whether they confer the place of honor to heroic or humble figures, to aristocrats or to peasants, these windows present the Vendeans as saintly victims, and the republicans as odious assassins. In this graphic fusion of the political and the religious, women's special vulnerability is undeniable. As sexual objects of an invading army, they were sometimes pressured into unwanted marriages—often the alternative to outright rape or execution. They had their share of the physical privations, brutality, and murder endemic to both sexes during war. For many of them, the sight of their children wracked by hunger and sickness was the most unbearable form of torture.

Motherhood forced women to make choices specific to their sex and gender. After the birth of her first child, Mme de La Rochejaquelein chose not to breast-feed: "I gave my daughter to be nursed to a peasant woman . . . I wanted to follow M. de Lescure at any price, be it to prison, if he were put there, be it to the war."[23] Similarly, during the time of her migrant existence, Mme de La Bouëre entrusted the daughter she was still nursing to the care of a young woman who had just lost her own child.

Mme de Bonchamps, already the mother of two small children, remained at the family château when her husband was persuaded by a group of peasants to be their military leader. "I was pregnant," she wrote, "and that prevented me from following my husband."[24] Her narrative of the errant, chaotic life she endured with her children after General Bonchamps's untimely death offers a wrenching picture of a mother's calvary. First she saw her beloved son Herménée succumb to smallpox. Then she struggled against man and nature to keep her two other children alive, only to lose a second child. Later, she hid in the hollow of a tree for three days and three nights, holding in her lap her one surviving child while she herself almost died from smallpox.

General Bonchamps's widow was subsequently captured and imprisoned. At first she believed her captors would do her no harm since her husband was known to have spared the lives of 5,000 republican prisoners after the battle of Saint-Florent. But contrary to her expectations, she was condemned to death. While Mme de Bonchamps was waiting to be sent to the guillotine, history took a curious turn. One of the republicans who had been saved by her husband—a certain M. Haudaudine from Nantes—addressed a petition to the Convention on her behalf, signed by numerous others whose lives had been spared at Saint-Florent, and the Convention chose to grant her pardon.

Yet there were still formalities to be overcome before Mme de Bonchamps was released. The local judges were reluctant to give their famous captive the letters of pardon issued by the tribunal of Nantes. Finally Mme de Bonchamps hit upon a compelling strategy: she sent her little daughter, aged three or four, to her captors to demand the "letters of pardon for Mama"—a phrase she had made her daughter repeat a dozen times. As recounted by Mme de Bonchamps, with assistance from her "editor" Mme de Genlis, the scene is a small comic masterpiece.

> The judges found my daughter extremely sweet, and one of them . . . said to her that he knew she had a voice that charmed all those detained in prison, and that he would give her the letters of pardon on the condition that she sing for them her prettiest song.
>
> My daughter wanted to please the judges . . . and she sang with all her might the following refrain: "Long live the King, Down with the Republic!"
>
> If she had been a few years older, we would have been—both of us—sent to the guillotine. . . . They laughed, made a few patriotic comments about the detestable education these unfortunate children of fanatical royalists receive, and yet accorded the letters of pardon which my daughter carried triumphantly back to me.[25]

Such happy triumphs were rare in women's reminiscences of the Vendean Wars; for the most part, they recorded grim memories of victimization and defeat. Famous battles provided the spine of their narratives: Cholet, Saint-Florent, Thouars were names that echoed in the Vendée like Austerlitz and Waterloo on a national level. And attached to that sequence of regional victories and defeats were the private sorrows that harrowed each narrator—the loss of their husbands, children, mothers, fathers, brothers, and sisters. For women, those losses were often more momentous than the loss of a battle. Theirs is a saga that crosses the lines of the public and the private, the collective and the personal. When one has joined one's fate to a horde of 80,000 civilians protected by 40,000 or so soldiers; when one has followed itinerant troops through the thicketed *bocage* and across the waters of the Loire; when one has hidden out in friendly farms or camped on the edge of battlefields and doubled back to avoid the enemy, only to witness the crushing defeat of one's army and the razing of one's homeland, then one's individual history and military history appear inextricable.

What saved many of them from giving in to despair was their sense of belonging to a heroic community, self-selected on the grounds of loyalty to prerevolutionary religious and political forms. Their support of refractory priests, who went into hiding and continued to perform mass in secret, and their proclaimed commitment to the family of a dead king inspirited their resistance. Most of the memoirists expressed pride in the sense of solidarity that permeated their ranks—a spirit that transcended the traditional boundaries of sex and class. It is certainly ironic that the notion of "fraternity" extolled by the Revolution was so well exemplified by those Vendean men and women, both peasants and aristocrats, who formed a common cause against the Revolution. And it is a sad commentary on human history that such comradeship between the sexes and classes generally finds its fullest expression during wartime, in the face of an enemy.

For the past two hundred years, the Vendean Wars have cast their shadow upon this region of France and contributed to its identity. As François Furet notes, "such longevity in the memory of misfortune" can be attributed both to the great dimensions of the catastrophe and to the great depth of the conflict between religious tradition and secular revolutionary goals.[26] Increasingly, the Vendée has come to represent in the popular imagination the martyrdom of a stalwart people loyal to Old Regime values. And in this cultural legacy, the cries of women have added a distinctive mournful chorus to the communal song of lament.

The ship *Diane* that brought the Marquise de La Tour du Pin to America. *Reproduced from* Recollections of the Revolution and the Empire (*New York: Brentano's, 1920*)

11

EXILE:
LONDON, ST. PETERSBURG,
AND UPSTATE NEW YORK

WHILE MILLIONS OF FRENCH MEN AND WOMEN were suffering the birth pangs of a new nation, numerous citizens fled their homeland for countries as close as Switzerland and Belgium, or as far as Russia and the United States. The first wave of emigration began right after the storming of the Bastille with the ostentatious departure of the Comte d'Artois, Louis XVI's youngest brother, and many other grandees hostile to the prospect of change. A second wave carried off the top military, naval, and judicial officers, and then thousands of priests who refused to swear allegiance to the Civil Constitution. Leaving France was not prohibited during the first two years of the Revolution, but after the king's forced return from Varennes and the formation of an army aimed at delivering him, the national deputies began to enact laws against the émigrés. On October 31, 1791, emigration was defined as a crime subject to the death penalty and the confiscation of one's property. During the next decade, until the amnesty accorded by Bonaparte in 1802, the names of 140,000 émigrés would be placed on official lists declaring them enemies of the nation.

Women's experience with exile had distinctly female parameters: often they were obliged to accompany their émigré husbands or fathers, or they were enjoined to remain behind to look after the family property while their husbands and fathers fled. In each instance, they were catapulted into new responsibilities. Whatever hardships they were obliged to endure—and these were clearly legion—exile also opened unanticipated opportunities for women. The novelty of travel to countries beyond their native land, the necessity of earning a living and developing a greater sense of independence, even the obligation to stay at home and become the head of the household may not have seemed like advantages at the time, yet these circumstances undoubtedly contributed to the deepening of their lives and to the interest sparked by the stories they were able to tell in their later years.

Approximately 25 percent of women's eyewitness accounts of the Revolution focus heavily on the experience of exile: Boigne, Coigny, Dauger, Ducrest, Du Montet, Durey de Noinville, Falaiseau, Franclieu, Genlis (*Précis*), Gontaut, La Boutetière de Saint-Mars, Lage de Volude, La Roque, La Tour du Pin, Médel, Ménerville, Molé Léger, Saulx-Tavannes, and Vigée-Lebrun. Of these, all were aristocrats, except for the painter Elisabeth Vigée-Lebrun and Georgette Ducrest, niece of the writer Mme de Genlis, both of whom were treated as social equals in the upper echelons of émigré society. The word "émigré," Mme de Ménerville reminds us, was almost a title in many circles outside France, whereas in France it carried a criminal stigma.

In several respects, Mme de Ménerville is representative of the many upper-class women who went into exile. We saw her last in chapter 2 at the January 1790 meeting of the Charité Maternelle in the queen's apartments at the Tuileries. Twenty months later, she left Paris with her two daughters Annette and Virginie and two servants, all ensconced in a large Berlin carriage. The decision to leave had been made for her by her mother, her husband, and her doctor: once again pregnant, she was judged too fragile to endure another winter of revolutionary turmoil, especially since a warrant had been issued for her husband's arrest.

Mme de Ménerville and her husband set up housekeeping at Tournay in Belgium, where they began to frequent a society of "very young and very gay" émigrés. From this period she retained happy memories of a communal life marked by simplicity and a sense of fraternity. In February 1792, she gave birth to a much-desired son, namedLouis-Léopold-Gustave for the kings of France, Tuscany, and Sweden. She nursed him successfully and regained her health, but their reversal in fortune, as well as that of the monarchs for whom her son was named, is summed up in a wrenching statement: a year later "the child and the three sovereigns no longer existed."[1]

From this poiont on, the Ménerville family saga goes downhill. With the invasion of the French army warring against the combined forces of Prussia and Austria, they were obliged to leave Belgium and to join the flow of émigrés wandering further north. On the road in their carriage they passed those less fortunate than themselves: "Many of the poorest émigrés went on foot, carrying their little children in their arms. . . . Women, burdened with belongings they could no longer carry, sold them along the way."

In the little city of Bréda near the Hague, they were well received by the Dutch, who cried with them at the news of Louis XVI's execution, wore black with them as a sign of mourning, and repeated "with astonishment and dread 'The King is dead.' " Mme de Ménerville pays a special tribute to the Dutch for their hospitality:

> I have traveled a great deal with children; everywhere they inspire an interest which reflects back on the young mother, making her smile in the midst of tears. . . . It is in Holland above all that this interest in children and old people expresses itself in the most touching manner. That excellent people gave me many proofs [of their kindness].

The life at Bréda was not very expensive and the Ménervilles could easily have tolerated exile there, but with the threat of the French army pushing closer and closer, they moved on again, and at each move "the packages became lighter."

With the many precipitous moves, the increasingly dreadful news from France, and a difficult fourth pregnancy, Mme de Ménerville's health deteriorated so dramatically that she scarcely left her bed. In January 1794, she gave birth to another daughter, Elisa, "who did not seem destined to live a long time" because her mother's milk dried up after six weeks. Yet, jumping ahead fifty years, the author tells us: "This dear child . . . became the consolation of my life."

The news from home could not have been more disheartening Mme de Ménerville's mother, the energetic Mme Fougeret who had founded the Charité Maternelle, wrote that all the family members remaining in France—mother, father, three daughters, an aunt and several cousins—were together in the prison of La Bourbe; shortly thereafter M. Fougeret was guillotined.

Deeply saddened by the news of her father's death, Mme de Ménerville, her husband, and children crossed the channel to London in December 1794. After three years in exile, their resources had been depleted, and she began to work for pay. Unlike most émigré men of their class, many of the women had a number of saleable skills.

> All the women worked and sold their goods in a public depot where they were exhibited. I imitated this example and painted many fans for a merchant in the City who sent them to Portugal. I made tapestries for another who sent them to Russia. I gave French lessons . . . I embroidered dresses, which was the most lucrative.

It is instructive to watch this formerly protected woman, once totally dominated by her elders, husband, and doctor, emerge as the breadwinner of the family. What would have been beneath her in Paris became a source of pride and connection to the other émigrée women grouped in mutually supporting clusters throughout London. In joining the work force, these émigrées were, in fact, paralleling a pattern increasingly familiar to their less privileged sisters at home since, with the disruptions of the Revolution and the wars, women's work took on a greater importance both inside and outside France.

A similar story is told by Mme de La Roque, who started life as a member of a rich and powerful class, and was brought "by misfortune, to that which earns its daily bread by dint of labor." In January 1792, her father and brother joined the royalist army, while she and her mother settled in the German city of Aix-la-Chapelle (Aachen). With the advance of the revolutionary armies, they moved farther and farther north to Bremen, and were less and less welcomed by the German population. From this period, Mme de La Roque remembered a sign written on the doors of a German city stating "No Jews or émigrés allowed to sojourn here."[2]

With the sale of their silver and the family diamonds, they embarked for London, where their itinerant life ceased and their work life began. The father stayed at home and did housework, ostensibly to prevent the children from ruining their aristocratic hands, while the women went out to work. They did embroidery, worked at engraving, and made straw hats, which turned into an astonishing success. At one point, they had as many as fifty women, including a duchess, working for them.

At fifteen, the narrator became engaged to the Baron de La Roque, whom she married four years later in the Protestant church according to the Anglican rites, so that their children would have all the rights of British citizens. As a mother, Mme de La Roque had a fully different life from the ladies of her own mother's generation; she envied them their grace of style and freedom in regard to their offspring, whose care had been entrusted to maids and tutors, whereas she was "the nurse, the maid, the teacher" of her children. Her ten years in exile would be remembered as a period of humiliation and misery, so intensely painful that she declared in one passionate outburst, "I would rather throw my head to the scaffold than to exile.[3]

The future Comtesse de Dauger was only six when her family left France in September 1789. At first, at Aix-la-Chapelle, a lighthearted atmosphere prevailed among the numerous French émigrés. Two years later, the Dauger family moved to the Dutch city of Maastrich, then back to Germany, finally settling, for economic reasons, in Westphalia, a region described as "more savage than civilized."[4]

There the family realized they had to work. "My mother told us that one day, and from then on we courageously began to earn our living by piece work. . . . We made an enormous number of mittens; that's what sold the most easily." She and her sister also invented a form of floral paper cut-outs, which, unfortunately, did not bring in sufficient money to warrant the long hours required for their production. They made straw hats and embroidered silk shawls, leather slippers, and belts. Her sister gave drawing lessons in a school run by German nuns, and she gave lessons in cutting out clothes at her home. Her father rented land for a garden "which he raked himself with his servant."[5] Obviously some aspects of their former aristocratic life did not disappear since they were still served by this faithful retainer, who even risked his life by going back to France for business on their behalf.

Mme de Ménerville, Mme de La Roque, and Mme de Dauger all returned to France after the Revolution. Mme de Ménerville found herself prematurely old, exhausted by her work years, and greatly reduced in fortune. She lived out the rest of her long, embittered life in Versailles, to which many former émigrés had repaired because it was cheaper than living in Paris.

Mme de La Roque set foot on French soil with an "indescribable feeling" of tenderness and fear, for she was still erecting scaffolds in her mind.[6] She was so used to English culture and language that she had difficulty readapting to her native land, an adjustment made all the more painful because she could never reconcile herself to her reduced station in life.

Mme de Dauger's history ended on a happier note. After ten years of exile, she returned to France at the age of sixteen, enchanted by the sounds of the French language and the friendly welcome extended her family. Her father was able to buy back his property at Quesnoy, and "everything seemed to return to life," as in the aftermath of a great storm.[7]

Of the many French women who went into exile—it is estimated that in 1794 there were 25,000 French men and women in London alone—precious few had any professional means of employment.[8] A very small number of actresses, singers, writers, painters, and dressmakers were able to earn a decent living abroad. The writer Mme de Genlis, governess to the children of the Duc d'Orléans, continued to supervise the education of his teenaged daughter in England, Switzerland, and Germany, while her father supported the Revolution in France, voted for the death of his cousin Louis XVI, and eventually was himself guillotined. Mme de Genlis was forced to hide out with her charge in a convent in Bremgarten for a full year, and, being without resources, she supported both of them in her capacity as a prolific author of novels, plays, and pedagogical works. Her greatest professional worry at this time was the absence of a nearby printing house. As she explained in a self-justifying work published right after the Revolution, "it was absolutely necessary, in order to subsist, to move near a printing house. . . . because I did not want to dispatch my manuscripts by post."[9] Eventually she placed Mlle d'Orléans in the care of her aunt, the Princesse de Conti, while she remained in exile on her own or with her niece, until Napoleon allowed her to return in 1800.

The actresses Mme Molé and Louise Fusil both found audiences outside their homeland, the former in Holland, the latter in Belgium, Scotland, and Russia. Wherever Fusil went, she found French women making use of whatever education or accomplishments they possessed, and passing them on to their students. She paints a lovely, if romanticized, tribute to the cultural penetration of French womanhood abroad:

> Welcomed with kindness in foreign countries, they brought with them that flowering of good taste, of urbanity, of politeness, which has always distinguished French women. Forced to have recourse to work or the arts, they turned them into an honorable means of existence for themselves and for their families.[10]

Mme Molé, who emigrated to the Hague with her actor husband, is more explicit on the differences between men and women in exile. "The men," she wrote, "could do nothing for us in that sad situation; but we were quite happy to do something for them. . . . Every woman who has received an education always has some skills . . . each of us undertook with high spirits what she felt she could do." These tasks included making costumes for Dutch theatrical companies, and teaching music, drawing, and embroidery. In the evening, the women gathered around a table lit by a lamp and did needlework together. Mme Molé attributes their fortitude to the affection they bore for their loved ones: "One has so much courage when one works for a cherished husband or any other person whom one loves!"[11] After many initial difficulties, the Molé couple was able to act again, albeit sporadically, once in an extremely successful play written by Mme Molé and performed before the invading French troops.

No one was more successful in plying her trade abroad than the painter Elisabeth Vigée-Lebrun, known before the Revolution for her portraits of Marie-Antoinette and members of the highest nobility. Fleeing Paris with her daughter the night of October 5, 1789, as Versailles was being invaded by 5,000 women, she found herself seated in a stagecoach across from a man who smelled like the plague and kept repeating the names of people destined to be strung up on lanterns, many of whom she knew personally. She remained in exile a full twelve years, from 1789 to 1801, during which time she was in great demand in Italian, Viennese, and Russian aristocratic society. She painted the queen of Naples and her daughter, Czar Alexander and Czarina Elisabeth, the queen of Prussia, and a wide assortment of wealthy lords and ladies.

In her memoirs written forty-five years after her flight from France, she maintained that she was obliged to remake her fortune because her art dealer husband, left behind in

Paris, had gambled away the considerable savings she had previously earned through the efforts of her brush. For the first three years of exile, she worked in Rome, having only to chose among the great personages clamoring for her portraits. In this respect, her fate contrasted markedly with most other émigrés and especially with those who poured out of France at the beginning of the Terror. This is the scene she witnessed in Turin at that time:

> Entering the city, what do I see, Good Lord! Streets, squares filled with men and women of every age, who were fleeing from the cities of France and coming to Turin to seek asylum. They were arriving by the thousands, and this spectacle was heart-breaking. Most of them were not carrying either packages or money or even bread, since they had not had the time to think of anything other than saving their lives. . . . The children were crying from hunger so as to break your heart. Several pregnant women who had never ridden in a cart had not been able to support the bumps and gave birth prematurely. You could not have seen anything more deplorable.[12]

The difference between Vigée-Lebrun's lot as an émigrée and that of her compatriots is striking: they traveled to Italy on foot, in carts, with every conceivable handicap, while she took off for Vienna with a private driver, followed by an attentive Polish count and countess in their own small coach. Her memories of her two and a half years in Vienna feature balls, concerts, dinners, plays, and friendships within the international set.

Despite her total identification with the privileged classes, she was not wholly insensitive to the lot of the less fortunate. She observed the absence of beggars in Vienna and the fact that even peasants were well dressed. At her first theatrical outing, she was surprised to find women in boxes knitting stockings; this strange custom practiced "without their having to look at their work and with prodigious speed" gladdened her heart once she discovered that the stockings were destined for the poor.[13]

Vigée-Lebrun thoroughly approved of Austrian "paternal government" with its forms of conspicuous charity; she remained to the end of her life thoroughly conservative in her politics, reserving her greatest sympathy for the victims of the Revolution.[14] When she saw in the newspaper the names of nine acquaintances who had been guillotined, she stopped reading newspapers altogether. The news of the executions of Louis XVI and of her beloved Marie-Antoinette, conveyed in a letter from her brother, contributed to her decision to push on even farther from her native land.

In April 1795, she left Vienna for Russia. She was not twenty-four hours in St. Petersburg when the French ambassador came to announce her presentation to Empress Catherine the Great on the very next day. Vigée-Lebrun recalled her discomfort at so prompt a meeting with the "autocrat of all the Russias" since she had with her only simple dresses unsuitable for a court presentation. But her clothes appeared to be of little importance to the empress, described in the following manner:

> I was at first astonished to find her so little; I had imagined she would be of prodigious height, as tall as her fame. She was very fat, but she still had a beautiful face, which her white hair, drawn up on top of her head, framed to perfection. Genius seemed to reside in her large, high forehead. Her eyes were both gentle and keen, her nose completely Greek, her skin very alive, and her physiognomy very mobile.[15]

Here the painter's eye, sensitive to the details of face and form, served the writer well. Throughout her memoirs, Vigée-Lebrun made use of the verbal portrait as a valuable adjunct to her narratives. Her vision of Russia focused on the international set which had brought good taste "in one leap" from Paris to St. Petersburg.

Even the actors and actresses were all French, although they did not equal "the great players which Paris then possessed." Her observations of life among the lower classes tend toward generalizations, even clichés. For example, "Russian people are ugly in general; but they have a bearing that is both simple and proud. . . . Russians are clever and intelligent, and they learn all trades with a prodigious facility. . . . The Russian people are generally honest . . . and extremely religious." Never do we hear comments about poor farmers or starving peasants or reproaches concerning the "slaves," the institution of which had long been abolished in other European countries. Her sense of injustice was primarily limited to members of her own privileged class destroyed or dislocated by the Revolution, or to her own family, which included a profligate husband and an ungrateful daughter.

Indeed, it is the story of her daughter's ill-advised marriage that reveals a hidden side of Vigée-Lebrun's nature. She tells it with the anguish of a suffering mother for whom the pain is still excruciating decades later. At seventeen, this beloved daughter fell in love with a man who was, according to her mother, "without talent, without fortune, and without name." Despite her strong objections, Mme Lebrun was finally compelled to write to her former husband in France (they were divorced in 1794) to request his written assent, without which the marriage could not take place. From the moment of her daughter's marriage (which ultimately turned out badly), the narrator writes that all the charm of her life was destroyed. It was this great unhappiness that persuaded her to travel once again as a form of distraction, first to Moscow and then back to France.

She left Russia in 1801 with the greatest regret, returning to Paris by way of Berlin, Dresden, and Frankfort. Despite her tragic memories of the Revolution, she was glad to come home to her family and friends and to the welcome of such notables as the celebrated painter Greuze and Mme Bonaparte. The old life of balls, dinners, theater outings began anew, but she found Parisian life less gay than in the past: the streets seemed narrower after her familiarity with those of St. Petersburg and Berlin, and she was especially disconcerted to see the words "liberty, fraternity, or death" still written on the walls.

She decided to go to England in the spring of 1802, the season when, like the Gypsies, she was most wont to decamp. Although she planned to stay but a few months, she remained there for almost three years. Exile, which had originated in necessity, became a chosen way of life. It provided a form of multiple liberation, at first from potential annihilation and an unsatisfactory marriage, and later from a society that may have been too confining for her independent spirit. Napoleon, known for his misogyny, is reputed to have said during her London period when England and France were intermittently at war, "Madame Le Brun has gone to see *her friends.*"

Vigée-Lebrun's remarkable life story inverted traditional male-female roles in many ways: she was the breadwinner of the family and the parent driven into exile because of her fame, whereas her husband remained behind in obscurity. Throughout her very long life (she died at eighty-seven) she supported herself on a very grand scale. Having discovered her calling early in life, she pursued it with unfailing passion. As she put it, "Painting and living have always been one and the same word for me."

As the most successful self-employed émigrée, Vigée-Lebrun was clearly an exception. It was far more common for the husband to emigrate, while the wife remained at home. Many women became adept at holding onto family possessions even in the face of laws mandating the confiscation of property belonging to their émigré husbands. Mme Journel's memoirs contain an interesting story to that effect about one of her aunts whose husband had emigrated. When his property was confiscated, the aunt took it upon herself to buy it back, though this maneuver obliged her to get a divorce, the institution of which had been legalized for the first time in 1792 and which "did not entail great formality when it was a question of an émigré."[16] Then, when her husband returned after the Revolution, she was afraid to confess that they were no longer husband and wife. It was not until the marriage of one of their children that he discovered the truth, since the marriage contract listed his daughter's dowry as given solely by his "ex-wife."

Some women put their lives at great risk when they chose to return to France for the express purpose of maintaining the family fortune. The Duchesse de Saulx-Tavannes gratefully recalled her mother's sacrifice in returning to Amiens with her two sisters, while she and her husband remained in England. Contrary to the treatment meted out to many of their aristocratic friends, the citizens of Amiens behaved very decently to her mother and sisters. When the duchess was finally able to return from the years in exile that had taken her to Belgium, England, and Russia, she found that "in Amiens, as in Burgundy and the Franche-Comté, the people had tried to soften . . . the laws, and although seals were placed on our possessions, my mother never found herself in extreme poverty." She considered herself "indebted" to her mother for what remained of the family patrimony, preserved "through many perils."[17]

Another woman who saved the family fortune at the risk of her life was Mme de Lameth, wife of a deputy to the Estates General and the mother of the memoirist Mme de Nicolay. Having gone to England with her family in the fall of 1792, Mme de Lameth read in a French newspaper that further punitive decrees had been passed concerning émigrés and their property. Accordingly, "she made the courageous decision to return to France," her daughter Mme de Nicolay recalled. "All of the fortune belonged to her; she thought that if she remained in exile we would be ruined. This return to her country compromised only herself; I was too young to run any risk and my father was to remain in England." Mme de Lameth returned to France with her seven-year-old daughter and was promptly arrested. Thrown into the Prison des Carmes, where many priests and other victims had been massacred in September of that year, she entrusted her daughter to a loyal man from Picardy. He placed her with a chambermaid, "who was going to be a mother in a few months, and, because of that circumstance, was not bothered."[18]

Mlle de Lameth was allowed to see her mother in prison thanks to the jail-keeper, a man easily swayed by a bottle of wine. The young girl was deeply shaken by the somber prison with its walls still stained by the blood of the September massacres. During this period, the most notable inhabitants of the town of Osny in the Pontoise where the Lameths had their chateau came to see Robespierre to ask him to free Mme de Lameth; they thought, wrongly, that Robespierre might be sensitive to the fate of the family that had shared its table so liberally with him during the early Revolution. Mme de Lameth was finally freed without Robespierre's intervention, and she returned to Osny, where her family was later reunited.

Of all the stories of emigration, dislocation, confiscation, loss of fortune, loss of lives, one stands out for the sheer excitement of its narrative and the winning personality of its narrator. It is the story of Mme de La Tour du Pin. By dint of her strength of character, resourcefulness, and high spirits, she became a model figure of the French woman in exile. She appeared as such in the memoirs of Mme d'Abrantès, Mme de Genlis, and Louise Fusil long before she finished her own autobiography, begun in 1820 at the age of fifty and written over the next quarter-century.

Born Henriette-Lucie Dillon into a family of English and Irish forebears on the paternal side and of favored French aristocrats on the maternal side, she succeeded her mother as lady-in-waiting to Marie-Antoinette after heir marriage to M. de Gouvernet, later the Marquis de La Tour du Pin. For two years she went every Sunday morning to Versailles to attend the queen in her bedchamber, prior to the weekly audience for members of the court and mass in the royal chapel. Like many close to the Crown, she regarded the queen and king with affection, without being blind to their weaknesses. The king, she remembered, was "a stout man, about five feet six or seven inches tall, square-shouldered and with the worst imaginable bearing. He looked like some peasant waddling behind his plough, with nothing proud or regal in his appearance. . . . yet in his Court attire he was really magnificent."[19]

As for her own self-portrait, she is equally honest, acknowledging that her reputation for beauty rested entirely on her figure and "forest of ash-blond hair" rather than her face, which "might have been considered ugly. . . . But my height and good figure, my clear and transparent complexion with its dazzling sheen made me stand out in any gathering."[20]

This was the carefree period of her adult life, set in the context of a happy marriage to the man of her choice and the general optimism that reigned at the end of the Enlightenment. The members of her class, she recalled, had never been more pleasure-seeking than during the spring of 1789 before the meeting of the Estates General. "They went toward the precipice, laughing and dancing all the way. . . . The word *Revolution* was never uttered. Anyone bold enough to have pronounced it would have been taken for a madman." Yet within a few cataclysmic months, the entire political order was shaken to the roots, and emigration became instantly "fashionable." Wealthy aristocrats used it as an excuse to escape their creditors, and young people looked on it "as a fortuitous excuse to travel. . . . No one yet suspected the consequences such a decision could have."[21]

Mme de La Tour du Pin came in direct contact with émigré society during the summer of 1791 when she traveled with her aunt, the influential Princesse d'Hénin, to Lausanne, leaving behind her newborn son Humbert in the care of his wet-nurse. Switzerland was already the home of numerous French émigrés—about 16,000 are estimated to have found asylum there, including a large number of priests, artisans, faithful servants, and modest aristocrats.[22] It appears, however, that French manners in their host country left much to be desired. "They all brought the airs and insolence of Parisian society into the midst of Swiss customs, which were then much simpler than they are today. They made fun of everything and were always surprised that there should exist in the world anything besides themselves and their ways."[23] Retrospectively the narrator recognized that she, too, had probably been guilty of the same misconduct.

Back in Paris, she was saddened to see the continued emigration of her many friends, including those she had known through her father-in-law during his short tenure as minister of war. "Nearly all the regiments in the army were in a state of revolt. Most of the officers . . . sent in their resignations and left France. To emigrate became a point of honor."[24] Soon her father-in-law resigned as well and crossed the channel to England.

Through the appointment of her officer husband as minister plenipotentiary to Holland, Mme de La Tour du Pin found herself unexpectedly abroad. At the Hague, in her twenty-second year, she thoroughly enjoyed the series of balls, suppers, and fêtes of every sort. Dressed in the latest French fashions, prepared for the pleasures of the dance, she was soon very much "in fashion," and became intoxicated with her own success.[25] But when Dumouriez was appointed minister of foreign affairs in March 1792, M. de La Tour du Pin was relieved of his post. His wife, temporarily alone in Holland, became more and more alarmed by the news from Paris and the even closer French invasion of Belgium. The flight of émigrés who had taken refuge in Brussels would be remembered as

> the saddest and most lamentable thing imaginable. . . . It is difficult to convey an idea of the tumult that ensued and the panic which overtook all those wretched people in their haste to flee. . . . Every available boat, carriage, and wagon was hired at an exhorbitant price to carry them to Liège or Maastrich. The wisest, and those most liberally endowed with funds, decided to cross over to England.

Though they continued to live abroad for the remainder of 1792, the La Tour du Pin family was not listed among the émigrés. Consequently, they had the option of returning to France without penalty, which is what the narrator and her father-in-law elected to do after the November Convention decrees ordering émigrés to come back within a given period or suffer the confiscation of their property. Henriette-Lucie's fears for her father-in-law's safety were only too well founded, for his life was to end on the scaffold in April 1794.

Mme de La Tour du Pin left the Hague in December 1792 to protect the house she owned in Paris and certain state bonds. Wrapped in several layers of furs, her small Humbert bundled up at her side like an Eskimo, she was determined to endure the difficult carriage journey in winter and all reverses of fortune "with courage and fortitude, unlike the émigrés from Paris" whom she had seen abroad. But, as she reminds us, in those days she was "as delicate, as fine, and as spoiled a lady as it was possible to be." Reverses of fortune were not imaginable beyond the loss of her elegant chambermaid and her footman-hairdresser.

What she found upon crossing the border was considerably more ominous, the Revolution "with all its dangers . . . dark and menacing." Travelers were required to have a passport for journeys inside, as well as outside, France. No one could enter the Paris suburbs without a special pass subject to verification at every National Guard post. Finally, after numerous bureaucratic ordeals, she was reunited with her husband in the suburb of Passy, not far from her father-in-law living in Auteuil. Her own father, Colonel Dillon, had returned from a mission in the Antilles and "was doing all he could to serve the King" during his imprisonment and trial. In time, Colonel Dillon would pay with his head for his service to the Crown.

In her account of the king's final days, Mme de La Tour du Pin highlighted the prevalent hope for a last-minute revolt. She recalled the horrendous morning of his execution when she stood with her husband at the window of their suburban house overlooking Paris:

> We listened for the sound of the muskets which would give us some hope that so great a crime would not be committed without opposition. In a state of shock, we hardly dared say a word to one another. . . . Alas! The deepest silence reigned over the regicide city. At half-past ten, the gates were opened and the life of the city resumed its normal course.

Afterward, they walked toward Paris, trying to keep their faces calm and their thoughts unuttered. The people they encountered scarcely spoke. "It was as if each carried the burden of a part of the crime which had just been committed." For all the countless words that have been written about the king's execution, none speaks more eloquently than the guilty silence described in this passage.

With the king gone and all former aristocrats threatened, M. and Mme de La Tour du Pin decided to leave Paris for the relative safety of the family château of Le Bouilh in the vicinity of Bordeaux. Their good friend, M. de Brouquens, was stationed there as director of food supplies for the army fighting in Spain, and could be of potential service. On April 1, 1793, they set out for the south of France, with "passports covered in visas, which were renewed at almost every relay stop."

The four months they spent at Le Bouihl remained in the narrator's memory as the most precious in her life. Pregnant with her second child, she spent the evenings either making baby clothes or learning history and literature under her husband's tutelage. "Our domestic happiness was purer and more complete than at any other moment of our past life together . . . in spite of all the dangers that surrounded us." Part of Mme de La Tour du Pin's strength was clearly buttressed by her attachment to her husband. Their ability to weather the storms together would be severely tested in the months to come.

During the summer, the château of Le Bouilh was sequestered by the government. Fearing that a garrison would be stationed there at the time of the baby's birth, and eager to be near a good accoucheur, the La Tours du Pin decided to move to a small, isolated house named Canoles put at their disposal by their friend, M. de Brouquens. He came to dine with them every day, bringing news of the turbulent political scene in Bordeaux, whose citizens had risen in partial revolt, only to be put down fiercely by the revolutionary army. The newly arrived representatives, Tallien and Claude Ysabeau, set up a revolutionary tribunal that led to the prompt execution of many suspects. It was in this fearful atmosphere that Henriette-Lucie gave birth to her second child, a daughter born in September and named Séraphine. The mother's anxiety was considerably more intense than the physical pains of labor. An hour after the baby's birth, "her father left us, and nothing allowed us to predict . . . when we would meet again."

It would be six months before they would be reunited, and then under the most dramatic circumstances. Mme de La Tour du Pin and her children kept a low profile, until the house arrest of M. de Brouquens forced her to find new, even less conspicuous lodgings. In the meantime, her husband had found shelter with a local locksmith willing to hide him, for a handsome sum, in a windowless space adjoining his own bedroom.

From her own perspective, the situation looked hopeless: "My husband was in hiding, my father and my father-in-law imprisoned, my house seized and my only friend, M. de Brouquens, under house arrest. At twenty-four years of age, with two young children, what was to become of me?"

Reading the account of Mme de La Tour du Pin's actions during this period, one is tempted to believe the saying that character is destiny. While equally well-born heads were falling all around her, she managed to save her own and those of her immediate family through sheer determination. First she wrote a letter to Mme de Fontenay, a beautiful young woman she had known four years earlier in Paris, who had come to Bordeaux to join Tallien under the assumed name of the Citizeness Theresa Cabarrus. She received Henriette-Lucie effusively and warned her that her only salvation would be in flight. Leave without her children and husband? Impossible! An interview with Tallien, arranged by his mistress, did nothing to advance Mme de La Tour du Pin's cause; indeed she was so offended by his willingness to write off her father and father-in-law as condemned enemies of the nation that she abruptly ended the meeting: "I have not come here, citizen, . . . to hear the death sentence of my relatives . . . I will not importune you further." Though her haughty words might well have turned against her, it was ultimately Tallien, favorably impressed by her boldness, who figured significantly in her successful escape to America.

At her wit's end, unable to sleep at night, lodging near enough to the Place Dauphine to hear the drum-roll that marked each execution, she feared that her milk would dry up and her health deteriorate just when she needed it the most. It was then, at the nadir of her despair, that she made the sudden decision to go to America, after reading in the paper the news of the upcoming departure of the ship Diana, released after a year's embargo.

She went straight to Mme de Fontenay and enlisted her help. She set in motion the plot that would bring her husband out of hiding. She went to find a ship-broker who would reserve passage on the Diana for the four members of her family. The following day she lunched with M. de Brouquens, who had just been released from house arrest. That lunch proved more fortuitous than she could have imagined, for Mme de Fontenay appeared at Canoles on the arm of Tallien, who tried to make amends for his earlier boorish behavior. Explaining that she wished to travel to Boston and then to Martinique for financial reasons, Mme de La Tour du Pin asked him for a passport for herself, her children, and her husband. Two hours after her return to Bordeaux, Tallien's secretary brought her the order directing the municipality of Bordeaux to issue a passport to Citizen Latour, his wife, and their two small children for the purpose of visiting Martinique on board the ship *Diana*.

Henriette-Lucie de La Tour du Pin spent the next three days in a state of nervous anxiety. She had entrusted the life of her husband to a man she scarcely knew, and when he did not arrive at the scheduled time, she spent the night in unspeakable anguish. She did not know that her husband was already sleeping in an unused room at the top of a secret stairway, having been hidden there earlier while she was out of the house. Their meeting the next morning after six months apart was never forgotten: "Life is marked by a few luminous memories that shine like stars on a dark night. The day of our reunion was one of them."

The La Tours du Pin still had other risks to run and obstacles to clear before they were on their way, but at the appointed moment they climbed into a dinghy, waved off by Mme de Fontenay with tears of joy in her eyes. The narrator recalled that event as the happiest moment in her life:

> When the captain seated himself at the tiller and shouted "Off," a feeling of inexpressible happiness
> flowed through me. Seated across from my husband, whose life I was saving, with my two children on
> my knees, nothing seemed impossible to me. Poverty, work, misery, nothing was difficult with him
> beside me.

The *Diana* was a small vessel of only 150 tons with a tall, solitary mast. There was no cargo except for twenty-five cases of goods which Mme de La Tour du Pin, with the help of her servant Zamore, had managed to put aboard. The entire crew consisted of five sailors, a cabin boy, the captain and his mate, both of whom came from Nantucket. In addition to her family, a friend named M. de Chambeau also managed to get passage at the eleventh hour. On such a small ship with so little cargo, the ship rolled furiously and the crossing was very grim. It seems to have been worst for M. de La Tour du Pin, who did not leave his bed for thirty days and took only tea and a few pieces of toasted biscuit soaked in sweet wine. As for his wife:

I cannot conceive how I was able to withstand the fatigue and the hunger. . . . Fortunately the movement of the ship lulled my poor little daughter. She slept nearly all day. But for that very reason, when she felt me beside her at night, she allowed me no peace. . . . For fear of rolling over on her in my sleep and smothering her, I had myself fastened to the bed frame by a piece of cloth stretched across my middle, which prevented me from turning or changing my position. . . . At first, this manner of sleeping was torture, but I soon grew used to it.

Once the proverbial princess and the pea, Henriette-Lucie now grew used to many "tortures" unthinkable in her previous existence. What is perhaps most admirable in her story is this ability to accept her changed circumstances. Deprived of servants for the first time in her life, she cared for her children and her sick husband alone, with little regard for the conventions common to her class. For example, although fashion still decreed excessive quantities of powder and pomade on one's hair, she wore only a little Madras kerchief around her head, and when she found her hair so tangled that she could not keep it in order, she took the scissors and cut it quite short. Her husband, clearly less adaptable than his wife, responded with undisguised anger. The haircut in the middle of the ocean constituted a symbolic break with the past: "I dropped my hair overboard and with it, all the frivolous ideas which my pretty blond curls had given rise to."

Two months after their departure, the *Diana* sailed into the Boston harbor. Her family's transports of joy were beyond measure, as they saw the flowering trees and luxuriant vegetation on each side of the narrow, mirror-smooth creek leading inland. Once on that friendly shore, the La Tours du Pin accepted the captain's invitation to lunch in one of the best inns, an experience remembered as an unsurpassed gustatory pleasure. In Boston they sold off half the cargo—clothing, materials, laces, a piano, porcelain, anything that might fetch money—and accompanied by M. de Chambeau, they traveled to Albany where they had letters of introduction to the affluent Renslaer and Schuyler families.

For Lucy, as she was called in the new land, America breathed the virtues of sincerity, industry, and thrift. Even in very good inns, the luxury of fresh sheets was still uncommon. "To ask for sheets that had not been used by others would have been considered an incomprehensible whim, and when the bed was fairly wide, you would even be asked, without much ado, to share it with a bed-mate."[26] Lucy was intrigued by the construction of log cabins, which were used only for sheltering cattle in Switzerland, but which, in America, represented the first stage of a new settlement. She was enchanted by the great vistas of unspoiled nature, the magnificent forests and seemingly endless grasslands studded with mosses and vivid flowers. Through her eyes, we are able to reconstruct that vanished America which seems even more idyllic to us today than it did to her two hundred years ago.

With the help of General Schuyler and Mr. Renslaer, M. de La Tour du Pin began to look at farms for sale. He eventually purchased one 4 miles from Albany that consisted of 300 acres of crops, woodland, and pasture; a small kitchen garden filled with vegetables; and a fine orchard planted with ten-year-old cider apple trees. But as the owners did not want to move until after winter had set in, the La Tour du Pin family moved into a little wooden house in Troy for the fall. It was here one day at the end of September, when Lucy was out in the yard with a chopper in hand, busily cutting a leg of mutton to be roasted on the spit, that she heard a deep French voice remark behind her back: "Never was a leg of mutton spitted with greater majesty." The owner of the voice was none other than the bishop-diplomat Talleyrand. This incident and the story of his visit with her family made the rounds in France while they were both still in exile; it found its way into the memoirs of Mme d'Abrantès and Mme de Genlis, who invested their meeting with what Mme de La Tour du Pin called "stupid and ridiculously romantic circumstances." Later she would also be visited by the Duc de Liancourt, who wrote a beautiful tribute to her in his multivolume book about his travels in America.[27]

The La Tour du Pin family took up residence on their farm after the snow had fallen and the river had frozen. It was to be an experience unlike any other they would know in their long life together. On the day of their move, Lucy adopted the dress worn by the women on neighboring farms—a blue and black striped woolen skirt, and a little bodice of dark calico. This action won her immediate popularity among her neighbors. She also bought some moccasins from the Indians living in that area, the last survivors of the Mohawk. In time she came to know some of the Onondagas quite well, and even got used to their nakedness.

More significant was her encounter with the slaves purchased to work on the farm, three adult men, a woman, and her child. The first two were a son and father, Minck and Prime, the latter known for his "intelligence, industry and knowledge in agricultural matters." Prime was bought very cheaply because of his age, for it was no longer permitted to sell a slave older than fifty, and he was already forty-eight. The purchase of Judith showed greater humanity on the buyer's part, in that she was bought from a brutal master in order to be reunited with her husband. Along with their three-year-old daughter, this couple was given the unexpected comfort of a room in the granary entirely to themselves.[28]

Having given up any practices that would recall her former station, Lucy lived and worked like all the other farm owners in the area. She recognized that this renunciation of the past earned her far more respect than if she had tried to play the aristocrat. She worked with her servants on all the chores, including the fortnightly laundry divided up equally with Judith—she did her family's clothes, while Judith did those of the slaves. Although she found this laundering very tiring, she enjoyed the ironing, a skill she had learned in the château linen-room of her childhood. Her descriptions of life on the farm evoke not only the ceaseless activity of an energetic woman, but also the pride she took in producing only the best. In this she remained, as Peter Gay has noted, "the great lady she had always been."[29]

She took special pride in her dairy, producing butter twice a week in molds stamped with the family monogram. Arranged in a clean basket on a fine cloth, her neat pats of butter were much in demand by the local inhabitants, unused to such European refinements. She and her husband were also successful in producing and selling a fine apple cider, which fetched more than twice the customary price; the portion they kept for themselves was respectfully treated as if it had been the finest white wine produced at the château of Le Bouilh.

One anecdote that reveals the difference between Mme de La Tour du Pin's character and those of more conventional French émigrés concerns the visit of M. de Novion, a former officer in her husband's regiment. As he, too, was interested in buying a farm in the region, they set out on horseback to see the surrounding countryside. At one point, Lucy saw one of her Indian friends sitting in the undergrowth along the road, and she called to him to cut her a stick, since she had forgotten her whip. The story is too good to be told secondhand:

> Nothing could describe the surprise, the near horror, of M. de Novion when he saw a tall man emerging from the bushes and coming toward us with his hand held out to me: his entire clothing consisted of a strip of blue cloth between his legs. . . . His astonishment increased when he saw the familiarity that existed between the Indian and me and the calm way in which we engaged in a conversation of which he did not understand a single word. . . . I am certain that M. de Novion resolved, deep in his heart, never to live in a country where one was exposed to such encounters.[30]

The narrator's openness to people in cultures vastly different from her own, her curiosity and sociability, stood her in good stead in her adopted land. Her contacts extended from the stark Shaker community several miles away to the plush Renslaer family in Albany. Despite recurrent bouts of fever and a workload that would be considered weighty by any standard, she spent her second year on the farm very happy in her new life.

But then she was struck with an irreversible misfortune, "the cruelest and most terrible blow that any person could endure."[31] Her daughter Séraphine came down with a severe stomach illness and died within hours. They buried her in a small cemetery intended for the people on the farm. Mme de La Tour du Pin, who was to outlive all her children but one, considered this a major turning point in her life. She felt as if a voice cried out to her to interrogate her whole existence. Kneeling on her child's grave, she implored God to give her a little comfort in her distress. From that point on, she was able to turn to God for solace in her many trials and griefs.

Toward the end of the winter of 1795-96, a letter arrived from France announcing that Le Bouilh had been released from sequestration, but that the seals could not be removed in the owner's absence. If M. de La Tour du Pin did not return, the château would be offered for sale as national property. The Revolution, as such, was over, and France, under the rule of the Directory, was pursuing a policy of greater leniency toward former aristocrats, especially those like the La Tours du Pin who had left the country with a passport and had never been on the official list of émigrés.

Lucy and her husband responded differently to the letters urging their return. He was eager to go back, fired by ambition and hopes for a better life, in short, as she put it, "all the sentiments which animate the life of men." Her reaction reveals another mentality shaped by personal, political, and probably gender considerations. "France had left me only memories of horror. It was there I had lost my youth, crushed by countless, unforgettable terrors. Only two sentiments had remained alive in me . . . : love of my husband and love of my children." Despite her reluctance to return, she submitted to her husband's desire, with only one condition for their departure—that she be allowed to free their slaves. This, too is a story best told in her own words.

> I said to them with emotion: "My friends, we are going to return to Europe. What should we do with you?" The poor things were overwhelmed. Judith sank into a chair, sobbing; the three men hid their faces in their hands . . . I went on: "We have been so pleased with you that it is only fair for you to be rewarded. My husband has charged me to tell you that he gives you your freedom." Hearing this word, our good servants were so amazed that for a few seconds they could not speak. Then, falling on their knees at my feet, all four of them cried out: "Is it possible? Do you mean that we are free?" I replied: "Yes, upon my honor. From this moment you are as free as I am myself."

In the privacy of her home, she alone granted freedom to the five slaves, whose new status then had to be recognized legally. The traditional Western division between the private domain reserved for women and the public domain reserved for men has never been more obvious than in these two sequential acts of emancipation. The following day, her husband took the slaves before the justice in Albany for the ceremony of manumission. They were told to kneel in front of their master, "who laid his hand on the head of each as a sign of liberation, exactly as in ancient Rome." The narrator's observation that "All the Blacks of the town were there" gives us some small idea of the hopes aroused in the hearts of the Black community by this uncommon spectacle. One could say that the best ideals of the French Revolution, initially inspired by the earlier American War of Independence, had come home to roost.

On May 6, 1796, the La Tour du Pin family set sail for Europe. True to her new industriousness, Lucy established herself as wardrobe-mistress to the sailors on board: she made shirts, marked linens, hemmed cravats. With forty days of crossing, she had enough time to put the crew's entire wardrobe in order.

They returned to France via Spain, taking in the sights at Cadiz, Cordoba, and Madrid. Finally, they crossed the border into France after some anxious moments when the National Guard questioned M. de La Tour du Pin about the cause of his absence and his plans for the future. Their first experiences at Le Bouilh were also cause for consternation, as they had left the house well furnished and found it quite empty. "Not a single chair to sit on, not a table, nor a bed." But the next day, many of the village people, ashamed of having bought their furniture at auction, came to suggest that they buy the pieces back at reasonable prices, which enabled them to refurnish their house.

Her old maid Marguerite returned in time to help her with the delivery of her new daughter Charlotte, born on November 4, 1796. They lived comfortably enough at Le Bouilh until the following summer when it was necessary to go to Paris for business reasons. There they found that many émigrés had come back under borrowed names, even her aunt, the Princesse d'Hénin, who had taken that of a milliner. On the other hand, Mme de Staël had returned in open glory and was actively involved in politics under the protection of Paul Barras, one of the most influential of the five Directors. With their support, Talleyrand had been made minister of foreign affairs.

For a short period, Mme de La Tour du Pin enjoyed Parisian society once again. She went immediately to thank her benefactress Mme de Fontenay, now married to Tallien and the mother of their child. She saw Mme de Staël nearly every day, for she was working for a policy of compromise with the royalists, who were beginning to speak openly of their plans and hopes with what Mme de La Tour du Pin considered an extreme lack of prudence. This royalist resurgence was partly responsible for the day known as 18 Fructidor (September 4, 1797)—a coup d'état that had severe consequences for all the émigrés.

As she sat nursing her daughter, Henriette-Lucie heard the noise of troops assembling on the boulevard, and deemed it prudent to call on Mme de Staël for information. There she found Benjamin Constant, Mme de Staël's lover and an influential political writer. He informed her that the Directory had just voted a decree ordering all returned émigrés to leave Paris within twenty-four hours and France within a week. She rushed home to tell her husband. Two courses were open to them: they could ask for a passport to Spain and travel by way of Le Bouilh, or they could go to England. They opted for the latter, since Mme d'Hénin was also returning there and since Henriette-Lucie could hope for help from some of her numerous Dillon relatives. Within days, they had crossed the channel and embarked upon another long period of exile. Indeed, the La Tours du Pin would not return to their native land until the coup d'état of 18 Brumaire (9/10 November, 1799) which brought Napoleon to power. Even then, they would not become permanent residents of France, for M. de La Tour du Pin eventually entered the Foreign Service, which obliged them to spend many years in Italy under both pleasant and trying circumstances. Throughout a marriage that lasted half a century, Mme de La Tour du Pin demonstrated those qualities of loyalty and courage that were recognized by her husband in a loving tribute written shortly before his death: "It is quite impossible to conceive of any sacrifice too great for the devotion of which she is capable."[32]

But it was another man, the Duc de Liancourt, her visitor in America, who understood Mme de La Tour du Pin's special place within the larger panorama of stalwart French women abroad.

It was they who showed, in that cruel revolution, the greatest firmness, the greatest attachment to their
duty, the greatest constancy in their feelings. It is they who propped up the courage of many men. . . .
Madame de Gouvernet [de La Tour du Pin] is at the head of this group; it was because of her that her
husband was saved, that he exited from France, that he was able to preserve a little money. To her are
due the happy days, the gaity, the pleasure with which he endured a life little made, I believe, for his
tastes and habits.[33]

As was the case for many émigrée women, exile tested Mme de La Tour du Pin's
mettle and proved her more resilient than could have been expected from her overly
privileged upbringing. She was part of that corps of women compelled to leave their
homeland, who ultimately did honor to it by projecting a high-quality image of the French
character and its products. Mme de La Tour du Pin's elegant pats of butter and superior
cider, Mme de Ménerville's petit point and painted fans, Mme de La Roque's engravings
and embroidery, Mme de Dauger's mittens and straw hats, not to mention Mme Vigée-
Lebrun's masterpieces of portraiture, paralleled the spread of French revolutionary ideas
throughout the Western world and won for France widespread admirers of its wares. The
dissemination of numerous French products on the world market dates back to the French
Revolution, and to the émigrée women who produced them.

Conversely, in returning to France, they often brought with them new ideas, other
languages, tales of foreign lands, and a spirit of female independence that was out of
keeping with the tenor of the times. Indeed, under the notoriously misogynist emperor
who reigned for the first fourteen years of the nineteenth century, some of the most
independent spirits were constrained to further exile, for example, Germaine de Staël by
his explicit order and Elisabeth Vigée-Lebrun by her own choice. More often, the women
adapted to the limitations of their social roles and reduced fortunes, satisfied to be once
more safely at home.

Among the many political realities generated and popularized by the Revolution,
massive emigration must be counted as one of them. Since then, violent revolutionary
conflict has almost always produced hordes of victims on the run, seeking havens far
from the land of their birth. Vigée-Lebrun's description of the stream of French men and
women pouring into Turin, La Tour du Pin's memory of the frantic escape of the French
émigrés from Brussels—these scenes are all too easy for us to envision today, given our
unwelcome familiarity with the photos and films of refugee convoys during World War II
and the more recent media images of civil wars in Asia, Africa, Eastern Europe, and the
Middle East. French history of two hundred years ago is sadly close to our own. A chilling
reminder of that similarity is found in the signs posted in some German cities classing
Jews and émigrés as undesirables, according to reports by both Mme de La Roque and the
Duchesse d'Escars.

The French emigration, it can be argued, was largely a class phenomenon brought
about by an excess of wealth on the part of those arbitrarily born to privilege. Moreover,
as Mme de Staël reminds us, the Revolution might have been quite different if numerous
members of the highest nobility had not gone into exile as early as the summer and fall of
1789. Yet for most of those who experienced it, exile was not a matter of choice, especially
for the women. They were clearly victims of political decisions in which they had no say,

although they were sometimes propelled into personal decision-making roles that would have been unthinkable in their former lives. The Duchesse d'Escars remembered that when she and her two children were ordered to leave the city of Mayence by the German Elector who had at first welcomed the émigrés, "it was a great event for me. For the first time in my life, I had to make a serious decision on my own."[34] In many instances, their new independence and determined efforts to provide for themselves and for their families made it possible for them to survive in unfamiliar and even hostile settings, though not so hostile as their homeland. Their ambivalent feelings when they reentered France is captured in the words of Elisabeth Vigée-Lebrun:

> I shall not try to paint what I felt inside when I set foot on French soil from which I had been absent for twelve years. . . . I mourned the friends I had lost on the scaffold; but I was going to see those who still remained. This France, to which I was returning, had been the scene of atrocious crimes; but this France was my native land.[35]

A personification of Republican France. Reproduced from Ernest E Henderson, Symbol and Satire in the French Revolution (New York: Knickerbocker Press, 1912)

12

REFLECTIONS, PERSONAL
AND POLITICAL

Ceux qui n'ont pas vécu alors ne peuvent décider de ces temps de tourmente.
("Those who were not living then cannot judge those tormented times.")
—Alexandrine des Echerolles, 1843

THE WOMEN IN THIS BOOK have been my companions for a very long time. I have grown accustomed to their presence in the corners of my mind where they continuously appeal for my attention, and I have come to see myself as a medium for their resurrection. Of course, it is commonplace for biographical writers to become involved with their subjects. To begin with, we have elective affinities with the people we choose to write about—affinities that usually become strengthened in the course of our work. Belle Gale Chevigny, following Jacques Lacan, calls this sense of identification a "mirroring self" and suggest that it is especially prevalent when women write about other women.[1]

But why, I ask myself, have I chosen to identify with French women who lived two centuries ago, and were predominately elitists? The simplest and truest answer lies in their strength as givers of testimony. I was drawn into their lives by the stories they left behind, eloquent and moving accounts of survival on the cusp of catastrophe.

Almost all the women memoirists echoed Mme Vallon's assessment of the Revolution as "an execrable word that should be written only in blood."[2] Despite their immense differences in social status and political position, they had all been immersed in the same bloodbath, had all become kin to one another through the ceremony of violence that had slain their nearest and dearest. For them, violence and bloodshed were the Revolution's defining features. They would have been outraged by the argument of more distant observers, such as the contemporary French historian Dominique Godineau, that the

Revolution should not be measured by "the number of heads cut off and drops of blood spilled."[3] To dismiss the life toll as a mere consequence of what historian Lynn Hunt has called "the still unfulfilled promise of a leap into the future" would have been considered a sacrilege.[4] Instead, unlike neutral observers, they force us to see the Revolution as an expression of not only the best, but also the worst, in human nature.

They ask us to remember those who were slaughtered simply because they had been born into the nobility or had grown up in the Vendée or had chosen the priesthood. This sense of injustice was forcefully expressed by Mme de La Villirouët in a letter she wrote protesting her detention in a Breton prison: "One should not regard as a crime my status of 'ex-noble': one does not preside at one's birth."[5] When I read that sentence for the first time, my mind jumped ahead 150 years to the European Jews doomed to destruction in Nazi Germany because of their birth as Jews, or because of their grandparents' birth as Jews. It may seem strange to think of French aristocrats and European Jews in the same context, given their disparate starting points on the social and political spectrum; yet from the perspective of the survivor their stories have this in common—each had experienced unimaginable suffering under the auspices of a government which had designated their kind as undesirables. Of course, to twentieth-century observers familiar with the machine gun and the gas chambers, the guillotine appears antiquated and relatively benign: one could still die as an individual with a modicum of dignity. After the unparalleled horrors of the Holocaust, it takes a leap of the imagination to enter into the full phenomenological terror experienced by the women of 1789.

In both political moments, the concept of the "other" as scapegoat was used to effect devastation. Consider this scene from a play written by the Citizeness Villiers, which was produced in Dijon in March 1794, under the title "The Republican Mother." The concept of the republican mother responsible for instilling civic virtues in her children was one of the most cherished ideals of both the French and the American Revolutions. Here the mother teaches her children the difference between themselves and the "aristocrats." "Aristocrat," she says, "means an enemy of the revolution; it is a person who hates it, who wants to injure it." To her children's reminder that she had taught them to love their fellow creatures, she responds:

> Aristocrats are not our fellow creatures ["semblables"]. Those cowards for whom liberty has no appeal, who delight in their baseness and degradation; those tigers who have no fear of tearing the breast of their country to pieces in order to defend odious prerogatives; those traitors, who put on the mask of patriotism in order to deceive us all the better, to betray us all the more. No, thank heaven, all those vile beings, the shame and scourge of humanity, are not our fellow creatures, and we owe them only scorn, hatred and harshness.[6]

With such instruction the children promise to hate aristocrats with all their heart.

It should be remembered that the word "aristocrat" had extended beyond its original class meaning to encompass all who did not support the Revolution with sufficient fervor. One had the duty to despise and punish them, to think of them as different from oneself. The French word "semblable," translated as "fellow creature," literally means "alike"— the one who is like you. Once a particular group of people has been designated by a vengeful government as "not like," as "them out there," as culpable outcasts—be it French aristocrats, Vendeans, Jews, Gypsies, Armenians, Kurds, Muslims, or Hindus—the results can be barbaric. Categorizing others as fundamentally different, as beyond the pale of a common humanity, makes it possible for even well-meaning people to perpetrate inhuman acts.

The survivors of the French Revolution, like the survivors of World War II and other contemporary victims of mass destruction, wrote with an urgent need to inscribe the cruelties and injustices they had witnessed. So indelible was the stain of bloodshed, so deep the wounds they bore, that their memoirs often read like religious testimonials. The gravest sin would have been to forget.

For these women, their personal trials and sorrows represented the deepest reality of the Revolution. While the men of 1789 were concerned with their public images and tended to suppress private emotions in their memoirs, the women had no such compunctions. They did not consider their private lives "irrelevant to the founding of a new nation," as Lynn Hunt has written in her appraisal of men's memoirs.[7] Why should they? Had they not been idealized as republican *mothers*? Raising children for the fatherland (la patrie) and educating sons for their roles as future citizens were considered the rightful activities of patriotic women. This said, many of them may have perceived the term "republican mother" as an oxymoron, given the different loyalties such a combination of words implied. Loyalty to their children and other family members sometimes conflicted with loyalty to the state, as in the case of women whose sons, husbands, fathers, and brothers had emigrated or deserted.

Only three of the women memoirists fully accepted both parts of the expression "republican mother": Mme Roland, Mme Cavaignac, and especially Mme Le Bas. The last took to heart her husband's final words—that she should inspire within their son the patriotic sentiments for which his father had died. Most of the other memoirists considered the Revolution a malevolent intruder in their private lives, come to rupture the fabric of personal relationships which they prized above all else.

Indeed, their memoirs were often written alongside or through the stories of their family members and close friends. Perhaps this suggests, as certain scholars have maintained, that women's sense of self is intimately meshed within relationships, and that their texts, like their lives, reflect more permeable identity boundaries than those found in men.[8] Or perhaps, the literary use of intermediaries was merely a subterfuge employed by French women at a time when society mandated feminine self-effacement.[9] More likely, they wrote about their families—husbands, children, fathers, mothers, brothers, and sisters—because this was what they knew best and cared about most passionately. Rarely did women set aside their private concerns to ponder the collective course of the nation. Only Mme de Staël, and, to a lesser extent, Mme Roland and Mme de Tourzel, had the broader, more abstract view commonly associated with men's approach to public life, perhaps because all three were situated near the seat of power.

Yet, as we have seen, most of the memoirists found ways to confront the public face of the Revolution, to raise their disenfranchised voices, to negotiate a system designed to repress them. I think of Théroigne de Méricourt marching in Amazon trousers in republican demonstrations, of Renée Bordereau fighting in an army that forbade the service of women, of Mme Roland writing her husband's circulars, of Mme de La Villirouët orchestrating the release of sixty-six coprisoners. I think of Mlle Puzela slipping through bureaucratic loopholes to remain in prison with her father, of Mme Le Bas persuading Robespierre to bring home her soldier husband, of Mme de Staël deterring the police from discovering her lover, of Mme de La Tour du Pin extracting a passport from Tallien, and of all those women who held onto the family property while their husbands were in exile.

If the Revolution brought with it the increasing intrusion of government into private life, the women did not accept that intrusion passively. They fought back with courage and cunning to defend what they judged to be their territory—the private terrain where life begins and cries out for nourishment. In their annals, the protection of life was the primary motivation behind their behavior. When they had to admit that some women had been life-destroyers, these were seen as exceptions, "unnatural" women, traitors to their sex. They portrayed themselves as heroines in an epic of survival: they succor their offspring; protect their husbands, brothers, and sisters; and shield their fathers with their own bodies. The image of women intervening between men in order to "mitigate the effects of masculine conflict" eventually became an iconographic trope.[10] Revolutionary paintings and engravings represented women in the act of deterring bloodshed, as in David's famous classical painting *The Intervention of the Sabine Women* in the Louvre, and the popular engravings of Mlle de Sombreuil defending her father in prison.

When, in its early years, the Revolution promoted the humanitarian ideals of a broad social agenda, many of the memoirists were its friends. The republicans Mme Roland, Mme de Staël, Mme Le Bas, Mlle Robespierre, Mme Cavaignac, Théroigne de Méricourt, the young Mme Juillerat-Chasseur, and Marie-Victoire Monnard counted themselves among the partisans of the Revolution from 1789 to 1792. But as the Revolution took on more menacing tones, as it began to feed on the lives of both royalists and republicans, almost all the women memoirists turned against it. Their written memories add suffering faces to the canvas of lofty thinkers and fiery orators who dominate traditional historiography of the Revolution. They give flesh and blood to the people—not the "people" construed by Robespierre and Danton as a sovereign community, nor "man" with his rights and responsibilities, nor even the tricolored mobs that destroyed the Bastille and brought the king and queen to Paris from Versailles, but individual people, female and male, old and young, Parisians and provincials, aristocrats and peasants, with their personal grievances and hopes. Most of them mourned the loss of friends and relatives and the disappearance of an entire way of life; they hoped their children and grandchildren would be spared the political turmoil they had known. Both Mme Roland and Mme Vallon—women of totally different political persuasions—expressed the hope that their daughters would be able to devote themselves exclusively to the peaceful joys of private life. If, like Mme Vallon and Mme de La Tour du Pin, they turned inward with renewed commitment to their families after the trials of revolution, it was partially because they had learned to view the public arena occupied by men with deep distrust.

Moreover, they had witnessed the silencing of the few women activists, such as Olympe de Gouges and Mme Roland, who had stuck their necks out and then literally lost their heads. Official government policy after the execution of Marie-Antoinette was to squelch any expression of women's political voice, as if female power should finally have been laid to rest with the queen's remains. Even the republican women's clubs were closed as part of the backlash against the feminine principle, deemed thoroughly incompatible with the masculine ideals of robust energy and stoic courage. While some female groups still participated in periodic food riots and others agitated for the restoration of their churches, most women evinced no desire to penetrate the collective public space reserved exclusively for men. In the society that emerged from the Revolution, women were enjoined, like Rosie the Riveter after World War II, to return to domesticity.

Yet, belatedly, a few of these women found a way to speak out from their domestic habitat, to rewrite history according to their autobiographical scripts. "We were there, too!" they insisted. "And our story is not the same as your story." Devoid of political rights, they claimed the right to remember and to transmit their memories, however personal, to their descendants. Though they have never been fully appreciated for their historical, literary, and moral worth, their memoirs still constitute a valuable verbal legacy. Now, as then, we need to be reminded that innocent people are often the victims of political causes—even such intrinsically good ones as the French Revolution—and we need to ask, over and over, how such victimization can be held in check. We who have a political voice unknown to the women of 1789 would do well to keep them in mind as we make our way through a world that has not yet learned to prevent, much less minimize, the human costs of radical social change.

NOTES

CHAPTER 1
INTRODUCTION: MEMORY AND MEMOIRS

1. Alfred Fierro lists 1,502 entries in his *Bibliographie critique des mémoires sur la Révolution écrits ou traduits en français* (Paris: Service des Travaux historiques de la Ville de Paris, 1989), of which 138 are women, but a careful study of his list indicates that many of these are not memoirs in the more limited English sense of the word: a first-person retrospective account of one's life and the historical events one has witnessed. I have eliminated from my study those works listed by Fierro that are (1) "false memoirs" written by someone other than the subject, (2) biographies unless they are based largely on the subject's own words, and (3) works in which the Revolution is virtually nonexistent, but I have retained the few collections of diaries and letters that contain authentic eyewitness accounts of the Revolution. Odile Krakovitch's summary of Fierro's 138 women's "memoirs" lists these works according to dates of publication, political opinions, historical value, provincial regions and foreign countries, and women born from the popular classes. 0. Krakovitch, "Analyse critique des mémoires sur la révolution écrits par les femmes," *Les Femmes et la Révolution française: L'Effet 89*, 3 vols. (Toulouse: Presses Universitaires du Mirail, 1991), 3:123-29. All translations are my own.
2. Mme de Fausselandry, *Mémoires de Mme la vicomtesse de Fars Fausselandry, ou Souvenirs d'une octogénaire*, 3 vols. (Paris: Ledoyen, 1830), 1:343.
3. Although a select few of these works found their way into print in the immediate aftermath of the Revolution (for example, the memoirs of Mme Roland and an early memoir of Mme de Genlis), the first big wave of publication occurred between 1815 and 1865, when many of the authors were still alive or recently dead, and the second wave between 1865 and 1914, when the centennial of the Revolution produced a renewed interest in such manuscripts. A much smaller number has trickled into publication since 1914. See Fierro, *Bibliographie*, p. 10, and Krakovitch, "Analyse critique," 3:127-29.
4. Jean-Paul Bertaud, *La Vie en France au temps de la Révolution (1789-1795)* (Paris: Hachette, 1983), p. 220; and Elisabeth Badinter, *Emilie, Emilie ou l'ambition féminine au XV IIIe siècle* (Paris: Flammarion, 1983), p. 14.
5. These words come from the English title of Françoise Basch's insightful *Femmes victoriennes*, translated by Anthony Rudolf as *Relative Creatures: Victorian Women in Society and the Novel* (New York: Schocken Books, 1974).
6. For a discussion of this issue, see Marilyn Yalom, "Adèle Hugo, Witness of Her Husband's Life," in *Revealing Lives: Autobiography, Biography, and Gender*, ed. Susan Groag Bell and Marilyn Yalom (Albany: State University of New York Press, 1990), pp. 53-63.

7. Denis Bertholet, *Les Français par eux-mêmes, 1815-1885* (Paris: Olivier Orban, 1991), pp. 70-78.

8. Karl Mannheim, "The Problem of Generations," in *Essays on the Sociology of Knowledge*, ed. and trans. Paul Kecskemeti (New York: Oxford University Press, 1952), pp. 276-322. Whereas Mannheim focused largely on the imprinting that occurred in childhood and adolescence, in accordance with the psychoanalytic emphasis of his times, I extend the notion of "generation" into adulthood, in accordance with the self-definitions of the memoirists themselves. The issue of generations, as applied to U.S. children of World War II, is cogently presented by William M. Tuttle in *Their War, Too: America's Homefront Children during the Second World War* (New York: Oxford University Press, 1993).

9. Considerably more women fought on the side of the Republic than against it. For vignettes of those on both sides, see Jeanne Bouvier, *Les Femmes pendant la Révolution* (Paris: E. Figuère, 1931), pp. 198-211. The names of seventy women who served in the republican army have been identified by Léon Hennet in his *Histoire de la Révolution*, vol. 1, chapter VIII, as cited by R. Brice in *Les Femmes et les Armées de la Révolution et de l'Empire, 1792-1815* (Paris: L'Edition Moderne, 1913), p. 311. The best-known women who fought on the side of the counterrevolutionaries in the west of France appear in Nicole Vray, *Les Femmes dans la tourmente* (Rennes: Editions Ouest-France, 1988), pp. 107-10.

10. Lynn Z. Bloom makes this point in relation to Japanese internment camp narratives in "Reunion and Reinterpretation: Group Biography in Process," *biography* 13 (Summer 1990):222-23.

11. Historians who have examined some of these texts with profit include Paule-Marie Duhet, *Les Femmes et la Révolution, 1789-1794* (Paris: Julliard, 1971); Darlene Levy, Harriet Applewhite, and Mary Durham Johnson, *Women in Revolutionary Paris, 1789-1794* (Urbana: University of Illinois Press, 1979); and Catherine Marand-Fouquet, *La Femme au temps de la Révolution* (Paris: Stock-Laurence Pernoud, 1989).

12. Jean Tulard, Preface to Fierro, *Bibliographie*, p. 7.

13. This French distinction between victims and accomplices, or victims and executioners, becomes common in this period, as in Alexandrine des Echerolles's assertion that France had been divided "into only two classes: executioners or victims." Alexandrine des Echerolles, *Une famille noble sous la Terreur* (Paris: E. Plon, 1879), Preface to the first edition, p. xiv.

14. Benoîte Groult, Preface to Marilyn Yalom, *Le Temps des orages: Aristocrates, bourgeoises, et paysannes racontent* (Paris: Maren Sell, 1989), p. 1.

15. See Jacques Voisine, "Naissance et évolution du terme 'autobiographie,'" *La Littérature comparée en Europe orientale* (Budapest: Akademia Kiado, 1963), pp. 278-86.

16. Annette Rosa, *Citoyennes: Les Femmes et la Révolution française* (Paris: Messidor, 1988), p. 54.

17. I am grateful to Keith Baker of Stanford University for this connection between women's memoirs and the hopes of the early Revolution.

18. The paucity of memoirs authored by female religious figures is striking, especially in contrast to the numerous accounts left by priests. Fierro lists fifty-five texts written by

refractory priests in the introduction to his bibliography, but only four are attributed to nuns: the short memoirs of Sister Besnard focusing on the closing of the convents in Angers in 1794; the memoirs of Sister Théotiste Valombray, whose authorship is highly problematic since the work was probably written or rewritten by the novelist Elise Moreau; the memoirs of Sister Jeanne Le Royer, which were shaped by her priest/editor/biographer; and the diary of Sister Gabrielle Gauchat, authored during the Terror from September 1792 to June 1795. Fierro, *Bibliographie.* In my annotated bibliography, I have added the autobiographical narrative of Sainte Jeanne-Antide Thouret, brought to my attention by Claude Langlois, the author of *Le catholicisme au féminin* (Paris: Les Editions du Cerf, 1984).

19. Marie-Catherine Vallon, *Mémoires de Madame Vallon* (Paris: Emile Paul, 1913), pp. 1-2.

20. Marquise de La Rochejaquelein, *Mémoires de la Marquise de La Rochejaquelein, 1782-1857* (Paris: Mercure de France, 1984), p. 37.

21. Angélique de Maussion, *Rescapés de Thermidor* (Paris: Nouvelles éditions latines, 1975), p. 7.

CHAPTER 2
THE YEAR 1789, IN WOMEN'S WORDS

1. Mme de Geniis, *Mémoires sur le XVIIIe siècle et la Révolution française,* 10 vols. (Paris: Ladvocat, 1825), 3:257-59.

2. Marquise de La Tour du Pin, *Journal d'une femme de cinquante ans, 1778-1815* , 4 vols. ed. Aymar de Liedekerke-Beaufort (Paris: Librairie Chapelot, 1913), 1:119.

3. Marquise de Villeneuve-Arifat, "Souvenirs d'enfance et de jeunesse de la marquise de Villeneuve-Arifat," ed. Henri Courteault, *Revue des études historiques* (1901):45-47.

4. Mme Cavaignac, *Les Mémoires d'une inconnue* (Paris: Plon, Nourrit, 1894), p. 52.

5. Louise Fusil, *Souvenirs d'une actrice,* 3 vols. (Paris: Dumont, 1841-46), 1:3.

6. Mme de Chastenay, *Mémoires de Madame de Chastenay (1771-1815)* (Paris: Librairie Académique Perrin: 1987), p. 75.

7. Charlotte Robespierre, *Mémoires de Charlotte Robespierre, précédes d'une introduction par Laponneraye et suivis de pièces justificatives* (Paris: au depot   central, 1835), pp. 69-70.

8. Mme de Fausselandry, *Mémoires de Mme la vicomtesse de Fars Fausselandry, ou Souvenirs d'une octogénaire,* 3 vols. (Paris: Ledoyen, 1830), 1:249-50.

9. Mme d'Abrantès, *Mémoires complets et authentiques de Laure Junot Duchesse d'Abrantès. Souvenirs historiques sur Napoléon, la Révolution, le Directoire, le Consulat, l'Empire, la Restauration, la Révolution de 1830 et les premières années du règne de Louis-Philippe,* 13 vols. (Paris: Jean de Bonnot, 1967-68), 1:93.

10. Mme de Staël, *Considérations sur la Révolution française* (Paris: Tallandier, 1983), p. 140.

11. Ibid., pp. 161-62.

12. Chastenay, *Mémoires,* p. 95.

13. Ferdinand Strobl von Ravelsberg, *Les Confessions de Théroigne de Méricourt . . . extrait*

du procès-verbal inédit (Paris: L. Westhausser, 1892), pp. 254-55.

14. Staël, *Considérations*, p. 168.

15. Mme de Ménerville, *Souvenirs d'émigration* (Paris: P. Roger, 1934), p. 20.

16. This and the preceding quotation are from La Tour du Pin, *Journal*, 1:192-95.

17. Alexandrine des Echerolles, *Une famille noble sous la Terreur* (Paris: E. Plon, 1879), p. 9.

18. Marie-Victoire Monnard, "Les souvenirs d'une femme du peuple à Creil," *Bulletin d'histoire et d'archéologie de Senlis*, 1 (1926), 69-70.

19. Mme Roland, *Mémoires de Madame Roland* (Paris: Mercure de France, 1986), p. 336.

20. Ibid.

21. Mme Campan, *Mémoires de Madame Campan* (Paris: Mercure de France, 1988), pp. 206-7. The princess died June 19, 1787; the dauphin, during the night of June 3-4, 1789.

22. *La Duchesse de Tourzel, Mémoires de Madame la Duchesse de Tourzel*, ed. Jean Chalon (Paris: Mercure de France, 1986), p. 20.

23. Madame Vigée-Lebrun, *Souvenirs*, 2 vols. (Paris: des femmes, 1984), 1:138-39.

24. La Marquise de La Rochejaquelein, *Mémoires de la Marquise de La Rochejaquelein, 1772-1857* (Paris: Mercure de France, 1984), p. 72.

25. Ménerville, *Souvenirs*, pp. 21-22.

26. Ibid., p. 28.

27. Tourzel, *Mémoires*, p. 25.

28. Staël, *Considérations*, p. 212.

29. Chastenay, *Mémoires,* p. 102.

30. Tourzel, *Mémoires*, p. 28.

31. Chastenay, *Mémoires*, p. 102.

32. Ibid.

33. Ibid., p. 103.

34. On the publication of these "memoirs," the Marquise de Lage de Volude, who had been the Princesse de Lamballe's official companion, called the work "an abominable obscenity, written by a woman of whom we have never heard, and who could certainly not have known her interior, nor even her barn-yard." La Marquise de Lage de Volude, *Souvenirs d'imigration . . 1792-1794* (Evreux: Auguste Hérissey, 1869), p. 59.

35. Elisabeth Guénard, *Mémoires historiques de Madame Marie-ThérèseLouise de Carignan, princesse de Lamballe* (Paris: Lerouge, 1801), 4:67-68.

36. Marie-Louise Lenoël, Femme Cheret, *Evénement de Paris et de Versailles. Par une des Dames qui a eu l'honneur d'être de la Députation* à *l'Assemblée Générale* (Paris: Chez Garnery & Volland, Libraire, Quai des Augustins, no. 25, 1790)

37. O.H. Hufton, *The Poor of Eighteenth-Century France* (Oxford: Oxford University Press, 1974), p. 318.

38. Ménerville, *Souvenirs*, pp. 37-39.

39. For a fuller discussion of Rousseau's role in the advocacy of breast-feeding, see Mary Jacobus, "Incorruptible Milk: Breast-feeding and the French Revolution," in *Rebel Daughters*, ed. Sara E. Melzer and Leslie W. Rabine (New York: Oxford University

Press, 1992), pp. 5475, esp. pp. 56-61.

40. The ideology and rules governing the Charité Maternelle are found in Jeanne Bouvier, *Les Femmes pendant la Révolution* (Paris: E. Figuère, 1931), pp. 72-86 (quotation from p. 77).

41. Sara Ruddick, "Maternal Thinking," in *Rethinking the Family: Some Feminist Questions*, ed. Barrie Thorne and Marilyn Yalom (New York: Longman, 1982), pp. 76-94, esp. p. 79.

42. Lynn Hunt, "The Unstable Boundaries of the French Revolution," in *A History of Private Life*, 5 vols., ed. Philippe Ariès and Georges Duby (Cambridge: Harvard University Press, 1990), 4:13-45.

43. Ménerville, *Souvenirs*, p. 21.

CHAPTER 3
THE FALL OF THE ROYAL FAMILY:
WITNESSED BY THE DUCHESSE DE TOURZEL

1. Mme la Duchesse de Tourzel, *Les Mémoires de la Duchesse de Tourzel* (Paris: Mercure de France, 1986), ed. Jean Chalon, Introduction, p. 14. All quotations are my translations from this edition.

2. Pauline de Tourzel, comtesse de Béarn, *Souvenirs de quarante ans (1789-1830)* (Paris: J. Lecoffre, 1861).

3. Mme Campan, *Mémoires de Madame Campan, Première Femme de Chambre de Marie-Antoinette* (Paris: Mercure de France, 1988), p. 218.

4. Tourzel, *Mémoires*, p. 31.

5. Ibid., p. 43.

6. Ibid., p. 53.

7. This and the following quotations are from ibid., p. 65.

8. Ibid., p. 74.

9. Ibid., pp. 96-97.

10. Ibid., pp. 99-100.

11. Ibid., p. 101.

12. Ibid., pp. 101-2.

13. Returning from the royal family's abortive flight to Varennes in spring 1791, Mme de Tourzel heard the republican deputy Antoine Barnave refer to the Festival of the Federation as a missed opportunity for the monarchy; he said to the king's sister Madame Elisabeth, "We would have been lost if you had known how to take advantage of it." Ibid., p. 208.

14. Ibid., p. 135.

15. Jeremy Popkin, "The Prerevolutionary Origins of Political Journalism," in *The French Revolution and the Creation of Modern Political Culture*, ed. Keith Baker (Oxford: Pergamon Press, 1987), pp. 203-23.

16. Robert Darnton, *Bohème littéraire et Révolution: Le Monde des livres au xviii siècle* (Paris: Gallimard, 1983), p. 41. See also Jean-Paul Bertaud, *La Vie quotidienne en France au temps de la Révolution (1789-1795)* (Paris: Hachette, 1983), p. 128.

17. Ouzi Elyada, "La Mère Duchesne: Masques populaires et guerre pamphlétaire, 1789-1791," *Annales historiques de la Révolution française* 271 (January-March, 1988): 1-16.

18. Tourzel, *Mémoires*, p. 139.

19. Ibid., p. 144.

20. Ibid., pp. 172-73.

21. Ibid., p. 191.

22. Jean Chalon, *Chère Marie-Antoinette* (Paris: Librairie Académique Perrin, 1988), p. 319.

23. Tourzel, *Mémoires*, pp. 199-200.

24. Ibid., p. 200.

25. Ibid., p. 203.

26. Ibid., pp. 207, 209, 210, 211.

27. The republican pamphleteer Olympe de Gouges, for one, expressed prevailing popular sentiments in two letters addressed separately to the king and queen. To the king she wrote: "Sire, you haven't a moment to lose. Send your couriers to the foreign powers and declare to them that you embrace the cause of your country." To the queen she addressed an equally vehement epistle that began, "Madame, you cannot hide the fact that you are no longer the same in the eyes of the French." For the definitive biography of Olympe de Gouges, see Olivier Blanc, *Olympe de Gouges* (Paris: Editions Syros, 1981). For a selection of her texts, see Benoîte Groult, *Olympe de Gouges: Oeuvres* (Paris: Mercure de France, 1986).

28. Tourzel, *Mémoires*, p. 223.

29. Ibid., p. 238.

30. Ibid., p. 239.

31. For an analysis of this demonstration, see Darline G. Levy and Harriet B. Applewhite, "Women, Radicalization, and the Fall of the French Monarchy," *Women and Politics in the Age of the Democratic Revolution*, ed. Darline G. Levy and Harriet B. Applewhite (Ann Arbor: University of Michigan Press, 1990), pp. 81-107.

32. Tourzel, *Mémoires*, p. 324.

33. Ibid., pp. 327-28.

34. Ibid., p. 328.

35. Campan, *Mémoires*, pp. 327-28.

36. Marquise de La Rochejaquelein, *Mémoires de la marquise de La Rochejaquelein, 1772-1857* (Paris: Mercure de France, 1984), pp. 101-3.

37. This and the preceding citations are from Marie-Victoire Monnard, "Les souvenirs d'une femme du peuple à Creil," *Bulletin d'histoire et d'archéologie de Senlis,* 1 (1926): 28-30.

38. Tourzel, *Mémoires*, p. 376.

39. Ibid., p. 382.

40. Ibid., pp. 387, 389.

41. Ibid., p. 389.

42. Ibid.

43. Ibid., p. 391.

44. Ibid., pp. 394-95.

45. La Ferronays, Introduction to Tourzel, *Mémoires de Madame la duchesse de Tourzel, gouvernante des Enfants de France pendant les années 1789, 1790, 1791, 1792, 1793, 1794, 1795, publiés par M. le duc Des Cars* (Paris: E. Plon, 1883), 2 vols. 2:1-2.

CHAPTER 4
THE KING AND THE QUEEN IN THE FACE OF DEATH:
WITNESSED BY MADAME ROYALE AND ROSALIE LAMORLIÈRE

1. [Duchesse d'Angoulême] *Mémoires particuliers, formant, avec l'ouvrage de M. Hüe et le journal de Cléry, l'histoire complète de la captivité de la famille royale à la Tour du Temple* (Paris: Audot, 1817). Both Jean-Baptiste Hanet, known as Cléry, and François Hüe, members of the king's entourage, published accounts of their attendance on the dauphin in the Temple prior to the publication of the Duchesse d'Angoulême's memoirs. J.-B. Cléry, *Journal de ce qui s'est passé à la tour du Temple* (London: l'auteur, 1798). F. Hüe, *The Last Years of the Reign and Life of Louis XVI*, trans. R. C. Dallas (London: Cadell and Davies, 1806).

2. Rosalie Lamorlière, "La Dernière Prison de Marie-Antoinette" in *Récits des grands jours de l'histoire* (Paris: H. Gautier, 1897), pp. 75-91, followed by an appendix containing Rosalie Lamorlière's conversation with Mme Henriette Simon-Viennot.

3. Later editions sometimes also included the Duchesse d'Angoulême's short account of the flight to Varennes, which she had given in 1796 shortly after her arrival in Vienna to Weber, her mother's "milk brother," and which he subsequently inserted into his own memoirs. Joseph Weber, *Mémoires concernant Marie-Antoinette* (London: Impr. Daponte et Vogel, G. Schulze, 1804-1809), 3 vols.

4. Joseph Turquan, *Madame, Duchesse d'Angoulême (1778-1851)* (Paris: Emile Paul, 1909), pp. 54-55.

5. Angoulême, *Mémoires*, p. 3.

6. Ibid., p. 9.

7. Ibid., pp. 23-25.

8. Ibid., p. 37.

9. Ibid., p. 41.

10. Ibid., pp. 71-72.

11. Pierre de Zurich, *Une femme heureuse: Madame de La Briche, 1755-1844. Sa famille, son salon, le château du Marais* (Paris: E. de Boccard, 1934), pp. 336-38.

12. Mme la Comtesse de Béarn, née Pauline de Tourzel, *Souvenirs de quarante ans (1789-1830)* (Paris: Victor Sarlit, 1868), p. 195.

13. Among the most noteworthy of these biographies, see J. M. Gassier, *L'Antigone française, ou Mémoires historiques sur Marie-Thérèse-Charlotte de France* (Paris: Aubry, 1814); Joseph Turquan, *Madame*; and André Castelot, *Le Secret de Madame Royale* (Paris: Sfelt, 1949).

14. Precious little information about the life of Rosalie Lamorlière can be found in the interview by Mme Henriette Simon-Viennot published at the end of Lamorlière's memoirs; this same interview had already appeared earlier in Simon-Viennot's justificatory book on Marie-Antoinette, *Marie-Antoinette devant le dix-neuvième*

siècle (Paris: J. Ange, Editeur, 1838).

15. Mme Simon-Viennot received this information from Mme Jolivet, who had visited her imprisoned painter-husband in the Conciergerie, ibid., p. 323.

16. Lafont d'Aussonne (abbe), *Mémoires secrets et universels des malheurs et de la mort de la reine de France* (Paris: Petit, 1824).

17. For recent studies, see Chantal Thomas, *La Reine scélérate: Marie-Antoinette dans les pamphlets* (Paris: Seuil, 1989); and Lynn Hunt, *The Many Bodies of Marie-Antoinette: Political Pornography and the Problem of the Feminine in the French Revolution* (Baltimore: Johns Hopkins University Press, 1990).

18. Simon-Viennot, *Marie-Antoinette*, p. 359.

19. Lamorlière, "Dernière Prison," p. 78.

20. Ibid., p. 84.

21. Ibid., pp. 79, 84.

22. Ibid., p. 85.

23. Ibid., pp. 85-86.

24. Ibid., pp. 88-89.

25. Ibid., pp. 89-90.

26. Ibid., pp. 90-91.

27. Words of de Rouy, the elder, cited by Jean Chalon, *Chère Marie-Antoinette* (Paris: Perrin, 1988), p. 470 n.

28. Lamorlière, "Dernière Prison," p. 91.

29. Ibid., App., p. 92.

30. J. M. Thompson, *The French Revolution* (New York: Oxford University Press, 1966, 1st ed. 1943), p. 472.

31. For some important feminist works that have promoted this view, see Paule-Marie Duhet, *Les Femmes et la Révolution 1789-1794* (Paris: Julliard, 1971); Joan B. Landes, *Women and the Public Sphere in the Age of the French Revolution* (Ithaca, N.Y.: Cornell University Press, 1988); and Thomas, *La Reine scélérate*.

32. Simon Schama, *Citizens: A Chronicle of the French Revolution* (New York: Knopf, 1989), pp. 799-800. Thompson, *French Revolution*, p. 473.

33. Carolly Erickson, *To the Scaffold: The Life of Marie Antoinette* (New York: William Morrow, 1991).

CHAPTER 5

THE REPUBLIC VINDICATED AND VIOLATED:
STARRING MADAME ROLAND

1. Mme Roland, *Mémoires de Madame Roland*, ed. Paul de Roux (Paris: Mercure de France, 1986). Mme Roland's memoirs were first published in 1795 in a version titled *Appel à l'impartiale postérité*, and again in 1800 in a collection of her husband's works. Both of these publications, edited by two of Mme Roland's closest male friends, eliminated or changed passages from her original manuscript that were considered detrimental to the author's glory and embarrassing to her surviving daughter Eudora.

In 1820, her still-altered memoirs appeared as the lead title in A. Berville and F. Barrière's series, *Mémoires relatifs à la Révolution française*, an anthology of fifty-three volumes (Paris: Baudouin fils, 1820-27).

2. Ferdinand Strobl von Ravelsberg, *Les Confessions de Théroigne de Méricourt* (Paris: L.Westhausser, 1892); Mme de Geniis, *Précis de la conduite de Mme de Geniis, depuis la Révolution* (Hamburg: B. G. Hoffmann, 1796); Charlotte Robespierre, *Mémoires de Charlotte Robespierre sur ses deux frères précédés d'une introduction par Laponneraye et suivis de pièces justificatives* (Paris: au dépôt central, 1835).

3. Elisabeth Le Bas, "Manuscrit de Mme Le Bas" in *Autour de Robespierre. Le Conventionnel Le Bas*, ed. Stéfane Paul [pseudonym of Paul Coutant] (Paris: Flammarion, 1901) pp. 102-50; Sophie Grandchamp, *Souvenirs*, app. to Claude Perroud's 1905 edition of Mme Roland's memoirs (see note 5); Mme Cavaignac, *Les Mémoires d'une inconnue* (Paris: Plon, Nourrit, 1894).

4. Mme de Staël, *Considérations sur la Révolution française*, 3 vols. (Paris: Delaunay, 1818). Several other republican women, such as Suzanne Juillerat-Chasseur, recall that their early patriotic convictions were destroyed by the Terror. The memoirs of Thérèse Figueur Sutter, who fought in the army on the republican side in the south of France after 1792, are of doubtful authenticity.

5. Mme Roland, *Mémoires de Mme Roland*, 2 vols., ed. Claude Perroud (Paris: Plon, Nourrit et Cie, 1905).

6. Roland, *Mémoires* (1986), p. 98. All translations are from this edition.

7. Ibid., pp. 98-99.

8. Ibid., pp. 201-2.

9. For this insight into autobiographies of childhood, I am grateful to Richard N. Coe, *When the Grass Was Taller* (New Haven: Yale University Press, 1984).

10. Ibid., pp. 48, 57.

11. Ibid., p. 185.

12. Ibid., p. 62.

13. Ibid., p. 63.

14. Preceding quotation ibid., p. 304. Letter to Sophie Cannet, February 5, 1776, in *Lettres de Madame Roland*, ed. Claude Perroud, 4 vols. (Paris: Imprimerie Nationale, 1900-15), vol. 1, p. 271.

15. Grandchamp, *Souvenirs*, pp. 461-97.

16. Roland, *Mémoires*, p. 132.

17. Ibid., p. 63.

18. Ibid., p. 137.

19. Ibid., pp. 333, 99.

20. Ibid., p. 342.

21. This and the preceding quotations are from ibid., p. 64.

22. Ibid.

23. Ibid., p. 65.

24. This and the preceding quotations are from ibid., pp. 65-66.

25. Ibid., p. 66.

26. Ibid., pp. 68, 158. Dorinda Outram, *The Body and the French Revolution: Sex, Class*

and Political Culture (New Haven: Yale University Press, 1990), p. 133.

27. Roland, *Mémoires*, p. 168.

28. Ibid., p. 69.

29. Ibid., p. 71.

30. Ibid., p. 73.

31. Ibid., p. 74.

32. Ibid., pp. 76, 77.

33. Ibid., p. 77.

34. Ibid., pp. 79-80.

35. Ibid., p. 84.

36. Ibid., pp. 86-87.

37. Ibid., p. 90.

38. Ibid., p. 92. Danton's words cited by C. A. Dauban, *Etude sur Madame Roland et son temps* (Paris: Henri Plon, 1864), p. CL.

39. Roland, *Mémoires*, pp. 93, 155.

40. Ibid., pp. 94, 184, 176.

41. Guy Chaussinand-Nogaret, *Mme Roland: Une Femme en Révolution*, (Paris: Seuil, 1985), p. 275. The best biography of Mme Roland in English is still Gita May, *Mme Roland and the Age of Revolution* (New York: Columbia University Press, 1970).

42. Outram, *The Body*, p. 138.

43. Mme Roland hoped to write the annals of her century, to become the Mrs. Macaulay of her country, the Tacitus of France (Roland, *Mémoires*, p. 338). Her passion for Tacitus and her desire to become a historian are expressed in a letter dated September 28, 1793, to her friend the geographer Edmé Mentell.

44. Cavaignac, *Souvenirs*, p. 30.

45. *Lettres autographes de Mme Roland addressées à Bancal-des-Issarts* (Paris: Eugène Renduel, 1835). The introduction by Sainte-Beuve is reproduced in his *Nouvelle Galérie de femmes célèbres* (Paris: Garnier Frères, 1872), pp. xvii-lix.

46. Louise Colet, *Charlotte Corday et Madame Roland* (Paris: Berquet et Pétion, Editeurs, 1842).

47. Alphonse de Lamartine, *Histoire des Girondins*, 8 vols. (Paris: Furne, 1847), 2:3. For a discussion of Lamartine's evolving attitude to Mme Roland, see A. Court, "Lamartine et Madame Roland" in R. Bellet, ed., *La Femme au XIXe siècle* (Lyons: Presses Universitaires de Lyons, 1978).

48. *Grands Hommes et grands faits de la Révolution française* (1789-1804) (Paris: Ancienne librairie Furne, 1889), p. 124. Elisabeth Badinter, *Paroles d'hommes* (1790-1793) (Paris: P.O.L, 1989), p. 11.

49. *Le Moniteur*, November 19, 1793.

50. Grandchamp, *Souvenirs*, pp. 492-95.

CHAPTER 6
THE OTHER ROBESPIERRE

51. Two decades after Charlotte's death, when historical romance was much in vogue,

the Comtesse Dash (pseudonym for the Vicomtesse de Poillöüe de Saint-Mars) wrote a fanciful novel loosely based on Charlotte's life, *Mademoiselle Robespierre*, 2 vols. (Paris: Coulon-Pineau, 1855). At the end of the nineteenth century she appeared again in the scholarly work of G. d'Orcey, "La Soeur de Robespierre, épisode de la Terreur,» in the *Revue Britannique* (Paris, 1893), vol. 6. She is presented as the classic spinster in Max Gallo's *Robespierre the Incorruptible: A Psychobiography* (New York: Herder & Herder, 1971, originally *Maximilien Robespierre: Histoire d'une solitude* [Paris: Librairie Académique Perrin, 1968]), as well as in J. Tulard, J.-F. Fayard, A. Fierro, *Histoire et dictionnaire de la Révolution Française, 1789-1799* (Paris: Robert Laffont, 1987). Charlotte Robespierre's *Mémoires sur ses deux frères* was reprinted (Paris: Présence de la Révolution, 1987) on the basis of the first edition (Paris: au dépôt central, Faubourg Saint-Denis, no. 16, 1835). My translations are from the 1835 edition.

52. Hector Fleischmann, *Charlotte Robespierre et ses Mémoires* (Paris: A. Michel, 1910), p. 11.

53. Robespierre, *Mémoires*, p. 46.

54. Ibid., p. 51.

55. Ibid., pp. 56-57.

56. Ibid., pp. 57-59.

57. Ibid., p. 73.

58. Villier's statement is reproduced in Louis Jacob, *Robespierre vu par ses contemporains* (Paris: Librairie Armand Colin, 1938), p. 86. See Patrice Gueniffey, "Robespierre," in *The Critical Dictionary of the French Revolution*, ed. François Furet and Mona Ozouf (Cambridge: The Belknap Press of Harvard University Press, 1989), p. 299.

59. The complete letter is found in Fleischmann, *Charlotte Robespierre*, pp. 27-29.

60. These two articles are reproduced in Jacob, *Robespierre*, pp. 91-95.

61. Robespierre, *Mémoires*, pp. 86-88.

62. Ibid., pp. 91-92.

63. Rosalie Jullien, *Journal d'une bourgeoise pendant la Révolution, 1791-1793*, ed. Edouard Lockroy (Paris: Calmann-Lévy, 1881), pp. 345-46.

64. Robespierre, *Mémoires*, p. 100.

65. Ibid., pp. 102, 105.

66. Ibid., pp. 109, 110.

67. Ibid., p. 115.

68. Reproduced in Fleischmann, *Charlotte Robespierre*, pp. 54-55.

69. Albert Laponneraye, *Cours public d'histoire de France* (Paris: Impr. de David et A. Amie, n.d.); *Histoire de la Révolution française depuis 1789 jusqu'en 1814*, 2 vols. (Paris: 16 rue du Faubourg Saint-Denis, 1838).

70. Robespierre, *Mémoires*, pp. 144-45.

71. Ibid., pp. 146-47.

72. Ibid., p. 143.

73. Fifteen years is the period designated by Laponneraye in his introduction to the 1835 edition of Charlotte's memoirs, but Fleischmann (*Charlotte Robespierre*, pp. 109-13.) says the pension lasted till her death, with the possible exception of the years 1823-

30.

74. Robespierre, *Mémoires*, p. 33.

75. Ibid., p. 172.

76. On the subject of women memoirists related to famous men, see Marilyn Yalom, "Adèle Hugo, Witness of Her Husband's Life," in *Revealing Lives: Autobiography, Biography, and Gender*, ed. Susan Groag Bell and Marilyn Yalom (Albany: State University of New York Press, 1990), pp. 53-63.

CHAPTER 7

THE WIDOW LE BAS

1. Paul Valéry, *Degas/Danse/Dessin* (Paris: Gallimard, 1965), p. 55.

2. Elisabeth Le Bas, "Manuscrit de Mme Le Bas" in *Autour de Robespierre. Le Conventionnel Le Bas*, ed. Stéfane-Paul [pseudonym of Paul Coutant] (Paris: Flammarion, 1901), pp. 102-50).

3. A similar example is found in a work written by Mme de Bourboulon, wife of the French minister to China in the mid-nineteenth century. One would scarcely guess from the male "author's" name on the cover (Achille Poussièlgue) and the title of the book (*Voyage en Chine et en Mongolie de M. de Bourboulon, Ministre de France, et de Mme de Bourboulon, 1860-1861*) that Mme de Bourboulon was the sole author of this fascinating travel memoir (Paris: Hachette, 1866).

4. Le Bas, "Manuscrit," p. 146.

5. Ibid., p. 102.

6. Ibid., pp. 102-5.

7. Ibid., p. 106.

8. Ibid., pp. 106-7.

9. Ibid., p. 104.

10. Ibid., pp. 108-9.

11. The 1982 film *Danton* by the Polish director A. Wadja takes this approach.

12. Le Bas, "Manuscrit," pp. 110-11.

13. Ibid., p. 113.

14. Ibid., p. 114.

15. Ibid., pp. 115-16.

16. Ibid., pp. 119-20.

17. Ibid., pp. 121-22.

18. Ibid., pp. 127-28.

19. Ibid., p. 128.

20. Ibid., p. 133.

21. Ibid.

22. Ibid., p. 136.

23. Ibid., p. 137.

24. Ibid., p. 138.

25. Ibid.

26. Ibid., pp. 139, 140.

27. Ibid., p. 139.

28. Ibid., p. 140.

29. Ibid., p. 141.

30. Ibid., pp. 142-43.

31. Byron, *Don Juan*, Stanza 194.

32. Karen Homey, *Neurosis and Human Growth* (New York: Norton, 1950).

CHAPTER 8
GERMAINE DE STAEL'S *CONSIDERATIONS OF THE FRENCH REVOLUTION*

1. Germaine de Staël, *Dix Années d'exil*, ed. Simone Balaye (Paris: Bibliothèque 10/18, 1966).

2. *Oeuvres complètes de Mme la baronne de Staël*, 17 vols. (Paris: Treuttel et Wurtz, 1820-21); and *Oeuvres inédites de Mme la baronne de Staël*, 3 vols. (Paris: Treuttel et Wurtz, 1821).

3. Mme de Staël, *Considérations sur la Revolution française*, ed. Jacques Godechot (Paris: Tallandier, 1983), p. 65. All my translations are from this edition.

4. Ibid., p. 63.

5. Ibid., p. 26.

6. Ibid., p. 82.

7. Ibid., p. 157.

8. The biography of Jacques Necker that Staël intended to write as a separate work ended up as Part 1 of the *Considérations*. Ibid., p. 86.

9. Ibid., p. 105.

10. Ibid., pp. 105-6.

11. Ibid., p. 101.

12. Mme de Ménerville, née Fougeret, *Souvenirs d'émigration* (Paris: ed. Pierre Rogers, 1934); and Angélique de Maussion, *Rescapés de Thermidor* (Paris: Nouvelles éditions latines, 1975).

13. Staël, *Considérations*, p. 108.

14. Ibid., pp. 110-11.

15. Ibid., p. 111.

16. Mme de Genlis, *Mémoires inédits de Madame la comtesse de Genlis, sur le XVIIIe siècle et la Révolution française*, 10 vols. (Paris: Ladvocat, 1825), 3:257.

17. This and the preceding quotations are from Staël, *Considerations*, pp. 128, 129.

18. Marquise de La Tour du Pin, *Journal d'une femme de cinquante ans*, 4 vols., ed. Aymar de Liedekerke-Beaufort (Paris: Impr. R. Chapelot, 1907-11), 1:181-82.

19. Ibid., p. 142.

20. Ibid., p. 160.

21. Ibid., p. 168.

22. Ibid., p. 175.

23. Ibid., pp. 175, 199, 177.

24. Ibid., p. 177.

25. Ibid., p. 181. Mme de Tourzel, *Mémoires* (Paris: Mercure de France, 1986), p. 219.

26. These and the following quotations are from Staël, *Considérations*, p. 227.

27. This and the preceding quotations are from p. 228.

28. Ibid., p. 229.

29. Ibid., p. 187.

30. Ibid., p. 191. Anne Soprani, *La Révolution et les femmes de 1789 à 1796* (Paris: MA Editions, 1988), p. 104.

31. Staël, *Considérations*, p. 226.

32. J. Christopher Herold, *Mistress to an Age: A Life of Madame de Staël* (New York: Bobbs-Merrill, 1958), p. 108.

33. Staël, *Considérations*, pp. 237-38.

34. Tourzel, *Mémoires*, p. 168.

35. Mme Roland, *Mémoires* (Paris: Mercure de France, 1986), pp. 127, 128.

36. Staël, *Considérations*, pp. 313-14.

37. The quotations in this paragraph are from ibid., pp. 240-41.

38. The quotations in this paragraph and the preceding one are from pp. 248-49.

39. This and the following quotations are from ibid., pp. 250, 253-56.

40. For a brilliant discussion of this subject, see Jean Starobinski, "The Authority of Feeling and the Origins of Psychological Criticism: Rousseau and Madame de Staël," *Literary Criticism and Psychology*, Yearbook of Comparative Criticism, vol. 7, ed. Joseph P. Strelka (University Park: Pennsylvania State University Press, 1976), pp. 69-97.

41. Staël, *Considérations*, p. 265.

42. Ibid.

43. Ibid., pp. 275-76.

44. René Girard, *Violence and the Sacred*, trans. Patrick Gregory (Baltimore: Johns Hopkins University Press, 1977). For an insightful application of Girard's theories, see Lynn Hunt, *The Family Romance of the French Revolution* (Berkeley: University of California Press, 1992), pp. 10-11, 14-15.

45. These and the following quotations are from Staël, *Considérations*, pp. 279, 281-86.

46. Linda Orr, "Outspoken Women and the Rightful Daughter of the Revolution: Madame de Staël's *Considérations sur la Révolution française*," in Rebel Daughters, ed. Sara E. Melzer and Leslie W. Rabine (New York: Oxford University Press, 1992), pp. 121-36.

47. Staël, *Considérations*, p. 601.

CHAPTER 9
PLIGHTS AND PLOYS IN THE PROVINCES:
MADAME VALLON AND ALEXANDRINE DES ECHEROLLES

1. Antoinette Carra de Vaux, "Cahiers de mémoires inédits de la baronne Carra de Vaux," *Bulletin de la Société des sciences et arts du Beaujolais*, 11 (1910): 282.

2. On the treatment of pregnant women in prison, see Dr. Max Billard, *Les Femmes*

enceintes devant le tribunal révolutionnaire (Paris: Librairie Académique Perrin, 1910).

3. Suzanne Juillerat-Chasseur, *Un épisode de la Terreur à Nîmes, extrait des souvenirs personnels de Madame Juillerat-Chasseur* (Montbéliard: Impr. montbéliardaise, 1902), pp. 72-73.

4. Alexandrine Lambert, *Souvenirs d'Alexandrine Pannelier d'Arsonval, baronne Lambert, avant and pendant la Révolution* (Versailles: Impr. Aubert, 1902), p. 23.

5. This and the following quotations are from ibid., pp. 26-29.

6. See Pierre Caron, "Les Arrestations des suspects a Paris entre le 10 août et le 2 septembre 1792," *Révolution Française*, 84 (1931): 107-26.

7. Mme Ranfer de Bretenières, "Dix-huit mois de ma vie: Histoire tragicomique de la maison de détention des femmes de D.," *La Révolution à Dijon: Paroles de femmes* (Dijon: Bibliothèque Municipale, 1989), pp. 25-26.

8. Victoire de Saint-Luc, *Victoire de Saint-Luc . . . journal de sa détention en 1793* (Paris: P. Tequi, 1905), pp. 115, 85, 116.

9. Marie-Catherine Vallon, *Mémoires de Madame Vallon, souvenirs de la Révolution dans le département du Loir-et-Cher* (Paris: Emile Paul, 1913), p. 81.

10. Ibid., p. 13.

11. Ibid., pp. 42, 63.

12. Ibid., pp. 67, 72.

13. Ibid., p. 76.

14. Ibid., pp. 84, 81.

15. Ibid., p. 95.

16. René Levasseur, *Mémoires de R. Levasseur (de la Sarthe), ex-conventionnel* (Paris: Messidor, 1989), p. 390. I am grateful to Donald Sutherland of the University of Maryland for this reference.

17. Vallon, *Mémoires*, p. 101.

18. This and the following quotations are from ibid., pp. 111, 116, 120, 126, 130, 135, 163, 180-82, 186, 188.

19. This and the following quotations are from ibid., pp. 208, 213, 217, 219, 224-26, 229.

20. Ibid., p. 12.

21. Alexandrine des Echerolles, *Une famille noble sous la Terreur* (Paris: E. Plon, 1879), p. 76.

22. This and the following quotations are from ibid., pp. 76, 78-79, 8384, 89-90, 94-103.

23. Ibid., p. 218.

24. *Les Citoyennes de Ville-Affranchie, aux Représentans du Peuple,* document no. 1660, Bibliothèque Marguerite Durand, Paris.

25. Simon Schama, *Citizens: A Chronicle of the French Revolution* (New York: Knopf, 1989), p. 783.

26. Echerolles, *Une famille noble,* p. 219.

27. These and the following quotations are from ibid., pp. 232, 237-39, 241.

28. Using a Freudian grid, Lynn Hunt analyzes the shift between a patriarchal and a fraternal mentality in *The Family Romance of the French Revolution* (Berkeley:

University of California Press, 1992).

29. Annette Rosa, Citoyennes: *Les Femmes et la Révolution française* (Paris: Messidor, 1988), pp. 83-87.

30. Marie-Victoire Monnard, "Les souvenirs d'une femme du people à Creil," *Bulletin d'histoire et d'archéologie de Senlis*, 1 (1926): 72.

31. See, for example, *Cahiers des Doléances des Femmes et autres textes, 1789*, ed. Paule-Marie Duhet (Paris: des femmes, 1981); *La Révolution à Dijon*, pp. 10-12, 18-20; and Rosalie Jullien, *Journal d'une bourgeoise pendant la Révolution*, 1791-1793, ed. Edouard Lockroy (Paris: Calmann-Lévy, 1881).

CHAPTER 10

THE WOMEN OF THE VENDEE

1. Comtesse de La Bouëre, *Souvenirs de la comtesse de La Bouëre, La Guerre de la Vendée, 1793-1796* (Paris: Plon, Nourrit, 1890), p. 2.

2. François Furet, *A Critical Dictionary of the French Revolution*, ed. François Furet and Mona Ozouf, trans. Arthur Goldhammer (Cambridge: Harvard University Press, 1989), p. 167.

3. Reynald Secher, *Le Génocide franco-français: La Vendée vengée* (Paris: Presses universitaires de France, 1986), p. 298.

4. Marquise de La Rochejaquelein, *Mémoires de la Marquise de La Rochejaquelein, 1772-1857* (Paris: Mercure de France, 1984); Mme de Bonchamps, *Mémoires de madame la marquise de Bonchamps, sur la Vendée, rédigés par Mme la comtesse de Genlis* (Paris: Baudouin frères, 1823), vol. 6; Madame de Sapinaud de Boishuguet, *Mémoires sur la Vendée*, 2 vols. (Paris: Baudouin frères, 1823).

5. Pauline Gontard des Chevalleries, baronne de Candé, *Une jeune fille à l'armée vendéenne. 1793. Souvenirs inédits . . . publiés et annotés par le vicomte Aurélien de Courson* (Paris: Librairie des Saints-Pères, 1930).

6. Julienne Goguet de Boisheraud, "Récit des tristes événements arrivés à Julienne Boishéraud," *Bulletin de la Société archéologique et historique de Nantes et de la Loire-Inférieure*, 68 (1928): 35-89.

7. Renée Bordereau, *Mémoires de Renée Bordereau dite Langevin touchant sa vie militaire dans la Vendée, rédigés par elle-même* (Paris: L.-G. Michaud, 1814).

8. Françoise Després, *Détails historiques sur les services de Françoise Després, employée dans les armées royales de la Vendée* (Paris: L.-G. Michaud, 1817).

9. Louise Barbier, "Les Souvenirs de Louise Barbier sur l'insurrection vendéenne," ed. Charles Arnault, *Société des sciences, lettres et beaux-arts de Cholet* (1937): 247-310.

10. Comtesse Turpin de Crissé, *Mémoires relatifs aux différentes missions royalistes de Madame la comtesse Turpin de Crissé*, in vol. 2 of *Mémoires secrets et inédits pour servir à l'histoire contemporaine*, ed. Alphonse de Beauchamp (Paris: Vernarel et Tenon, 1825).

11. La Rochejaquelein, *Mémoires*, p. 309.

12. This and the following quotations are from ibid., pp. 320, 334, 330, 350, 351, 383, 446, 484.

13. George Sand, *Oeuvres autobiographiques*, 2 vols., ed. Georges Lubin (Paris: Gallimard, 1970), 1:901.
14. Bordereau, *Mémoires*, p. 8.
15. This and the following quotations are from ibid., pp. 16-17, 7-9, 15, 29, 41.
16. La Bouëre, *Souvenirs*, pp. 111-12.
17. La Rochejaquelein, *Mémoires*, p. 249.
18. Marjorie Garbor, *Vested Interests: Cross-Dressing and Cultural Anxiety* (New York: Routledge, 1992), p. 131.
19. Nicole Vray, *Les Femmes dans la tourmente* (Rennes: Editions ouest-France, 1988), pp. 92-93. See also the accompanying notes to the La Rochejaquelein memoirs, p. 512.
20. This and the preceding quotations are from La Rochejaquelein, *Mémoires*, pp. 247, 248, 250.
21. Vray, *Les Femmes dans la tourmente*, pp. 95-96.
22. Vitrail et Guerre de Vendée (Paris: Inventaire Général, SPADEM, 1987).
23. La Rochejaquelein, *Mémoires*, p. 120.
24. Bonchamps, *Mémoires*, p. 26.
25. Ibid., pp. 86-87.
26. Furet, *Critical Dictionary*, p. 175.

CHAPTER 11 EXILE:
LONDON, ST. PETERSBURG, AND UPSTATE NEW YORK

1. Madame de Ménerville, *Souvenirs d'émigration* (Paris: P. Roger, 1934), pp. 56, 63. The following quotations are from pp. 77-78, 92, 54-55, 94, 123-24, 170.
2. Mme de La Roque, "Les Mémoires d'une Vivaraise émigrée sous la Révolution," *Revue du Vivarais* 53 (1949):12, 21.
3. Ibid., pp. 13, 21.
4. Comtesse de Dauger, *Souvenirs d'émigration* (Caen: Legost, 1858), P. 60.
5. Ibid., pp. 73, 75.
6. La Roque, *Mémoires*, p. 24.
7. Dauger, *Souvenirs*, p. 111.
8. This and many other facts about émigré society abroad can be found in Joseph Turquan, *Les Femmes de l'émigration* 2 vols. (Paris: Emile Paul, 1912).
9. Madame de Genlis, *Précis de la conduite de Mme de Geniis, depuis la Révolution* (Hamburg: B. G. Hoffmann, 1796), p. 153.
10. Louise Fusil, *Souvenirs d'une actrice*, 3 vols. (Paris: Dumont, 18411846), 1:124.
11. Julie Molé-Léger, "Souvenirs d'une actrice pendant l'émigration," *Carnet historique et littéraire*, 5 (1900), 334.
12. Elisabeth Vigée-Lebrun, *Souvenirs*, 2 vols., ed. Claudine Herrmann (Paris: des femmes, 1986), 1:258; 1:238.
13. Ibid., 1:280.
14. Ibid., 1:279.
15. These and the following quotations are from ibid., 1:305-6, 343-44, 335-37; 2:50,

106, 158.

16. Emilie Millon-Journel, *Papiers et souvenirs de Famille . . . Cahiers confidentiels de Madame Journel née Millon d'Ailly de Verneuil, de 1774 à 1833* (Montbrison: Impr. E. Brassart, 1940), p. 25.

17. Duchesse de Saulx-Tavannes, *Sur les routes de l'émigration. Mémoires de la duchesse de Saulx-Tavannes (1791-1806)* (Paris: C. Lévy, 1933), pp. 126, 146.

18. Mme de Nicolay's memoirs have never been fully published. Extracts have appeared in the *Mémoires de la Société historique et archéologique de l'arrondissement de Pontoise et du Vexin*, 40 (1930): 97-107. The quotations are from pp. 99, 100.

19. Marquise de La Tour du Pin, *Journal d'une femme de cinquante ans, 1778— 1815*, 4 vols., ed. Aymar de Liedekerke-Beaufort (Paris: Impr. R. Chapelot, 1907-11), 1:114. All translations are from this edition. For an excellent, but abridged, English translation see that of Felice Harcourt, *Memoirs of Madame de La Tour du Pin* (New York: McCall Publishing Co., 1971).

20. La Tour du Pin, *Journal*, 1:73-74.

21. Ibid., 1:160, 199.

22. Georges Andrey, "Les 'Émigrés' Français en Suisse (1789-1797)," in *La Révolution française vue des deux côtés du Rhin*, ed. André Dabezies (Aix-en-Provence: Publications de l'Université de Provence Aix-Marseilles, 1990), pp. 207-8.

23. La Tour du Pin, *Journal*, 1:262.

24. Ibid., 1:266.

25. This and the following quotations are from ibid., 1:280, 285-86, 290, 300, 303, 304-5, 307-9, 314, 330, 339, 365, 377, 381, 386.

26. This and the following quotations are from ibid., 2:17, 31, 32.

27. M. de La Rochefoucauld-Liancourt, *Voyages dans les Etats Unis d'Amerique fait de 1795-1798*, 8 vols. (Paris: Du Pont, 1799), 2:316-18.

28. La Tour du Pin, *Journal*, 2:46.

29. Peter Gay, Introduction, Harcourt, trans., *Memoirs of Madame de La Tour du Pin*, p. 4C.

30. La Tour du Pin, *Journal*, 2:61.

31. Ibid., 2:88. The following quotations are from 2:100-03, 131.

32. Quoted by Felice Harcourt, Introduction, *Escape from Terror: The Journal of Madame de La Tour du Pin* (London: Folio Society, 1979), p. 10.

33. La Rochefoucault-Liancourt, *Voyages*, 2:317.

34. Duchesse d'Escars, *Mémoires de la marquise de Nadaillac, duchesse d'Escars* (Paris, Emile Paul, 1912), p. 41.

35. Vigée-Lebrun, *Souvenirs*, 2:100.

CHAPTER 12
REFLECTIONS, PERSONAL AND POLITICAL

1. This discussion is taken from the Introduction to *Revealing Lives: Autobiography, Biography, and Gender*, ed. Susan Groag Bell and Marilyn Yalom (Albany: State University of New York Press, 1990), p. 3. See also Belle Gale Chevigny, "Daughters

Writing: Toward a Theory of Women's Biography", *Between Women: Biographers, Novelists, Critics, Teachers and Artists Write about Their Work on Women*, ed. Carol Ascher, Louise de Salvo, Sara Ruddick (Boston: Beacon Press, 1984), pp. 79-102; and Carolyn G. Heilbrun, *Writing a Woman's Life* (New York: W. W. Norton, 1988).

2. Marie-Catherine Vallon, *Mémoires de Madame Vallon, souvenirs de la Révolution dans le departemcnt du Loir-et-Cher* (Paris: Emile Paul, 1913), p. 81.

3. Dominique Godineau, *Citoyennes Tricoteuses: Les Femmes du peuple* à *Paris pendant la Révolution française* (Aix-en-Provence: Alinéa, 1988), p. 11.

4. Lynn Hunt, *The Family Romance of the French Revolution* (Berkeley: University of California Press, 1992), p. 194.

5. Mme de la Villirouët, *Une femme avocat, épisodes de la Révolution à Lamballe et à Paris. Mémoires de la comtesse de La Villirouët, née de Lambilly (1767-1813)* (Paris: J. Poisson, 1902), p. 33.

6. *La Révolution à Dijon: Paroles de femmes* (Dijon: Bibliothèque Municipale, 1989), p. 19.

7. Lynn Hunt, "The Unstable Boundaries of the French Revolution," *A History of Private Life*, 5 vols., ed. Philippe Ariès and Georges Duby (Cambridge: Harvard University Press, 1990), 4:36.

8. For an application of these psychological principles to literature, see Shari Benstock, *The Private Self* (Chapel Hill: University of North Carolina Press, 1988); and Joan Lidoff, "Autobiography in a Different Voice," *Approaches to Teaching Maxine Hong Kingston's "The Woman Warrior,"* ed. Shirley Geok-lin Lim (New York: Modern Language Association, 1991), pp. 116-20.

9. For an account of British women's writing from the same period that makes the same point, see Valerie Sanders, *The Private Lives of Victorian Women: Autobiography in Nineteenth-Century England* (New York: St. Martin's Press, 1990).

10. Hunt, *Family Romance*, p. 167.

ANNOTATED BIBLIOGRAPHY OF FRENCH WOMEN'S EYEWITNESS ACCOUNTS OF THE REVOLUTION

This bibliography of French women's memoirs, defined as retrospective accounts of an author's life and times, also contains selected examples of diaries, letters, a "baby book," a last testament, and a few biographies with autobiographical content. Original editions are cited here; later editions are often cited in the Notes.

1. ABRANTÈS (Laure Junot, duchesse d'), 1785-1838.

Mémoires de Mme la duchesse d'Abrantès ou Souvenirs historiques sur Napoléon, la Révolution, le Directoire, le Consulat, l'Empire et la Restauration. Paris: Ladvocat, 1831-35, 18 vols.

Author: Wife of the Napoleonic general Junot, known for her elevated social position during the Empire.

Work: In the first volume, Mme d'Abrantès recalls a few vivid childhood memories of the Estates General and of the young Bonaparte frequenting her Corsican-born mother.

2. ANGOULÊME (Marie-Thérèse-Charlotte de France, duchesse d'), 1778-1851.

Mémoires particuliers, formant, avec l'ouvrage de M. Hüe et le journal de Cléry, l'histoire complète de la captivité de la famille royale à la Tour du Temple. Paris: Audot, 1817.

Author: Surviving child of Louis XVI and Marie-Antoinette. Wife of the Duc d'Angoulême, her first cousin and heir apparent to the throne after 1815. Adult reputation as haughty, courageous, and most unfortunate in all aspects of her life.

Work: Short, moving account of her family's imprisonment in the Temple and successive deaths of her father, mother, aunt, and brother. Written in 1795, copied and "corrected" by Louis XVIII, first published anonymously in 1817 in a pirated version, succeeded by numerous editions.

3. BARBIER (Louise).

"Les Souvenirs de Louise Barbier sur l'insurrection vendéenne," ed. Charles Arnault. *Société des Sciences, lettres et beaux-arts de Cholet* (1937): 247-310.

Author: Innkeeper's daughter from Cholet, dressmaker, mother of eight.

Work: Describes flight from Cholet, when author was ten, after town had been burned by republican troops. With an antiroyalist father, two brothers in the republican army, and several members of her family massacred by republican troops, as well as memories of the royalist Chouans perpetrating similar massacres, this work shows horrors emanating from both political camps. It also provides examples of compassion exercised by both sides. Author's work is unfortunately buried in editor's notes.

4. BAULT (Madame).

Récit exact des derniers moments de la captivité de la Reine, depuis le 11 septembre 1793 jusqu'au 16 octobre suivant. Paris: Impr. de C. Ballard, 1817.

Author: Widow of the prison warden of the Conciergerie during half of Marie-Antoinette's captivity, mother of several children.

Work: Less colorful than the account dictated by Rosalie Lamorlière (see entry), Mme Bault's sixteen-page narrative adds a few new details on the queen's final imprisonment.

5. BÉARN (Pauline de Tourzel, comtesse de), 1771-1839.

Souvenirs de quarante ans (1789-1830), récits d'une dame de Madame la Dauphine. Paris: J. Lecoffre, 1861.

Author: Daughter of the Duchesse de Tourzel (see entry), married to the Comte de Béarn, mother of five.

Work: Written in 1832, the Comtesse de Béarn's memoirs cover the first years of the Revolution when she was at her mother's side at Versailles, the Tuileries, the Temple, and the Prison de la Force, from which she escaped during the September 1792 massacres.

6. BESNARD (Soeur).

"Relation de la détention et du voyage des religieuses d'Angers jusqu'à Lorient." *Revue d'Anjou*, 44 (1902): 257-92.

Author: Sister Besnard was a hospital worker at Beaufort.

Work: Recounts the arrest and transfer to Lorient of nuns from the convents of Angers, in 1794.

7. BOHM (Comtesse de), née de Girardin.

Les Prisons en 1793; par la comtesse de Bohm, née de Girardin. Paris: Bobée et Hingray, 1830.

Author: Wife of an émigré, mother of a son who shared her cell in the prison of Chantilly.

Work: Focuses on prison conditions, first in Chantilly, then in Paris, where she was incarcerated for a year beginning August 1793. Contains sustained description of prison life, means of communication between the women, reflections on nature, and many vignettes around a chosen theme.

8. BOIGNE (Eléonore-Adèle d'Osmond, comtesse de), 1781-1866.

Récits d'une tante. Mémoires de la comtesse de Boigne, née d'Osmond, publiés d'apres le manuscrit original par M. Charles Nicoullaud. Paris: Plon, 1907-8, 4 vols.

Author: Descendant of a distinguished aristocratic family that emigrated in 1792, married in England by her own choice for wealth and status in a union that proved incompatible, the Comtesse de Boigne became a witty and formidable member of Restoration society.

Work: Written after 1835, these memoirs of a high literary quality include 150 pages on the Revolution remembered by one who was only eight at its outbreak. Interesting chapters on émigré life in England.

9. BONCHAMPS (Marie-Marguerite-Renée de Scépeaux, marquise de), 1767-1845.

Mémoires de madame la marquise de Bonchamps, sur la Vendée, rédigés par Mme la comtesse de Genlis. Mémoires Relatifs à la Révolution Française, vol. 6. Paris: Baudouin freres, 1823.

Author: Widow of one of the Vendean generals, mother of three children, only one of whom survived the Revolution.

Work: Moving story of Mme de Bonchamps's personal history during the Vendean Wars, death of her husband from battle wounds, migrant period with the royalist army, loss of two children, imprisonment, final release. Edited and polished by Mme de Genlis.

10. BORDEREAU (Renée), called Langevin, 1770-1824?

Mémoires de Renée Bordereau dite Langevin touchant sa vie militaire dans la Vendée, rédigés par elle-même. Paris: L.-G. Michaud, 1814.

Author: Uneducated peasant girl in the royalist army. Wearing men's clothes, she became known as the Vendean Joan of Arc.

Work: Her memoirs were dictated in 1814 and "edited" by the author. Retaining her simple, gruff oral voice, they constitute a unique eyewitness account of the Vendean Wars over a six-year period from the perspective of an unusual participant.

11. BOURBON-CONTI, princesse Stéphanie-Louise de. Pseudonym for Anne-Louise-Françoise Delorme, Madame Billet, 1756-1825.

Mémoires historiques de Stéphanie-Louise de Bourbon-Conti, écrits par elle-même. Paris: l'auteur, an VI (1798), 2 vols.

Author: Member of a poor family from the town of Petit-Auvergne near Chateaubriand, this former servant invented a noble lineage as the sister of the Prince de Conti.

Work: Volume 2 contains interesting details on private life during the Revolution.

12. CAMPAN (Jeanne-Louise-Henriette Genet, Mme Berthollet) called Madame Campan, 1752-1822.

Mémoires sur la vie privée. de Marie-Antoinette, reine de France et de Navarre, suivis de souvenirs et anecdotes historiques sur les règnes de Louis XIV, de Louis XV et de Louis XVI. Paris: Baudouin freres, 1822, 3 vols.

Author: Marie-Antoinette's first lady-in-waiting; under Napoleon, director of the school for officers' daughters (from the Legion of Honor) at Ecouen.

Work: One of the most frequently cited accounts of the royal family's existence from 1789 to 1792. Intimate, witty, and highly readable.

13. CANDÉ (Pauline Gontard des Chevalleries, baronne de), 1776-1856?

Une jeune fille à *l'armée vendéenne. 1793. Souvenirs inédits de la baronne de Candé (née Gontard des Chevalleries), publiés et annotés par le vicomte Aurélien de Courson.* Paris: Librairie des Saints-Peres, 1930.

Author: Not yet nineteen in 1795 when she wrote this text, Pauline Gontard des Chevalleries was the daughter of an adored father who had emigrated in 1791, leaving behind his wife and two children to fend for themselves.

Work: Highly readable account of the counterrevolutionary wars as experienced in the Anjou region. Describes the early victories of the royalists, followed by those of the republicans, forcing the author, her mother, and sister to follow the Vendean army in its various moves. Narrative ends abruptly, presumably after the defeat of the émigré royalists at Quiberon in Brittany in July 1795.

14. CARRA DE VAUX (Antoinette- FrançoiseCésarine Des Roys, baronne), 1763-1849.

"Cahiers de mémoires inédits de la baronne Carra de Vaux, née Césarine Des Roys (1788-1804)." *Bulletin de la Société des sciences et arts du Beaujolais*, 11 (1910): 263-97.

Author: Daughter of a property intendant of the Duc d'Orléans, situated with husband on their properties in the Beaujolais region. Mother of five, aunt of poet Alphonse de Lamartine.

Work: Married in 1788, the author relates a history of Revolution in the Beaujolais, Lyons, and Nice, along with personal history of successive pregnancies, births, moves, and so on. Interesting account of husband's renouncing his feudal revenues in the face of threats by the populace and other changes wrought by revolution.

15. CASTELLANE (Louise-Adélaïde-Guyonne de Rohan-Chabot, Madame de), 1761-1805.

L'Education du maréchal de Castellane. Notes écrites par sa mère, publiées pour la Société des bibliophiles du Béarn. Pau: L. Ribaut, 1877.

Author: Aristocrat from Lower Pyrenees known for her intelligence and wit.

Work: Belongs to the genre of "baby books." From the point of view of a mother, it traces the educational progress of Boniface de Castellane, four years old in 1792, until 1801, revealing the liberal pedagogical ideas of an aristocratic family during the revolutionary period. It is, at the same time, a form of autobiography in that it traces the mother's history in relation to her son—her pregnancies, miscarriages, illnesses, hopes for her son's development and that of a hypothetical sister. The Revolution had a strong effect on their lives since her husband was imprisoned "in the time of Robespierre" and the family lost three-fourths of its fortune.

16. CAVAIGNAC (Marie-Julie de Corancez, Mme Jean-Baptiste), 1780-1849.

Les Mémoires d'une inconnue (Mme Cavaignac), publiés sur le manuscrit original, 1780-1816. Paris: Plon, Nourrit, 1894.

Author: Ardent republican, wife of regicide deputy Jean-Baptiste Cavaignac, mother of four.

Work: Valuable autobiography for its admixture of private and public life, as experienced and recorded by an unrepentant republican, who even defends the Terror. Nine years old at the outbreak of the Revolution, member of a comfortable and cultivated bourgeois family with fiercely republican sympathies, Marie-Julie would live to regret her marriage at seventeen to Cavaignac. Work offers many psychological insights on life in general, male-female and mother-child relations, griefs of old age, as well as historical témoignages.

17. CHASTENAY (Louise-Marie-Victorine, comtesse de), 1771-1855.

Mémoires de Madame de Chastenay (1771-1815), publiés par Alphonse Roserot. Paris: Plon, Nourrit, 1896, 2 vols.

Author: Well-known woman of letters, for whom the title of canoness was an entry into high society rather than the convent.

Work: The first volume is almost exclusively devoted to the Revolution as seen by the daughter of a liberal aristocrat elected to the Estates General, whose ideas changed after the first outbursts of violence. Excellent description of the Terror in Rouen between 1792 and 1794. Written between 1810 and 1817, work reflects Mme de Chastenay's well-situated position under Napoleon and her own witty character.

18. CHERET (Marie-Louise Lenoël, Femme).

Evénement de Paris et de Versailles. Par une des Dames qui a eu l'honneur d'être de la Députation à *l'Assemblée Générale*. Paris: Chez Garnery & Volland, Libraire, Quai des Augustins, no. 25, 1790.

Author: Parisian working-class woman.

Work: Seven-page pamphlet describing the women's march on Versailles, October 5-6, 1789, published by the author soon after the event. Recounts her participation in the deputation of twelve women who conferred with the king.

19. COIGNY (Anne-Françoise-Aimée de), 1769-1820.

Mémoires d'Aimée de Coigny. Introduction et notes par Etienne Lamy. Paris: Calmann-Lévy, 1902.

Author: Initially a partisan of the Revolution in the circle of the Duc d'Orléans, author fled to London in 1791.

Work: A compilation of memoirs, reflections, portraits, and notes covering the years of the monarchy, Revolution, Consulate, Empire, and Restoration. Exudes a cynical, sometimes witty tone with little that is personal.

20. DAUGER (Comtesse), née de Nédonchel, 1783—after 1858.

Souvenirs d'émigration. Caen: Legost, 1858.

Author: Granddaughter of minister of war under Louis XVI.

Work: Recounts childhood memories at Versailles and revolutionary tumult in Paris. Describes family's ten years as émigrés in Holland and Germany, with interesting section on village life in Westphalia where formerly rich aristocrats learned to work with their hands.

21. DELAHANTE (Alexandrine-Charlotte-Sophie Brossin de Saint-Didier, Madame Adrien), 1788-1860.

Souvenirs de Madame Delahante, née Alexandrine-Charlotte-Sophie Brossin de Saint-Didier, continués par sa fille, Sophie Delahante, baronne de Gravier. Evreux: Impr. C. Herissey, 1906-7, 2 vols.

Author: Member of minor provincial nobility; her daughter completed these unfinished memoirs.

Work: Early childhood memories of the Revolution offer an interesting picture of family retreating to the Normandy countryside while friends and relatives were led to the scaffold. Unusual observations on differences between Parisian and provincial life, and between treatment of girls and boys.

22. D'ESCARS (Rosalie de Rancher, marquise de Nadaillac, duchesse), 1761-1842.

Mémoires de la marquise de Nadaillac, duchesse d'Escars, suivis des Mémoires inédits du duc d'Escars, publiés par son arrière-petit-fils , le colonel marquis de Nadaillac. Paris: Emile Paul, 1912.

Author: Widow of Marquis de Nadaillac. Wife of the Duc des Cars. Mother of two children.

Work: Describes early emigration to Prussia and England. Widowed, she moved to Berlin, where she met and married the Duc d'Escars in 1796. Returning to France under the Empire, she and her husband were placed under house arrest for seven years, during which time they both wrote their separate memoirs.

23. DES ECHEROLLES (Alexandrine), 1777?-1843?

Quelques années de ma vie. Moulins: M. Place, 1843, 2 vols.

Author: Member of provincial aristocracy, raised by father and aunt. After revolution and father's second marriage, she went into permanent exile.

Work: Describes flight with her royalist father from their native Moulins to Lyons; siege of Lyons by republican armies, father's escape, aunt's arrest and execution, narrator's life in seclusion till end of Terror. Interesting, well-written record of teenage memories during revolution.

24. DESPRES (Françoise), 1746—?

Détails historiques sur les services de Françoise Després, employée dans les armées royales de la Vendée depuis 1793 jusqu'en 1815 , écrits par elle-même. Paris: L.-G. Michaud, 1817.

Author: Orphaned at an early age, Françoise Després was educated with her two brothers by a parish priest uncle and admitted to the institution of Saint-Cyr in 1775, where she worked in the infirmary.

Work: Describes the activities of a middle-aged woman serving the royalist armies in the Vendee as a courier and sometime leader of men. Unusual life and rare literacy on the part of an ordinary country woman.

25. DUCREST (Georgette), 1783—?

Mémoires sur l'impératrice Joséphine, ses contemporains, la cour de Navarre et de La Malmaison. Paris: Ladvocat, 1828, 3 vols.

Author: Niece of Mme de Geniis. (See entry.)

Work: After description of life as émigrée in London and return to France in 1800, work focuses on social and cultural life in France at highest levels.

26. DU MONTET (Alexandrine Prévost de La Boutetière de Saint Mars, baronne), 1785-1866.

Souvenirs de la baronne Du Montet (1785-1866). Paris: Plon, Nourrit, 1904.

Author: Daughter of an old and distinguished Vendean family. Mother also wrote memoirs. (See La Boutetière.)

Work: A few memories of emigration to Germany at age six, then to Vienna until 1801.

27. DU PARSCAU DU PLESSIX (Anna-Louise), 1769-1846.

"Extraits du 'Journal' fait par Anna-Louise Du Parscau Du Plessix, pendant les années 1792-1797 et 1800." *Bulletin diocésain d'histoire et d'archeologie, Diocèse de Quimper et de Léon* 24 (1925), 52-62, 296-308; 27 (1928), 21720, 290-96; 30 (1931), 34-42; 31 (1932), 81-84; 32 (1933), 121-39.

Author: Breton aristocrat.

Work: Journal extracts depict daily life in the Finistère region from the point of view of a pious woman whose family, friends, and way of life were successively battered by the Revolution.

28. DU PELOUX (Alphonse-Magdeleine Julien, Madame).

Journal de la captivité de la famille Du Peloux de Saint-Romain, en 1794, par Mme Alphonse-

Magdeleine du Peloux, née Julien. Publie par l'abbé A. Arsac. Montreuil-sur-Mer: Impr. Notre-Dame-des-Près, 1888.

Author: Provincial aristocrat, mother of one son, two daughters.

Work: Short history of family's arrest and incarceration in two provincial prisons. Graphic details that might evoke sympathy on the part of the modern reader are overlaid with class sentiments producing a counter-effect. For example, words overheard at prison entry that she and her family would be "game for the guillotine" are followed by her own contempt for the lower-class women with whom she was obliged to share space.

29. DURAS (Louise-Charlotte-Philippine de Noailles, duchesse de), 1745-1832.

Journal des prisons de mon père, de ma mère et des miennes, par Madame la duchesse de Duras, née Noailles. Paris: Plon, 1888.

Author: Member of the distinguished de Noailles family which lost several members to the guillotine, including her parents.

Work: Describes arrest in her (Oise) château in August 1793, imprisonment in Beauvais, Chantilly, and Paris, liberation in October 1794. Includes memoirs of Mme Latour, who had accompanied Mme de Duras's parents to prison and bore witness to their last days.

30. DUREY DE NOINVILLE (Pauline), 1778—after 1863.

"Les Émigrés pendant la Révolution. Souvenirs d'une octogénaire, présentés par Jacques Dinfreville." *Ecrits de Paris,* 1 (January—February 1973): 59-73 and 76-86.

Author: An eighty-three-year-old aristocrat.

Work: Selections from the unpublished memoirs of a woman who had emigrated to Germany at the beginning of the Revolution; her family was ruined by the seizure and sale of its possessions.

31. FALAISEAU (Adélaïde de Kerjean, marquise de), 1760-1812.

Dix ans de la vie d'une femme pendant l'émigration. Adélaïde de Kerjean, marquise de Falaiseau, d'après des lettres et des souvenirs de famille (Paris: Plon, 1893).

Author: Aristocrat in exile.

Work: A biography of the Marquise de Falaiseau written on the basis of her memoirs by Hervé de Broc. Recounts her years as an émigrée in London, Brussels, Holland, and Hamburg between 1791 and 1801.

32. FAUSSELANDRY (Louise de Peysac, marquise Antoine de Fars de), 1750?—after 1830.

Mémoires de Mme la vicomtesse de Fars Fausselandry, ou Souvenirs d'une octogénaire, événements, moeurs et anecdotes depuis le règne de Louis XV (1768) jusqu'aux ministères La Bourdonnaye et Polignac (1830). Paris: Ledoyen, 1830, 3 vols.

Author: Member of the provincial nobility, who survived the September prison massacres.

Work: Describes provincial childhood, short-lived marriage to the Vicomte de Peysac from whom she was separated during the rest of her life, young adulthood with her mother at the courts of Louis XV and XVI, the early Revolution, and the Terror. Memories of her uncle's election to the Estates General as a member of the clergy, her journalistic efforts to offer herself and a group of aristocrats as hostages for the king, her mother's death at the guillotine, her uncle's imprisonment and death during the September massacres, her own imprisonment in an effort to save him.

33. FRANCLIEU (Aglaé de), 1762-1858.

Mémoires de la chanoinesse de Franclieu, publiés par Jean Marchand. Paris: Firmin-Didot, 1930.

Author: Eighty-four years old in 1846 when she composed her memoirs, the canoness de Franclieu came from provincial nobility attached to the powerful Condé family.

Work: Anecdotal memories of childhood at the château de Chantilly, the early Revolution, emigration to Holland, Prague, Germany, Poland, and return to France in 1801.

34. FUSIL (Louise Fleury, Mme), 1774-1848.

Souvenirs d'une actrice, par Mme Louise Fusil. Paris: Dumont, 1841-1846, 3 vols.

Author: Well-known actress and singer, granddaughter of the famous actor Fleury.

Work: Completed in 1832, unusual description of the Revolution from the point of view of one who professed a nonpartisan stance. Story of her career in France, Belgium, and Scotland during the Revolution; after 1806 in Russia. Interesting observations on theater, art, and literature in the late eighteenth century.

35. GAUCHAT (Soeur Gabrielle), 1746-1805.

Journal d'une visitandine pendant la Terreur, ou Mémoires de la soeur Gabrielle Gauchat, précédés d'une introduction par M. l'abbé Godard. Paris: Librairie de Mme Vve Poussièlgue-Rusand, 1855.

Author: Born in Santo Domingo, of Creole origin, brought to France and called to the religious life at an early age, Sister Gabrielle entered the monastery of the Visitation at Langres in 1767.

Work: Journal kept between September 1792 and June 1795 by nun expelled from her order. Describes her efforts to practice religion secretly with other nuns and priests during the Terror.

36. GENLIS (Stéphanie-Félicité Ducrest de SaintAubain,
marquise de Sillery, comtesse de), 1746-1830.

*Mémoires inédits de Mme la comtesse de Genlis sur le XVIIIe siècle et la Révolution française,
depuis 1756 jusqu'à nos jours.* Paris: Ladvocat, 1825, 10 vols.

Author: Prolific woman, of letters, governess of the children of the Duc d'Orléans (Philippe-
Egalité), wife of the Marquis de Sillery who was guillotined with the Girondins.

Work: Long, often anecdotal, account of French society from the Revolution to 1825.
Describes author's early support of the Revolution, followed by emigration. Attempts
to valorize her role and that of the Duc d'Orléans.

37. GENLIS (See preceding entry)

Précis de la conduite de Madame de Geniis, depuis la Révolution. Hamburg: B. G. Hoffmann,
1796.

Author: (See preceding entry)

Work: Published in March 1796, work is a justification of author's conduct since 1789,
portraying her as a supporter of the Revolution, while deploring its excesses. Focuses
on years in exile as the governess and protector of the daughter of the Duc d'Orléans.

38. GIVRY (Marguerite-Victoire Pascaud, Madame de).

"Les Massacres de septembre 1792 a la prison des Carmes." *Le Carnet historique et littéraire,*
1 (1898): 381-94.

Author: Daughter of a secretary to the king, wife of mousquetaire in king's guard.

Work: Account of the September massacre in the Carmes Church, transformed into a
prison for the clergy. Most of the 180 refractory priests detained there were killed in
the garden by twenty to thirty assassins.

39. GOGUET DE BOISHERAUD (Julienne), 1765—?

"Récit des tristes événementsarrivés à Julienne Boishéraud." *Bulletin de la Société
archéologique et historique de Nantes et de la Loire-Inférieure,* 68 (1928): 35-89.

Author: An unmarried woman of approximately thirty in 1796 when she wrote her
memoirs, the author was the third child of a large family in the west of France.

Work: Forty-four-page manuscript recounting story of hardships experienced by author,
sisters, and mother after father and brothers emigrated. The women were incarcerated
in the Entrepôt prison in Nantes where her mother was one of the many prisoners
who were drowned. Author escaped, withdrawing to the country where she became
a dressmaker, then a servant. Rare deposition by a survivor of the Entrepôt prison.

40. GONTAUT (Joséphine de Montaut-Navailles, duchesse de),
1773-1857.

Mémoires de Madame la duchesse de Gontaut, gouvernante des enfants de France pendant la Restauration (1773-1836). Paris: Plon, 1891.

Author: Member of high nobility, governess of the royal children during the Restoration.

Work: Early chapters on revolutionary upheavals and author's friendship with the Duc d'Orléans's children are followed by account of emigration to London. Includes description of royalist military departure for Quiberon in Brittany.

41. GOUGES (Olympe de, pseudonym for Marie Gouze), 1748-1793.

"Testament politique d'Olympe de Gouges." In Marilyn Yalom, *Le Temps des orages: Aristocrates, bourgeoises, et paysannes racontent.* Paris: Maren Sell, 1989, pp. 245-52.

Author: Writer of plays, novels, and political brochures expressing patriotic and feminist ideas.

Work: Olympe de GOuge's "Political Testament" dated June 4, 1793. Having defended the king and criticized the excesses of the Revolution, she would be sent to the guillotine in November 1793.

42. GRANDCHAMP (Sophie).

"Les Souvenirs de Sophie Grandchamp." In Appendix to *Mémoires de Madame Roland*, ed. Claude Perroud. Paris: Plon-Nourrit et Cie, 1905, vol. 2.

Author: Known for her friendship with Mme Roland (see entry) and their mutual friend Louis-Augustin Bosc. A well-educated, sensitive, and effusive woman, who gave free lessons in astronomy, grammar, and literature.

Work: Written in 1806, this manuscript is found among the Roland Papers (ms. 9533, fol. 299-308) at the Bibliothèque Nationale, Paris. Beginning with February 1791, Mme Grandchamp traces her close association with Mme Roland in pages that at times resemble a novel of love; mutual rapture of the soul between the two women, mutual jealousy between Mme Grandchamp and M. Roland, "lovers' " quarrel and reunion in Mme Roland's prison, where Mme Grandchamp dedicated herself to her friend's glory by smuggling out her notebooks and stationing herself along the road leading to the guillotine so as to attest to Mme Roland's "firmness" of spirit on the day of her execution.

43. HORTENSE DE BEAUHARNAIS, 1781-1837.

Mémoires de la reine Hortense, publiés par le prince Napoléon. Paris: Plon, 1927, 3 vols.

Author: Daughter of Empress Joséphine from her first marriage, author became queen of

Holland under Napoleon.

Work: These authentic memoirs focus primarily on the period of the Empire but contain, in the first two chapters, memories of the Terror, her parents' imprisonment, her father's execution, and General Bonaparte's attentions to her widowed mother, Joséphine.

44. JOURNEL (Emilie Millon d'Ailly de Verneuil, Madame), 1774—after 1836.

Papiers et souvenirs de famille. Le fond de mon tiroir. Cahiers confidentiels de Madame journel née Millon d'Ailly de Verneuil, de 1774 à 1833. Montbrison: Imp. E. Brassart, 1940.

Author: World traveler, writer, thrice-married mother of three.

Work: These memoirs, written between 1833 and 1836, trace the history of the author's privileged childhood in the outskirts of Versailles under Louis XVI, her family's move in 1787 to the Ile de France. Describes revolutionary insurrection on the Ile de France, brief period of emigration to the United States in 1799, eight years in the French countryside under Napoleon, two years of literary work in Paris, and five years in Holland, plus later life in Guadaloupe.

45. JUILLERAT-CHASSEUR (Suzanne Chabaud de Latour, Madame), 1773-1850.

Un épisode de la Terreur à Nîmes, extrait des Souvenirs personnels de Madame Juillerat-Chasseur. Montbéliard: Impr. montbéliardaise, 1902.

Author: Unusual among memorialists as a Protestant observer of the Revolution in the provinces.

Work: Describes early "patriotism" of father and brother, followed by change of position in 1793 with treatment of the Girondins. Description of complex political and religious scene in Nimes from June 1790 till 1794.

46. JULLIEN (Rosalie Ducrollay, Madame MarcAntoine).

Journal d'une bourgeoise pendant la Révolution, 1791-1793, ed. Edouard Lockroy. Paris: Calmann-Levy, 1881.

Author: Wife of a supplementary deputy from the Dauphiny to the Legislative Assembly, exceptionally well educated.

Work: Collection of letters written between September 1785 and May 1793. Of special interest are those written from Paris, between 1789 and 1793, which describe with great enthusiasm the revolutionary events she witnessed at the Assembly, at the Jacobin Club, and at the Tuileries. Includes an account of a dinner in her home with the three Robespierre siblings.

47. LA BOUERE (Antoinette-Charlotte Leduc de Gazeau, comtesse de), 1770-1861.

Souvenirs de la comtesse de La Bouëre: La guerre de la Vendée (1793-1796), mémoires inédits publiés par Mme la comtesse de La Bouëre, belle-fille de l'auteur, préface par le marquis Costa de Beauregard. Paris: Plon, Nourrit, 1890.

Author: Wife of an officer in the Vendean army, mother of several children.

Work: Researched and written over half a century, these memoirs relate the Vendean War in the region between Angers, Cholet, and Nantes as experienced by a young woman who arrived in the Vendee for the first time in 1790. Interesting observations of the customs, architecture, furnishings, clothing, and everyday life among the Vendean peasants, as well as compelling narrative of a noble family fleeing from the republican army during the civil war.

48. LA BOUTETIERE DE SAINT-MARS (Adélaïde-Paule-Françoise, comtesse de la Fare), 1753-1823.

Mémoires de Madame la comtesse de La Boutetière de Saint-Mars, rapportant les principaux événements*de son émigration en 1791.* Angers: Impr. Lachèze et Dolbeau, 1884.

Author: Aristocrat in exile. (See Du Montet.)

Work: Written in 1816, these memoirs recall the author's emigration to successive locations in Germany and Austria between 1791 and 1801.

49. LA BRICHE (Adélaïde, Madame de), 1755-1844.

Une Femme Heureuse. Sa Famille. Son Salon. Le Château du Marais. D'après ses mémoires, sa correspondance, et d'autres documents inédits. Paris: E. de Boccard, 1934.

Author: Highly cultured aristocrat.

Work: A biography by Pierre de Zurich based on Mme de la Briche's unpublished memoirs, journals, and letters. Work focuses primarily on the private life of this widow and mother. Section on the Terror evokes her anxieties in 1793-94.

50. LA FAYETTE (Adrienne de Noailles, marquise de), 1759-1807, and LASTEYRIE (Virginie de La Fayette, marquise de), 1782-1849.

La Vie de Madame la Duchesse d'Ayen, in Vie de Madame de La Fayette par Mme de Lasteyrie, sa fille, précédée d'une Notice sur la vie de sa Mère, Mme la Duchesse d'Ayen. Paris: Leon Techener Fils, 1868.

Authors: Wife and daughter of the Marquis de La Fayette.

Work: This biography of Mme de La Fayette's mother belongs to the genre of biography-*cum*-autobiography not uncommon for women authors in the past. Written in the prison of Olmütz in 1798, where Mme de La Fayette had asked to be incarcerated with her husband, it traces the life of her adored mother from her birth in 1737 to her death on the scaffold. Mme de La Fayette's mother (the Duchesse d'Ayen), her grandmother (the Maréchale de Noailles), and her sister (the Vicomtesse de Noailles) were all executed on July 22, 1794. Mme de La Fayette inserts her own history and that of her famous husband in the interstices. Published by her daughter Mme de Lasteyrie, along with the latter's own biography of her mother, the two works constitute a unique example of trigenerational female life stories.

51. LA FAYETTE (Anastasie-Louise-Pauline de), comtesse de La Tour-Maubourg, 1777-1863.

"Arrestations de Mme de La Fayette et de sa fille au château de Chavaniac (1792). Souvenirs de Mlle Anastasie de La Fayette." *Nouvelle revue rétrospective*, 13 (1900): 363-406.

Author: Daughter of the Marquis and Marquise de La Fayette.

Work: Extracts from the account of a fifteen-year-old girl describing her mother's arrest in 1792 after her father went over to the Austrians.

52. LAGE DE VOLUDE (Béatrix-Etienne Renart de Fuchsamberg, marquise de), 1764-1842.

Souvenirs d'émigration . . . 1792-1794. Lettres à Mme la Comtesse de Montijo. Evreux: Auguste Hérissey, 1869.

Author: Companion of the Princesse de Lamballe, émigrée as of July 1789.

Work: Written in 1801-3 in the form of a letter, work covers period from July 14, 1792, to March 20, 1794. Traces author's illegal return to Paris from Coblenz and travel with false passport through France to see her sick mother and three children in Bordeaux. In constant danger of detection, she managed to embark aboard a vessel bound for America, which ended up in Spain. Work breaks off at this point.

53. LAMBALLE (Marie-Thérèse-Louise de Savoie Carignan, princesse de), 1749-1792.

Mémoires historiques de Marie-Thérèse-Louise de Carignan, princesse de Lamballe, publiés par Madame Guénard. Paris: Lerouge, 1801, 4 vols.

Author: Elisabeth Guénard, a prolific novelist and author of numerous "memoirs" of the royal entourage.

Work: These are not true memoirs but a biography of the Princesse de Lamballe, Marie-Antoinette's favorite. As a contemporary of her subjects, Madame Guénard frequently drew from personal memories.

54. LAMBERT (Alexandrine Pannelier d'Arsonval, baronne).

Souvenirs d'Alexandrine Pannelier d'Arsonval, baronne Lambert, avant et pendant la Révolution. Versailles: Impr. Aubert, 1902.

Author: Member of well-placed aristocratic family, niece of Mme Campan.

Work: Printed in fifty copies, work evokes author's childhood, with memories of Marie-Antoinette, Mme Campan, the Tuileries invasion of August 10, 1792, and family's retreat to Normandy during the Terror.

55. LAMORLIÈRE (Rosalie).

"La Dernière prison de Marie-Antoinette, relation de Rosalie Lamorlière." *Récits des grands jours de l'histoire,* 4 (1897): 75-96.

Author: Illiterate servant in the prison of the Conciergerie during Marie-Antoinette's captivity.

Work: Dictated to Lafont d'Aussonne in the 1830s, this short account of Marie-Antoinette's last days is remarkable for its sympathetic picture of the fallen queen separated from her children, under constant surveillance in prison, ultimately sent to her trial and death. Lamorlière's story retains her oral voice and compelling narrative style.

56. LA ROCHEJAQUELEIN (Marie-Louise-Victorine de Donnissan, marquise de Lescure, then marquise de La Rochejaquelein), 1772-1857.

Mémoires de Mme la marquise de La Rochejaquelein, écrits par elle-même. Paris: L.-G. Michaud, 1817.

Author: Best-known memoirist of the Vendean Wars, wife of one of the Vendean generals killed in battle.

Work: Recounts the insurrection in the Vendée between 1792 and 1795. Dramatic depiction of early royalist victories, later defeats, loss of her husband and three children, flight with mother into Brittany. Work of exceptional literary and historical merit.

57. LA ROQUE (Anne-Pauline de Taillevis de Jupeaux, baronne de), 1778-1877.

"Les Mémoires d'une Vivaraise émigrée sous la Révolution." *Revue du Vivarais,* 53 (1949): 11-31.

Author: Aristocrat originally from Vendôme.

Work: Describes emigration with her mother to Aix-la-Chapelle, while father and brother join émigré army. Family relocated to Dusseldorf, then London, where they became paid workers. Married the Baron de la Roque in 1797 and returned to France in 1802.

58. LA TOUR DU PIN GOUVERNET (HenrietteLucie Dillon, marquise de), 1770-1853.

Journal d'une femme de cinquante ans, 1778-1815, 4 vols., ed. Aymar de Liedekerke-Beaufort. Paris: Impr. R. Chapelot, 1907-11.

Author: Marie-Antoinette's lady-in-waiting; wife of officer and diplomat; mother of six children, all but one dying before her.

Work: Extremely readable account of the early Revolution at Versailles, Paris, and Normandy; period in hiding around Bordeaux, emigration to United States. Unique description of farm life in Albany, New York, as experienced by high-spirited émigrée. First part (1778-94) written in 1820; second part (1795-1815) in 1843.

59. LA VILLIROUET (Marie-Victoire de Lambilly, comtesse de Mouësan de), 1767-1813.

Une femme avocat, épisodes de la Révolution à Lamballe et à Paris. Mémoires de la comtesse de La Villirouët, née de Lambilly (1767-1813), ed. Comte de Bellevue. Paris: J. Poisson, 1902.

Author: Extremely literary and strong-willed member of the Breton aristocracy, mother of three.

Work: Account of her incarceration in the prison of Lamballe from 1793 to 1795 while husband was with royalist army; successful efforts to free herself and her coprisoners. Later arrest of husband and wife in Paris in 1799 and her successful plea in court on husband's behalf. Despite commentaries interspersed by a posthumous editor, Mme de La Villirouët's strong voice and personality are not attenuated.

60. LE BAS (Elisabeth Duplay, Madame Philippe), 1773-1859.

"Manuscrit de Mme Le Bas." In *Autour de Robespierre. Le Conventionnel Le Bas,* ed. Stéfane-Paul [pseudonym of Paul Coutant]. Paris: Flammarion, 1901, pp. 102-50.

Author: Daughter of the bourgeois furniture maker with whom Robespierre lodged in Paris, widow of the deputy Philippe Le Bas, mother of one son.

Work: Recounts the history of Elisabeth Duplay's romance with the deputy Le Bas, their short happiness, his death alongside Robespierre during the Thermidor coup, her imprisonment with a small baby, ostracism and poverty after her liberation. Memoirs written in 1842 when she was almost seventy reveal enduring republican loyalty.

61. LE ROYER (Jeanne, Soeur de la Nativité), 1731-1798.

Vie et révélations de la Soeur Nativité, religieuse converse au couvent des Urbanistes de Fougères, écrites sous sa dictée, suivie de sa vie intérieure, écrite aussi d'après elle-même par le rédacteur de ses Révélations et pour y servir de suite. Paris: Beauce, 1817, 3 vols.

Author: An obscure country nun, Sister Jeanne Le Royer dictated the story of her "life and revelations" to her priest.

Work: Recorded by the abbot Genet, this work is both the spiritual autobiography of a provincial nun and the biographical "praise song" written by her priest long after his flight from revolutionary France.

62. LOMENIE (Elisabeth-Louise-Sophie de Verges, vicomtesse de).

"Fragments des mémoires inédits de la vicomtesse de Loménie." *Mémoires de la société académique d'agriculture, des sciences, arts et belles lettres du département de l'Aube,* 46 (1882): 355-70.

Author: Aristocrat residing with family at the château de Brienne.

Work: Work recounts arrest of her father-in-law, husband, and brother-in-law at the château and their subsequent execution. Vivid depiction of a republican festival "for the martyrs of liberty" that she and the other women in her family were obliged to attend while their men were in prison.

63. MAUSSION (Angelique Fougeret, comtesse de), 1772-1851.

Rescapés de Thermidor. Paris: Nouvelles éditions latines, 1975.

Author: Daughter of Jean Fougeret, receiver general of finances, guillotined in 1794, and of Madame Fougeret, founder of the Société de la Charité Maternelle; sister of Madame de Ménerville (see entry); wife of the Comte de Maussion; mother of three sons. Amateur writer and artist.

Work: First part describes idyllic childhood in wealthy and well-placed family of jurists and administrators, followed by revolutionary upheaval, and incarceration of entire family (with the exception of Mme de Ménerville) in the convent of Port-Royal, where Mlle Fougeret lost her father to the guillotine and found a husband among the inmates.

64. MEDEL (Angélique de Ferrières, Madame de), 1754-1799.

"Le Journal d'émigration de Madame de Médel (1792-1794)." *Bulletins de la Société des Antiquaires de l'Ouest* 8 (1930): 661-78.

Author: Aristocrat from Poitiers who chose to join her husband in exile, while her brother, the Marquis de Ferrières, remained in France.

Work: Based on Mme de Médel's unpublished "Journal," Henri Carré wrote this account of her life as an émigrée in Belgium, Holland, and Germany, from January 1792 to 1799.

65. MENERVILLE (Elisa Fougeret, Madame de), 1768—?

Souvenirs d'Emigration. Paris: P. Roger, 1934.

Author: Member of illustrious Fougeret family (see entry for Maussion).

Work: Graphic descriptions of anxious existence during the first years of the Revolution, the 1789 women's march on Versailles that passed before her door, meetings of the Charité Maternelle founded by her mother, then her emigration with her family to Belgium, Holland, and England between 1791 and 1797. Unusual for her portrayal of upper-class émigrée women's work life in London.

66. MOLÉ-LEGER (Julie de La Vigne, Madame Molé, then comtesse de Valivon), 1767-1832.

"Souvenirs d'une actrice pendant l'émigration," *Carnet historique et littéraire*, 5 (1900: 332-357.

Author: An actress and sometime playwright.

Work: Selections from the largely unpublished memoirs of Mme Molé devoted to her adventures in Belgium and Holland where she and her actor husband emigrated in 1793. On the list of "suspect" actors, they fled from the invading French armies, yet performed before them in Amsterdam.

67. MONNARD (Marie-Victoire), 1777-1869.

"Les Souvenirs d'une femme du peuple à Creil," *Bulletin d'histoire et d'archéologie de Senlis*, 1 (1926-1927): 42-74, 2 (1928): 20-78.

Author: Working-class woman originally from the Oise.

Work: Describes her childhood in a family of modest farmers, then her apprenticeship to a bonnet-maker in Paris around 1790. Memories of numerous revolutionary events, such as the August 10 insurrection and September massacres in 1792 and the Festival of the Supreme Being in 1794.

68. NICOLAY (Marie de Lameth, marquise de), 1785—?

"Souvenirs de quatre-vingts ans (extraits des mémoires inédits de Mme de Nicolay, née de Lameth)." *Mémoires de la Société historique et archéologique de l'arrondissement de Pontoise et du Vexin,* 40 (1930): fascicule 1, 97-107.

Author: Daughter of the Comte de Lameth, deputy to the Estates General; wife of the Marquis de Nicolay.

Work: Short extracts from unpublished memoirs recounting childhood memories of the early Revolution when her father kept an open table for deputies from his region, including Robespierre. Period of emigration to England followed by mother's return to maintain property in the Pontoise. Mother put in prison, daughter farmed out, family eventually reunited.

69. PONS (Augustine-Eléonore de, marquise de Tourzel), 1775-1843.

Un épisode du temps de la Terreur. Paris: A. Vaton, 1857.

Author: Daughter of aristocrats imprisoned during the Revolution, wife of the Marquis de Tourzel (son of the Duchesse de Tourzel).

Work: Story of the author's imprisonment in the château de Chantilly, from September 1793 to October 1794.

70. PONTALBY (Marie-Elisabeth de), 1777-1867.

Souvenirs de Mme de Pontalby, dernière survivante des demoiselles de la maison royale de Saint-Louis de Saint-Cyr, recueillis et publiés par Fr. Joubert. Tours: A. Mame, 1869.

Author: Educator of young ladies.

Work: These memoirs, written when the author was over eighty, recount the last days of Saint-Cyr; this school founded by Louis XIV in the seventeenth century for daughters of the nobility was closed during the Revolution.

71. RANFER DE BRETENIERES (Madame).

"Dix-huit mois de ma vie: Histoire tragi-comique de la maison de détention des femmes de D." *La Révolution à Dijon: Paroles de Femmes* (Dijon: Bibliothèque Municipale de Dijon, 1989), pp. 25-26.

Author: Provincial aristocrat, whose mother had been imprisoned and whose son was suspected of having emigrated.

Work: Manuscript in the Municipal Library of Dijon; published extracts recount author's eighteen-month imprisonment in the Maison du Bon Pasteur, converted into a prison for the mothers, wives, and daughters of émigrés.

72. ROBESPIERRE (Charlotte), 1760-1834.

Mémoires de Charlotte Robespierre sur ses deux frères, précédés d'une introduction par Laponneraye et suivis de pièces justificatives. Paris: au dépôt central, 1835.

Author: Surviving member of the Robespierre family, after the death of her two brothers Maximilien and Augustin in the Thermidor coup.

Work: This memoir is a "praise song" of her two brothers, which attempts to restore the reputation of Maximilien as a great man. Records their sad childhood in Arras after the early loss of their parents, the separation of the children, Charlotte's happy early adult years as the mistress of Maximilien's house, his election to the Estates General, then Augustin's to the National Assembly, and their installation in Paris. Family caught up in revolutionary politics that led to interpersonal breakdown and ultimately her brothers' deaths. Work written when author was almost seventy, at the instigation of Laponneraye, a young admirer of her older brother.

73. ROLAND (Marie-Jeanne Phlipon, Madame), 1754-1793.

Appel à *l'impartiale postérité par la citoyenne Roland.* Paris: Louvet (an III) (1795), 4 vols.

Author: Best-known memoirist of the Revolution, extremely well-educated and highly literate wife of the minister of the interior, "muse" of the Girondin deputies, mother of one daughter.

Work: Written in prison in 1793 before she was executed, Mme Roland's manuscripts quickly became the most famous memoirs of the Revolution. They recount not only the history of her husband's political career and her covert involvement in revolutionary politics, but also the autobiography of her childhood and early adult years. Although the Rolands remained enthusiastic republicans, when they tried to oppose revolutionary violence they found themselves in direct opposition to Danton and Robespierre, who brought about their downfall and that of the entire Girondin faction.

74. SAINT-LUC (Victoire de), 1761-1794.

Victoire de Saint-Luc, dame de la Retraite, par Mme de Silguy, sa soeur; journal de sa détention en 1793. Paris: P. Tequi, 1905.

Author: Daughter of Breton noble family and member of religious community that did not take vows. Executed with parents in July 1794.

Work: Called by the author a "historical, tragi-comic journal" of her stay in the prison of Carhaix. Ironic description of prison life from October 1793 till February 1794.

75. SAPINAUD DE BOISHUGUET (JeanneAmbroise-Michel-Marie Talou de La Cartrie, Madame de).

Mémoires sur la Vendée. Paris: Baudouin frères, 1823, 2 vols.

Author: Wife of one of the Vendean generals.

Work: Describes the Vendean Wars from the point of view of an older woman whose husband was at the head of an army, while she wandered the countryside with other hapless women in hiding.

76. SAULX-TAVANNES (Aglaé-Marie-Louise de Choiseul-Gouffier, duchesse de), 1772-1861.

Sur les routes de l'émigration. Mémoires de la duchesse de Saulx-Tavannes (17911806), publiés avec une introduction et des notes par le marquis de Valous. Paris: C. Levy, 1933.

Author: Member of powerful Choiseul family, married at fourteen to the Comte de Tavannes, later Duc de Saulx.

Work: Recounts emigration with husband as of 1791 to Belgium, Holland, England, and then to Russia where her diplomat father had joined the court of Catherine the Great. Many interesting details on life of high-placed emigres in various countries that welcomed them.

77. STAEL-HOLSTEIN (Anne-Louise-Germaine Necker, baronne de), 1776-1817.

Considérations sur la Révolution française. Paris: Delaunay, 1818, 3 vols.

Author: Most famous and most esteemed woman writer of the generation of the Revolution, daughter of the Swiss-born minister Jacques Necker, wife of the Swedish Baron de Staël-Holstein, and mother of four children.

Work: A politicohistorical analysis of the Revolution that can also be read as Mme de Staël's partial autobiography, a biography of her father, and even as travel literature. As the daughter of Louis XVI's powerful liberal minister, Mme de Staël witnessed the workings of political office at close hand and supported the Revolution in its early efforts to create an English-style constitutional monarchy. Despite her flight from France in September 1792, and her residence abroad until 1795, de Staël remained loyal to the Revolution's basic ideals.

78. SUTTER (Thérèse Figueur, Madame Clément) 1774-1861.

Les Campagnes de Mademoiselle Thérèse Figueur, aujourd'hui Madame Veuve Sutter, ex-dragon aux 15e et 9e régimens, de 1793 à 1815, écrites sous sa dictée, par Saint-Germain-Leduc. Paris: Dauvin et Fontaine, 1842.

Author: Famous for having served in the republican army, with the Dragoons and the Hussards, between 1793 and 1800.

Work: Ostensibly dictated to Saint-Germain-Leduc, a minor writer, work reads more like a novel than authentic memoirs.

79. TARENTE (Louise-Emmanuelle de Châtillon, princesse de), 1763-1814.

Souvenirs de la princesse de Tarente, 1789-1792. Paris: H. Champion, 1901.

Author: Marie-Antoinette's devoted dame d'honneur, wife of Charles de La Trémoille (prince de Tarente), mother of one daughter.

Work: Covers first years of the Revolution, ending in 1792 when the princess was liberated from the Abbaye prison. Bears witness to her devotion to the queen, even under extreme duress. Interesting section on imprisonment during the September 1792 massacres.

80. THEROIGNE DE MERICOURT (pseudonym for Anne Josephe Terwagne), 1762-1817.

"Procès-verbal," June 3, 1791. Manuscript in the Imperial Archives, Vienna. Extracts published in Ferdinand Strobl von Ravelsberg, *Les Confessions de Théroigne de Méricourt.* Paris: L. Westhausser, 1892.

Author: Born of peasant stock in the Ardennes, one of the legendary women of the Revolution, placed in a mental institution from 1794 until her death.

Work: Written in Vienna in 1791 where she was imprisoned on trumped-up charges, this document recounts her troubled childhood, seduction by an Englishman, and involvement in the early Revolution. Memories of July 14, 1789, scenes at the Palais Royal and the National Assembly, the October Days at Versailles, and the republican society for men and women she founded with friends.

81. THOURET (Jeanne-Antide, Sainte), 1765-1826.

Lettres et Documents. Besançon: Imprimerie Jacques et Demontrond, 1962.

Author: Daughter of a farmer from the Franche-Comte.

Work: Describes her years as a novitiate in the Filles de la Charité, before the Revolution closed her order and sent her into exile. Later activities included the founding of a free school for girls in Besançon in 1799 and of the Congregation of les Soeurs de la Charité de Besançon in 1810.

82. TOURZEL (Louise-Félicité-Joséphine de Croy d'Havré, duchesse de), 1749-1832.

Mémoires de Madame la duchesse de Tourzel, gouvernante des Enfants de France pendant les années 1789, 1790, 1791, 1792, 1793, 1794, 1795, publiés par M. le duc Des Cars. Paris: E. Plon, 1883, 2 vols.

Author: Last governess of the children of Louis XVI and Marie-Antoinette, widow of the Marquis de Tourzel, mother of five.

Work: Major royalist memoirs for the period 1789 to 1792 when Mme de Tourzel was actively presiding over the two remaining royal children.

Includes spellbinding account of her time in prison during September massacres. Author of impeccable virtue and fine literary style.

83. TURPIN DE CRISSE (Emilie de Montulle, comtesse).

Mémoires relatifs aux différentes missions royalistes de Madame la comtesse Turpin de Crissé, et aux opérations de l'armée de la Haute-Bretagne et du Bas-Anjou, de 1794 à *1800.* In the *Mémoires secrets et inédits pour servir a l'histoire contemporaine,* 2 vols., ed. M Alph. de Beauchamp. Paris: Vernarel et Tenon, 1825, 2: 223-342.

Author: Provincial aristocrat.

Work: An account of the Vendean Wars written by Alphonse de Beauchamp on the basis of Mme Turpin de Crissé's notes. It focuses on the role she played as a mediator sent by the republicans to the royalist army in 1794. Interesting information on the use of women as negotiators of peace.

84. VALLON (Marie-Catherine Puzela, Madame), 1776-1851.

Mémoires de Madame Vallon, souvenirs de la Révolution dans le département du Loir-et-Cher, publiés par Guy Trouillard. Paris: Emile Paul, 1913.

Author: Bourgeois wife and mother residing in Saint-Cyr-du-Gault near Blois.

Work: Valuable account of private life in the department of Loir-et-Cher. Author recounts the turbulent revolutionary years when her father, a royalist notary, was arrested for counterrevolutionary activities and she accompanied him to prison.

85. VALOMBRAY (Christine de Saint-Vincent, comtesse de), Sister Théotiste, 1752-1832.

Les Mémoires d'une soeur de charité, publiés par Madame Gagne (Elise Moreau). Paris: Didier, 1870.

Author: Mme de Valombray was a member of the Ordre des Hospitalières and the director of a hospital in her home town of Mazières during the last fifteen years of her long life. Authorship is dubious; edited and heavily fictionalized by Elise Moreau, popular Christian writer of poetry, plays, and novels.

Work: Includes description of plight of nuns expelled from their orders by the Convention decree of March 1793

.86. VIGEE-LEBRUN (Marie-Louise-Elisabeth Vigée, Madame Lebrun), 1755-1842.

Souvenirs. Paris: H. Fournier, 1835-37, 3 vols.

Author: Most famous French woman painter of the eighteenth century, known for her portrais of Marie-Antoinette and members of the highest nobility; married and divorced; mother of one daughter.

Work: Highly readable autobiography covers her childhood, young adulthood, and flight from France in October 1789. Interesting account of her ten-year exile within the most elite circles of Italy, Austria, and Russia, by one who lived by her brush.

87. VILLENEUVE-ARIFAT (Aymardine-Aglaé-Louise-Gabrielle de Nicolay, marquise Maurice Jeande), 1773-1852.

"Souvenirs d'enfance et de jeunesse de la marquise de Villeneuve-Arifat," ed. Henri Courteault. Revue des études historiques, 67 (1901): 5-36, 14165, 225-69.

Author: Daughter of illustrious family of Parisian magistrates, widow living in Toulouse when she wrote her memoirs, after 1830.

Work: Work describes her parents' brilliant salons, her negative reactions as a young girl to the Revolution—the interminable political discussions, the Réveillon street demonstration that took place under her windows, a session of the National Assembly, her family's retreat to Neuilly. Text stops abruptly in the middle of a sentence, concerning the year 1793.

ABOUT THE AUTHOR

MARILYN YALOM was decorated as an Officier des Palmes Academiques by the French Government, and is the author of several popular nonfiction books, including *How the French Invented Love: Nine Hundred Years of Passion and Romance*, *A History of the Wife*, and *Birth of the Chess Queen: A History.* A former professor of French literature, and Deputy Director of the Institute for Research on Women and Gender at Stanford University, Yalom was educated at Wellesley College, the Sorbonne, Harvard, and Johns Hopkins. She lives in Palo Alto, California with her husband, the psychiatrist and author Irvin D. Yalom.

NOTES